SHARED RESPONSIBILITY
Families and Social Policy

SHARED RESPONSIBILITY
Families and Social Policy

ROBERT M. MORONEY

ALDINE
Publishing Company
New York

ABOUT THE AUTHOR

Robert M. Moroney is Professor of Social Work and Social Planning, School of Social Work, Arizona State University. Dr. Moroney has been a major contributor to numberous journals and books on social work, planning, and evaluation and is the author of "The Family and the State: Considerations for Social Policy." He is currently the Editor of *The Urban and Social Change Review* and is an active member of various task forces and advisory boards on both the local and federal levels.

Aldine Publishing Company
200 Saw Mill River Road
Hawthorne, New York 10532

Library of Congress Cataloging in Publication Data

Moroney, Robert, 1936–
    Shared responsibility

    Bibliography: p.
    Includes index.
    1. Family policy—United States. 2. Public
welfare—United States. 3. Aged—United States—
Family relationships. 4. Mentally handicapped
children—United States—Family relationships. I. Title.
HV699.M59 1986   362.8′2   85-20950
ISBN 0-202-36041-5 (lib. bdg.)
ISBN 0-202-36042-3 (pbk.)

Printed in the United States of America
10 9 8 7 6 5 4 3 2 1

For my mother, Helen

and in memory of my father, Michael

CONTENTS

THE SOCIAL WELFARE RESPONSE: RESOURCES   91

THE PROFESSIONAL RESPONSE: THE CAREGIVING   121
FUNCTION

RECOMMENDATIONS AND IMPLICATIONS FOR THE   143
FUTURE

FAMILY RESPONSIBILITY: AN EPILOG   171

PREFACE

A major role of any policy analyst is to provide relevant and timely information to decision makers so that they can more effectively go about the business of formulating policies. The analyst attempts to clarify and sharpen the discussion by presenting evidence and tracing through the implications of taking or not taking certain actions. Although it is recognized that the shaping of the questions that guide the analysis may reflect a bias or value position, this activity, the cornerstone of the policy process, is not *prescription* but *description*. The aim of the analysis is to raise a variety of questions from a range of sources, and, to the extent possible, to provide the necessary corrective to the bias.

I mention this in anticipation of possible charges that by introducing at the beginning of this book the idea that both families and the State have responsibility for the provision of care to dependent members, I will have predetermined the outcome of the study. In response, I would like to point out that this analysis begins where a previous analysis ended (Moroney, 1976). In 1974 I was invited by the Joseph Rountree Memorial Trust and the Department of Health and Social Services (United Kingdom) to conduct an inquiry into a number of sensitive policy areas. In general, they were concerned with the claim that families today are less willing and less capable than families in the past to provide care for their severely dependent members and are transferring this responsibility in greater numbers to the State. If this were occurring, they believed that the short- and long-range consequences of such transfers needed to be examined, since these transfers were said to be caused by an expanding Welfare State.

That inquiry began by raising four sets of questions. Is there evidence to support the charge that families are giving up the caregiving function? Have there been shifts in expectations or behavior on the part of families and professionals that have not been fully recognized but that have significant implications for future social policies? Is it possible that, in allocating greater amounts of social welfare resources, families are discouraged from continuing their participation in the caring function? As policies are enacted and eventually translated into programs, are they based on a realistic understanding of the family?

Focusing on two types of families, those caring for frail elderly parents and those caring for severely mentally retarded children, it became clear that there was little hard evidence that health and welfare services were being misused or that they were undermining family responsibility. In practice, the major beneficiaries were dependent persons who had either no family or none within reach. Families who decided to provide care for handicapped children and elderly parents experienced considerable hardship and stress; few, if any, supportive services were available. I concluded that when families cared, society, in general, and the State, in particular, benefited (at least in terms of keeping expenditures down), but that these families were penalized. Little in the way of exchange or shared responsibility was found in existing social policies and programs.

This book, then, begins with tne notion of shared responsibility and attempts to identify ways that might bring about a more equitable exchange. Even though the analysis begins with this framework, a great deal of attention has been given to the documentation of American policies and practice in terms of their overall emphasis. Are they structured so that the emphasis is on substitution or are they balanced to include the possibility of family support?

Still, a personal bias has emerged over the past 10 years. The bias, however, should be understood as one that identifies me as an advocate for a significant part of the population—families caring for dependent members, especially those members who are handicapped. This, I feel, is a legitimate role for the analyst as long as he or she does not also begin this sorting out with a predetermined solution. Recommendations must flow from analysis rather than analysis being used to support a particular policy.

This work was supported, in part, by a contract from the Division of Special Mental Health Programs of the National Institute of Mental Health (contract No. 278-77-0016-SM) and was originally published in a shortened version as a NIMH Monograph (*Families, Social Services and Social Policy: The Issue of Shared Responsibility*, 1980).

Many colleagues gave shape to the analysis with concepts, insights, and a philosophy of social welfare. These include Mary Lystad of the National Institute of Mental Health, Robert Morris and Charles Schottland of the Heller School, Brandeis University; Al Kahn and Sheila Kamermann of Columbia University; Nicholas Hobbs and Paul Dokecki of Vanderbilt University; and, finally, although we never met, Richard Titmuss of the London School of Economics, who gave direction to so many of us through his seminal works. Many of these people were willing to read the manuscript in various stages, and were generous in reacting to the strategy of the study. The opinions expressed, of course, are not their responsibility.

Robert M. Moroney

FAMILIES, SOCIAL SERVICES, AND SOCIAL POLICY

This book is an attempt to explore a number of key questions that have become the subject of intense public debate. The general issue is the relationship between families and the State. More specifically, it is concerned with the appropriateness of State intervention in family life. Under what conditions is intervention appropriate? For what purposes? In which areas of family life? What is appropriate for the family to carry out; what should families be required to do? What should be shared by both families and the State?

These questions are raised within a framework that builds on a number of key assumptions. The most basic is that the structure of the welfare state has been shaped by a number of beliefs concerning the responsibilities families are expected to carry for the care of the socially dependent and the conditions under which these responsibilities are to be shared or taken over by society. Admittedly, this framework assumes that both the family and the State are responsible for the provision of care to dependent members. The legitimacy of this general proposition is rarely contested. Serious problems and disagreements emerge, however, when attempts are made to translate the idea of shared responsibility into specific social policies and programs, for then it becomes necessary to define which functions are appropriate to each. What does sharing mean in real terms, and what is to be shared? What do families want the State to provide, and conversely, how does the State view the family? While these questions may, at first glance, be set aside as philosophical and far removed from the day-to-day workings of government, the search for answers can provide insight into how policies have evolved, the shape they have taken, and, most important,

1

the kinds of policies and programs that are likely to emerge in the future. This book will attempt to address these issues not in a global or comprehensive manner, but through the analysis of a discrete set of activities—the interactions between families and social welfare institutions.

The inquiry begins with some bias because it assumes some degree of exchange exists. This position can be defended on a number of grounds. There is an exchange operating already, although its emphasis and dimensions are unclear. It is evident that the State is benefiting from the amount of social care provided by families. In fact, such care exceeds by far the social care provided by the organized health and social services. It is impossible, furthermore, to assign a monetary value to these family "services," and it is inconceivable to estimate the costs involved if the State were to increase its caring function. For example, leaving aside the social cost, could the State afford to pay families caring for handicapped members a sum equal to the cost of care in institutions, or even the current rate paid to community care providers?

As will be discussed later in greater detail, the admission to institutions of persons who are severely physically or mentally handicapped has been prevented or delayed because their families care. Many families, often with the help of friends and neighbors, have provided what only can be described as a staggering amount of care at significant social, physical, and emotional costs. In this sense, the family has been a major resource for the social welfare system.

There is growing evidence that the exchange is far from bilateral or equitable. Even though over one half of all government expenditures go to social welfare efforts, a percentage that many feel cannot be increased, a disproportionate amount of these resources is channeled to individuals without families or whose families are unwilling to assume responsibility for their care. In other words, a relatively small number of individuals receive a large share of the services. Families are being penalized when they care and rewarded when they stop caring. It is not being suggested that this practice is based on explicit policies. It is argued, however, that this trend has significant short- and long-term implications that need to be exposed and discussed.

Although the questions posed at the beginning of this chapter may be viewed as more appropriate to a social philosopher or political theorist, they are of real concern to legislators and professionals in the human services. While the language of the debate may be different, while the issues are likely to be discussed in the context of specific and concrete policies, these more fundamental questions are central. Over the past few years, a number of new centers have emerged both inside and outside of academic institutions. In one form or another, their emphasis is the analysis of the effect or impact of public policies on families and family well-being. A few centers are attempting a comprehensive examination of public policies on specific population groups, e.g., families with young children. Others limit their analyses to a set of policies and not target groups, e.g., housing, employment, taxes, and income maintenance. During this same period, a number of academic institutions have established programs at the postdoctoral level for those individuals who see the family as a worthwhile field for research. That all these centers receive considerable funding from governmental or foundation sources is another indication of growing interest in the family. It should be noted that a significant amount of this support is developmental; each is grappling with the problem of finding an appropriate methodology or framework for such analysis.

This interest has also produced a loose coalition of individuals and organizations drawn together under the rubric of family policy; it includes representatives from both the political right and left. These developments are growing, suggesting the emergence of a new social movement. While these activities may be beneficial to families, they need to be closely monitored. Terms continue to be ill-defined, and even the concept of family remains unclear. What families? Policies for all or only some families? These questions were not anticipated in the planning for the first White House Conference on this issue. As groups interested in strengthening the American family came together during the conference (actually the White House Conference was a series of state and regional conferences), it became clear that there was little agreement as to what should be done. As the sessions evolved, the discussion moved beyond the rhetoric of family support, and contradictory agendas were debated (Steiner, 1981).

For example, many of those concerned with the status of American families seemed to be reacting to the social upheavals of the past twenty years, such as the emergence of the Civil Rights movement and its consequences. Initially the poor and blacks organized to attack the existing social welfare system. Criticism gave way to demands and eventually to threats of violence. Closely related were the unrest and the disturbances that occurred on the country's college campuses. Furthermore, the feminist movement gained momentum, placing new demands on the educational system and the employment sector, and putting significant pressure on some families in terms of changing roles, functions, and expectations. On a smaller scale, experiments in less traditional life-styles were taking place. These included communal living arrangements, cohabitation outside marriage, and homosexual "marriages." Such trends were confusing to people who did not understand them, reflected values they could not relate to or accept, and in general were unsettling. They were interpreted as threatening to traditional societal institutions and basic values. It is conceivable that part of the discomfort can be attributed to the fact that rapid change makes the future unpredictable, and the inability to predict is viewed as a lack of control in our lives. Some have observed these changes and blame the "family" for them. In their opinion, the family has defaulted in its responsibility to provide the necessary stabilizing influence in society. The family should, it is argued, guarantee continuity and the orderly transmission of appropriate values. Those who believe this see the necessity for family policies that will reverse the trends and restore the family to its earlier state. The family, thus, is both the cause of and the solution to the problem.

Others take a different view, suggesting that society as a whole is changing and the family is merely adapting to these shifts. In moving to an industrial and then a postindustrial society, families have had to make accommodations. The family initially lost its economic function to the industrial sector, retaining the residual functions of reproduction and care of the socially dependent: children, the old, and the sick. This evolution eventually created a family structure more suited to people's needs than earlier forms, which were likely to be characterized as more complete economic and political units composed of a number of subfamilies whose needs were met through an interdependent extended kin system. The extended family was both unnecessary and counterproductive to a highly mechanized labor market. The nuclear family, however, composed of husband, wife, and children, independent of its kin-related families, was viewed as the ideal structure for meeting the demands of geographical and occupational mobility. Over time, remaining functions began to be shared by other institutions. For example, the socialization of children was seen as a function that legitimately should be shared by the educational system. Changes in the family are, then, adaptations to external demands, and the mere fact that families still exist attests to their resiliency. Policies should be developed that strengthen this major stabilizing influence. Despite the fact that research over the past 20 years has seriously questioned such a conclusion, a significant number of people accept it.

Although large numbers of people have been and continue to be convinced that family deterioration has occurred and that the damage must be reversed, the evidence usually cited is not convincing; it is at least open to a number of different interpretations. The divorce rate has increased to the point where 30 to 40% of all first marriages end in divorce (Califano, 1976). Whereas in 1960 one in every 20 women giving birth was not married, the figure today has risen to one in eight. It is estimated that one million youth run away from home each year, and that suicide is the second leading cause of death among young people between the ages of 15 and 24. One teenager in 20 has a drinking problem and, if present trends continue, one of every nine youngsters will have been to juvenile court by age 18. Although these statistics may be misleading indicators of family disorganization and deterioration and will be discussed later, they are offered as "proof" of it by many. Some would argue further that these trends are associated with the increased participation of mothers in the work force. Today, over one half of mothers with school-age children work outside their homes, proportions that have more than doubled in the last 25 years.

With this background, it is easy to understand the recent and growing wave of nostalgia about family life in the past. People are told through the media that life was less complex and that appropriate values were respected. Youth accepted adult authority and roles were not blurred. In general, it was a better time to live.

In fairness, though, this picture of the past is highly selective, with certain aspects emphasized and others ignored. If life was better, it was also shorter. Life expectancy at the beginning of the nineteenth century was estimated to have been 35 years. At the beginning of the twentieth century it had been raised to 47 years. Today it has reached 70 years. One hundred years ago more children were born, probably two to three times more per family, but significant numbers of these children did not survive to young adulthood. For example, it has been estimated that one child in five died before the age of one, and one in three died before reaching their fifth year.

People today complain that aged parents are shunted off to nursing homes or retirement homes by their adult children, and that severely handicapped children are sent to institutions by their parents. Families in the past are believed to have been more caring, more responsible. The data, as incomplete as they are, however, do not support this. First, most families did not face this troublesome decision. Fewer people survived to old age, and most children born with severe handicapping conditions died very young. Furthermore, there is evidence that when families had to provide care, the handicapped member suffered. Care was given, but often at considerable emotional cost (Rosenheim, 1965). Finally, the extent of urban and rural poverty in the nineteenth century was staggering.

It might be argued that when most people speak of "returning to the past," they are primarily complaining that life today is too complex, and that the current rate of social change is unsettling. One social scientist describes this as the "world we have lost syndrome" (Laslett, 1976). It is inconceivable that anyone would really want to give up our improved standard of living for the dreary and relatively short life the majority of people preceding us endured, and that, of course, creates a dilemma.

FAMILIES AND SOCIAL POLICY: THE CONTEXT FOR DISCUSSION

In the best tradition of the modern welfare state, this country has repeatedly expressed a commitment to the basic needs of its people, producing a series of policies, programs, and services that are often contradictory and counterproductive when assessed holistically. This does not mean that specific policies individually have not been of value. Rather, the specific intervention has often created new problems in other areas or operated at cross-purposes to other policies. More often than not, the secondary effects are neither intended nor anticipated. Some examples are well known; e.g., the disruption of family life through the Aid to Families with Dependent Children Program (AFDC). The program as structured penalizes two-parent families and encourages fathers to desert. Ten years ago, the Senate Finance Committee and the House Ways and Means Committee discussed procedures to enforce child support payments, to establish paternity for dependent children, and to require mothers to cooperate in locating fathers. As one observer noted, "This requirement is not only an invasion of privacy; it acts to split poor families apart by pitting women against men within the family unit" (Stack and Semmel, 1974). We can find similar situations in the area of housing and deinstitutionalization. Many housing policies have had unintentional negative effects on local informal support networks, and physically separated children from their aged parents. The policies were, in fact, quite successful in providing adequate shelter to those who previously had been living in substandard physical environments (Young and Wilmott, 1975; Hearings before the Subcommittee on Executive Reorganization, Pt. 9, p. 2030, Pt. 11, p. 2837, 1966).

The recent emphasis on efforts to reduce hospital care for the mentally ill and the mentally retarded, defensible on both therapeutic and financial grounds, has brought with it increased pressure on families. The reduction of institutional places and increased discharges to the community have not been balanced with a comparable expansion of residential care places and community support services. Many families now find themselves under considerable stress, with few external resources available to assist them (Moroney, 1976). These and other inconsistencies in social policy are addressed throughout this book.

There have been continuous and often bitter debates around these issues. The disagreement can be reduced to a number of fundamental questions. Should services be provided as a right or only made available to individuals and families when they demonstrate their inability, usually financial, to meet their basic needs? Should benefits be provided to the total population or restricted to specific target groups, usually defined as "at risk"? Should the State develop mechanisms to continuously improve and promote the quality of life, or should it restrict its activity to guaranteeing some agreed-upon minimum level of welfare? Should it actively seek to prevent or minimize stressful situations, both environmental and personal, or should it react to problems and crises as they arise?

On one level these questions are shaped by financial considerations, on the other by disagreements on basic values. Arguments are offered supporting the thesis that the country can afford only so much social welfare. Resources are limited and need to be given to those with the greatest need. Selective provision rather than universal coverage is viewed as more effective and less costly. In fact, selective provision is more likely to result in more services and higher levels of benefits for those truly in need and are not "wasted" on those individuals and families who can manage on their own. Finally, by introducing means testing or other criteria for eligibility determination, potentially excessive demand or use is minimized, and the State indirectly encourages individual initiative and responsibility. This position is countered with the argument that a residual approach, one that basically reacts to crises or problems after they have occurred, is shortsighted, and that present economies might result in tremendous future demands. Furthermore, policies and services developed from this stance tend to stigmatize recipients, segregate them from the mainstream of life, and strengthen an already fragmented service delivery system.

These questions and concerns are value laden. They are presented in normative terms to emphasize the idea that policy formulation cannot be equated with technical decision making and that the process is open to disagreement. Questions of what the State should do or must do presuppose some degree of consensus as to the desired nature of a specific society, including the relationships among individuals and between individuals and formal institutions. On another level, and after the first two questions are resolved, analysts have a role to play. They can translate goals into resources and generate particular courses of action to achieve those goals. Unfortunately, the criteria for choosing among alternatives are often economic, and the implications of policies are not traced through sufficiently.

Despite this ambivalence and disagreement, there tends to emerge a general consensus that when policies are proposed, the family should be considered in all deliberations. Most, if not all, argue that families should be protected and strengthened as a basic social institution. For some, this position is philosophical and moral; for others, it is a political necessity. Reasons aside, the family continues to be very much a part of the social welfare debate. Even a cursory review of the past 40 years shows that social legislation has been promoted on the premise that it would benefit family life and, in so doing, benefit the country. In turn, opponents counter with the argument that such action, if taken, would weaken the family. Because little rigorous analysis accompanies these claims and countercharges, for the sake of argument it does not matter which group is "right" on a specific issue. Nor is it possible to determine what the motives are of the various groups involved, since motives are at best inputed from an individualized perception of what is "good." Regardless, the notion that the family will benefit or be harmed becomes a key part of the debate.

Almost 10 years ago, Carter in a major campaign address stated that "Families are America's most precious resource and most important institution. Families have the most fundamental, powerful and lasting influence on our lives. The strength of our families is the key determinant of the health and well-being of our nation, of our communities and of our lives as individuals" (Califano, 1976). Following the election, welfare reform emerged as a top priority for legislative action. The rationale presented was to the point, and it argued that existing welfare policies were detrimental to family life. Proposed reforms were necessary to restore families to positions of strength. This concern for restructuring the system, however, has not been unique to one political party, nor is it a new subject for political debate. Eight years earlier, the Nixon Administration introduced slightly different proposals with the argument that the welfare system had been "successful in breaking up homes, robbing millions of the joys of childhood, contributing to social unrest, and undermining family life in general" (A Message from the President, 1969). Before this the Kennedy Administration suggested amendments that would refocus efforts on the family and family life (office memorandum on "Administration Actions necessary to Improve Our Welfare Programs," 1962).

Each of these criticisms generated a series of reforms that were intended to overcome the deficiencies of the public assistance programs that evolved from the Social Security Act of 1935. This legislation in turn had been promoted as a major break from the Poor Law tradition, an innovation to strengthen the quality of family life by providing a protective floor against the risks of income loss through unemployment, death of the wage earner, disability, or unemployment. The designers of the earlier reform saw a guaranteed income as enabling families to remain intact. The merits or limitations of these policies will be addressed later. They have been introduced here to emphasize that each measure was introduced with the explicit assumption that it would benefit families.

Take another example. In 1971, the Office of Child Development proposed that universal day-care, available for all families and not just the poor, was both a right and a service with the potential of "improving the well-being of the total family" (Office of Human Development, 1971). The Administration disagreed, and in his veto of the proposed Comprehensive Child Development Act, the President argued that universal day care would "diminish parental authority and involvement with children." Furthermore, he suggested that such public provision would be harmful to the family and would not "cement the family in its rightful position as the keystone of our civilization" (Presidential Veto Message of the Comprehensive Child Development Act of 1971). Four years later, the Child and Family Service Act of 1975 was introduced, and a unique campaign was waged to discredit it. Some charged that, if the act passed, children would be raised in a "Soviet-style system of communal child care," and that "it would take the responsibility of parents to raise their children and give it to the government." And what principles did this legislation propose? In the preamble it states that "The Congress finds that the family is the primary and most fundamental influence on children; child and family service programs must build upon and strengthen the role of the family and must be provided on a voluntary basis only to children whose parents or legal guardians request such services with a view toward offering families the options they believe to be most appropriate for their particular needs" (House of Representatives, 1976).

This listing could go on with examples drawn from the areas of housing, mental health and mental retardation, family planning, employment and manpower, and even various proposals for tax reform. Legislation is defended on the principle of strengthening family life and attacked by opponents on the assumption that it has harmed or will harm families.

FAMILIES, SOCIAL WELFARE, AND THE CURRENT DEBATE

Assuming that these positions are more than political rhetoric, it is necessary to search for their rationale and to unravel their implications. The family is viewed by many as a social institution under attack, one that has been weakened over the preceding decades, one that is in danger of annihilation. How real is this concern for families? As importantly, why the concern, and what families are being discussed? Regardless of ideological or political preference, many agree that the breakdown is occurring and that it is the best interest of society that the family be restored to its earlier position. The underlying assumption is, of course, that previously the family was stronger. There tends to be less agreement, however, on the causes of the perceived breakdown or on ways to reverse the trend.

Historically, this concern is not new. For example, the issue of family responsibility for the care of dependent persons—e.g., children, the handicapped, the elderly—has been the subject of continuous debate over the past 350 years. Most social welfare programs have been developed on the premise that the family constituted the first line of responsibility when individuals had their self-maintaining capacities impaired or threatened. It was further expected that families would support these persons until the situation became overwhelming, and only then would society, through either the public or private sector, intervene.

This approach has been based on the principle that family life is and should be a private matter, an area that the State should not encroach upon. The family was and is viewed as the last sanctuary that individuals could retreat to, and as a fragile institution in need of protection (Bane, 1976). The appropriate role of the State, then, was to develop policies that would protect and strengthen families, more often than not resulting in intervention only when absolutely necessary. "Necessary" involvement was, however, unclear and subject to various interpretations.

There seems to have been agreement that society, through the State, had the right and responsibility to step in when individuals could no longer meet their own needs and did not have resources to fall back on. As early as the seventeenth century, the Poor Law made provision for widows with children through its outdoor relief policy. Children could be and were removed from their families and apprenticed if the State felt the family environment was not suitable. Today, this principle has been interpreted to cover the State's right to intervene in a family situation in which a child has been or is in danger of being abused or neglected. The child is accepted by society as an individual with certain rights, one of which is the protection from physical harm. Furthermore, few today feel that the State interferes with individual privacy if it moves an isolated elderly person to a nursing home when he or she is unable to meet basic survival needs. To the contrary, people are shocked and angry when they hear of an elderly person starving or freezing to death unattended. The emphasis in these situations is on the need to protect the individual who might harm himself or others or be harmed. In clear-cut cases, the State becomes a substitute family in that it provides for some basic survival needs.

The State has also assumed a degree of responsibility in less extreme situations, where it is thought that families or individuals are unable to cope adequately. In practice, each generation appears to define what form of intervention is appropriate and under what conditions, but each generation does not discard past policies and develop its own. The process is incremental, characterized more by marginal adjustments than by radical change. Examples are the numerous income mainte-nance, food stamp, manpower, and educational programs. Intervention usually takes place after a crisis or breakdown, whether individual or structural. While in the earlier period of the Poor Law, services were made available only as a last resort, forcing families to admit to pa-thology or "family bankruptcy," the current role of the State is still seen as marginal, though not as repressive or personally demeaning. Legislation, by and large, still views social welfare as a system that should be concerned with a relatively small proportion of the population, a residual group unable or unwilling to meet its own needs (Titmuss, 1963). In general, then, the State has been reluctant to interfere with the family's rights and responsibilities for self-determination.

This residual approach, consistent with earlier social philosophies of laissez-faire and social Darwinism, is gradually becoming balanced with the belief that society, especially as represented by government, should assume more direct responsibility for assuring that basic social and economic needs be met. However, this evolution, incorporating many of the earlier Poor Law policies, has produced a number of un-certainties, and the line dividing society's increased responsibilities through its social welfare institutions and the family's appropriate functions has become less clear.

For example, over 50 years ago, the federal government established a program of social insurance and public assistance that provided retired persons a guaranteed income. Implicitly, the principle was established that adult children were not to be held responsible for the economic needs of their parents, a position that ran counter to previous policies.

In practice, however, the principle was not totally accepted. A number of states still have various statutes regulating filial responsibility (though they are not enforced in most situations), and early drafts of recent welfare reform proposals state that adult children have a duty to care for their infirm parents.

The State has also assumed major responsibility for the education of children and youth. It has justified this intervention, a policy strengthened by legal requirements, from a human investment rationale; i.e., children are the adults of the future and will be responsible for the social and economic well-being of the next generation. And yet, it has been reluctant to expand this intervention to preschool programs, despite the fact that the same rationale could be used for developmentally oriented day care.

FAMILIES AS SOCIAL SERVICES

A major unifying theme throughout this book is that the family can be defined as a social service. Although the concept is ambiguous, and some find the definition demeaning to such a basic societal institution, it can provide a framework for identifying needed social policies and developing effective and responsive services. The essence of these policies and services is a commitment to the principle that families and other social institutions need to interact in providing support and services to individuals and groups.

Social services have come to be defined as those services designed to aid individuals and groups meet their basic needs, enhance their social functioning, develop their potential, and promote their general well-being (Wilensky and Lebeaux, 1965; Kahn, 1973). The starting point, then, is that families are a social service in that they, as well as the community, society, and the State, carry out these functions for family members. Furthermore, families are providing more social care to dependent members than are the health and welfare agencies. It is not argued that families are "better social services," and that de facto they are better equipped to carry out these functions. Any such statement tends to elicit sharp criticisms and examples of families that are not capable of providing such services or of individuals who have been harmed by relatives. For example, more people are becoming aware of the rising numbers of reported child-abuse or spouse-battering cases. However, in general, most families are functioning well in caring for children and other dependent family members.

There is an American tendency to establish dichotomies, to argue that either families or the State should assume primary responsibility.

For example, 25 years ago, professionals advised families with severely retarded children to place them in institutions. It was better for the child; it was better for the other children; it was better for the parents. Those parents who wanted to keep the child home often were told that they had neither the skills, knowledge, nor resources required to assist the child in reaching his or her potential. Many ambivalent parents were made to feel guilty if they resisted institutional care, and were led to believe that such a decision would not be in the best interests of the handicapped member in terms of his or her physical and social well-being. A second and equally convincing argument for institution-alization was that in providing home care, intense strains are placed on the total family unit, creating problems for the other children or between parents. Recently, however, the pendulum seems to have swung to the opposite side. Professionals now seem to feel that com-munity care, including family care, is superior to institutional care. Their current thinking is that institutional care is not in the best interests of the child or family as a whole, and, as in the 1950's, much pressure is brought to bear on parents. While there have been exceptions to these polar positions, there has been a tendency to see solutions in either/ or terms rather than accept the value of diversity. In some situations families can provide better care, and in others the State is the more appropriate caregiver. Therefore, there should be a range of policies, and specific policies may have multiple purposes.

Policies may then be located on a continuum whose end points are extreme forms of substitution (the State becoming the family for the individual) and total lack of State involvement in family life. The needs of families and individuals vary in time and over time, and ideally the State would respond to those variations with policies that support fam-ilies when they need support and substitute for families when they are incapable of meeting the needs of their members. Even this postulation is incomplete, since it suggests a progression from no services to sup-portive services to substitute services, the last only when the family breaks down. In many cases, a family in crisis may need some other social institution to temporarily assume the total caring function for a child or a frail elderly parent, but would reassume primary responsibility after the crisis has been dealt with. From this point of view, both func-tions (support and substitution) are necessary, and neither can be of-fered as more important or more desirable than the other.

The overriding question guiding this study is: What is the most de-sirable, effective, and feasible division of responsibility between the family and extrafamilial institutions in meeting the needs of individuals, and in what ways can these institutions relate to each other to maximize benefits? Although the question is raised in such a way that certain biases are introduced at the beginning of the analysis, that it presupposes the value of a relationship based on bilateral exchanges, and that it will also result in certain literature having greater weight than other sources, the result need not be prescriptive nor the outcome necessarily predetermined (Moroney, 1976).

This policy question can be broken down into the following dimensions:

To what extent is the State giving support to families in the areas of child care, socialization, care of the elderly or handicapped? Who is seen by the family and the organized welfare system as responsible in these areas and to what degree? What are the attitudes of families toward professionals and professionals toward families in the provision of social care? What are the gaps, if any, between the needs of families and actual services provided? What are the implications of these questions for policy formulation and service development? What criteria are useful for evaluating these policies and services in the context of family care? Is it possible to adjust policies to differences among families in terms of economic, racial, and ethnic variations?

A POLICY FRAMEWORK

Rein (1970: xii) suggested that social policy can be defined as the "study of the history, politics, philosophy, sociology, and economics of the social services." His point is well taken in that no single academic or professional discipline can be expected to provide sufficient insight or the most appropriate framework for analyzing most social problems and then recommend effective policies and programs. He goes on to say that the analyst must "trespass on academic and professional domains in which he may have no special competence." The policy analyst's unique contribution becomes one of identifying and understanding approaches used in the different disciplines and then synthesizing these into some whole. More often than not, policy analysis relies on available data and existing research rather than on the collection of new data. What tends to distinguish this from traditional research is the way the questions are formed and the specific purposes of the analysis.

The policy questions raised in the preceding section dealing with desirable, effective, and feasible division of responsibility between families and other institutions are different from a more standard research question that sets out to determine the relationships between variables, e.g., the effects of maternal employment on child development. The former hopes to produce something that legislators or administrators can easily translate into action, while the latter provides a better understanding of certain relationships. Policy analysis relies heavily on research, while research can stand by itself, although Bronfenbrenner (1974) has suggested that social science relies on social policy for vitality and validity. A further distinction is that policy analysis, to be useful, must to responsive to the needs of policymakers, who are often under considerable time pressures. The researcher who informs a decision maker, that the specific information needed is not available and cannot be had for one or two years or more soon loses his or her audience. While the best possible information may not exist, there is value in reexamining what is available and drawing from it reasonable policy responses. The argument used is that the information can provide some direction, transcending intuition.

This book attempts such analysis, and is based on a review and synthesis of major research dealing with the family as a social service over the last 15 years. Given that the family is accepted as an appropriate focus for academic disciplines such as philosophy, sociology, anthropology, political science, economics, and history, as well as the professional fields of medicine, social work, psychology, law, and education, the research was considerable. The initial phase of the study attempted to identify and pull together indicators associated with the caring function. In general, they dealt with family structure and family types. Specific indicators included family size, mobility, female participation in the labor force, dependency ratios, emerging new forms of families, the prevalence of three and four generational families, and symptoms of family disorganization. While these indicators are descriptive, implications of trends are drawn as they relate to the family's capacity to function as a social service.

Studies of the attitudes and values people hold about various caring functions were then reviewed. Policy formulation is dependent on general attitudes and beliefs. If consensus seems to exist, the process is facilitated; if not, the policymakers must determine whether there is a need for education and information that may generate a consensus. This review relies heavily on various opinion research efforts which touch on how people in general view family-State relationships.

Literature primarily from the human services field was then reviewed (e.g., mental health, mental retardation, health, rehabilitation, and social welfare) and analyzed along the following dimensions: Do the services support or substitute for the family? If there is a transfer of the caring function from the family, is the transfer complete, temporary, or permanent? These studies were also evaluated to identify how various professionals interact with families, and their roles and functions in the provision of social care to family members, e.g., a partnership, or the family as secondary to the professional, supportive to the professional, or supported by the professional. Finally, are families receiving social services defined in normal or pathological terms?

To further refine the analysis and identify practical points of intervention, two groupings of families—those providing care to handicapped children and those providing care to the handicapped elderly—were examined in greater detail. This analysis allows a better understanding of the general questions raised above; an identification of the constellation of institutions, policies, and programs interacting with these families; a working description of the nature of the relationships and the quality of care provided in the home; and some notion of strengths, deficiencies, and needs that should be addressed in future policies.

PLAN OF THE BOOK

Chapter 1 has presented the general focus of research as a study of the relationship between families and State in the provision of social care to dependent persons. The questions that have been raised are difficult to analyze, even to answer, so there is no set methodology to fall back on. This, however, has been described as the challenge of policy analysis, a challenge that is both frustrating and exciting. Rather than beginning with the collection of new data (for example, through a large-scale survey), a more efficient, productive, and politically responsive approach would be the analysis of existing information. The nature of the issue requires that the study be exploratory, not hypotheses testing, and the end product is a discussion of what may be done given what is already known.

Chapter 2 builds on Chapter 1 and discusses the critical issue of dependency and family responsibility, the cornerstone of shared responsibility. Chapter 3 explores the concept of the family as a primary social service. It covers approaches to defining families and the changing nature of the family over time. Chapter 4 provides descriptive material of two at-risk groups, their characteristics, and needs. Chapter 5 builds on the preceding chapter and discusses the more general issues of social welfare, i.e., financing patterns and problems in organizing and delivering supportive services. The question of professional response to families is dealt with in Chapter 6. Chapter 7 discusses the general issue of shared responsibility, while the final chapter reexamines the policy questions raised in Chapter 2—family responsibility, dependency, and support systems.

2 FAMILY RESPONSIBILITY

In the preceding chapter it was argued that our social welfare system is built on both explicit and implicit assumptions about families and family responsibility. As expressed in social policies and social services, these assumptions are often based on myth, ideology, and economic necessity, with little regard for fact. To expand the theoretical framework guiding this inquiry, the issue of family responsibility must be addressed in more depth.

IDEOLOGICAL DISAGREEMENTS

These contradictions and ambiguities are clearly seen in public debate over the past decade. Sir Keith Joseph, a leading theorist for the Conservative Party in the United Kingdom, suggests that:

> They (the family and civilized values) are the foundation on which the nation is built; they are being undermined. If we cannot restore them to health, our nation can be utterly ruined, what ever economic policies we might try to follow. . . . The socialist method would try to take away from the family and its members the responsibilities which give it cohesion. Parents are being divested of their duty to provide for their family economically, of their responsibility for education, health, upbringing, morality, advice and guidance, of saving for old age, for housing. When you take responsibility away from people, you make them irresponsible (*The Guardian*, 1974:5).

In this country, both the Carter and Reagan administrations have argued that the social welfare system has harmed rather than helped

families. These charges are leveled at the social policies formulated in
the New deal of the 1930's and expanded in the Great Society of the
1960's.

Beginning in the 1930's, it was suggested that a succession of identified needs warranted public action in that they could not be effectively
met through individual action. Social insurance and Medicare are examples of this principle in action. It was also argued that family life was
enhanced by periodically relieving the family of certain tasks, and provision was made for homemaker services for the frail elderly and respite
care for parents with mentally retarded children. Finally, the common
belief held that professional skill and professionally derived standards
were central to efficient and effective service delivery.

Within this framework there was a belief in family integrity, and it
was assumed that families recognized their natural obligations to care
for one another. It was also believed, however, that families were
weakened or experiencing stress because of modernization, industrialization, and urbanization. These shifts in the economy created risks
and consequences that negatively affected the quality of family life,
requiring the State to create a system to minimize these risks.

Today, the opposite argument has gained considerable momentum.
The position of the administration, supported by neoconservatives and
the New Right, is that government efforts to improve the quality of life
of individuals and families are both undesirable and harmful in that
they invariably weaken families and create dependency. A recent example of this position is the argument that minorities are in a worse
position today than they were before the social programs of the 1960's.
If high levels of social expenditures had not been available, minorities
would have sought and found jobs, participated in the nation's economic growth, and found ways to be enterprising. Instead, they are
even more dependent on the public sector and further removed from
the American mainstream today than they were two decades ago.

Furthermore, these advocates conclude that families should not be
relieved of traditional caring tasks. When more and more social services
are provided to more and more families, families begin to feel that they
are neither capable of nor expected to continue their traditional responsibilities, and the inevitable response to this pressure is that they
give up more and more of them. An example is the position of the
New Right on social expenditures. Under the banner of "pro family"
they argued that:

> . . . families are strong when they have a function to perform, and when
> government takes over the functions of a family, then as sure as the night

follows the day, families are going to disentegrate and fall apart, because they have no reason to exist . . . today, we have well intentioned causes saying that we'll provide your food and we'll take care of your health, and we'll provide you with everything you really need, and then you can be a strong family. It doesn't work that way. We have seen the results of that kind of misguided policy now. Families are strong when they have a job to do (Marshner, 1981:63).

Finally, it is commonly argued that professionals are suspect in what they can actually do. This is the position of Christopher Lasch (1977) and Jacques Donzelot (1979), who argue that professionals are self-serving and invariably create dependency.

During the period 1932–1970 the State assumed a proactive stance to minimize risk and enhance social functioning. Today, this role and function is being redefined, and the State is increasingly assuming a reactive stance, i.e., it intervenes only when it is absolutely necessary. Proponents of both positions argue that their formulation of the welfare state is the most effective way to strengthen the family.

HISTORICAL INFLUENCES

To understand how opposing and almost polar positions can be argued simultaneously, we need to explore the underpinnings of each. How is it one group can argue that proactive social welfare measures are the solution while another can argue that the solution is to dismantle that same social welfare system?

In part, each is concerned with a different problem, and in part, each interprets events of the past by looking through a different set of glasses. While each group agrees that *social change* is the key to the puzzle, each disagrees about the nature of the change. Those arguing for a proactive State feel that social welfare will buffer *changes in societal structures and institutions* that are harmful to families. They accept the inevitability of these changes (i.e., those caused by industrialization and modernization) and attempt to build a new institution to help families function to their fullest human potential. Those arguing for a reactive and minimalist State see the need to cut back on social welfare measures because they have *caused the family to change.* If the cause of the change is removed (i.e., the welfare state), families will return to their earlier position of strength.

These perspectives are tied to the notion of community as it is today and as it was in the past. Before modernization and urbanization, families were the basic institutions of social life. As Demos (1983) suggests:

Families were the building blocks from which all larger units of social organizations could be fashioned. A family was itself a little society. . . . The family performed a multitude of functions, both for the individual and for the aggregate to which it belonged. Thus, most of what children received by way of formal education was centered around the home hearth; likewise their training in particular vocations, in religious worship, and in what we would call good citizenship. Illness was also a matter of home care (p. 164).

Warren (1978), building on Toennies concept of *Gemeinschaft* (communication is dominated by personal relationships and marked by its informality and spontaneity), describes earlier or premodern communities as self-sufficient. Families produced their own food, made their own clothing, socialized their own children, and provided necessary social and physical care for dependent members.

These earlier communities tended to be homogeneous, in that families had similar characteristics and held similar values. There was a strong belief in mutual support and community responsibility. If an individual family experienced a problem, other families stepped in. All of us can relate to the classic example of the "barn raising," where the total community came together to build a home or barn for a new family or for an established family when theirs burned down. As depicted in literature and in the cinema, families willingly gave of their time and resources to help one of their own. They did so with the understanding that if they needed help, they would receive it.

Is this what the administration and the New Right have in mind when they speak of the family reassuming its functions? Is self-sufficiency synonymous with strong families? How realistic is this scenario?

First, this form of community was not the norm for all communities. When they existed, they were agrarian. Family life in urban areas was quite different. As far back as seventeenth century England we find the State establishing in law, with its accompanying sanctions, the principles of filial and parental responsibility. The common wisdom was that families were divesting themselves of their "natural responsibility" to care for their dependent members. Later, in the nineteenth century, the State decided that even harsher measures were necessary to coerce the family to care for its vulnerable members. We find the following statement in the Report of the Royal Commission of 1832:

It appears from the whole Evidence that the clause of the 43rd Eliz., which directs the parents and children of the impotent to be assessed for their support, is very seldom enforced. In any ordinary state of society, we much doubt the wisdom of such enactment. The duty of supporting parents and children in old age or infirmity is so strongly enforced by our natural feelings, that it is well performed, even among savages, and almost always so in a nation deserving the name of civilized. We believe that England is the only European country in which it is neglected (Report of the Royal Commission of 1832).

But England was not the only country experiencing this "deterioration" of the family. The American colonies adopted the Elizabethan Poor Law including the family responsibility clauses. By 1836, all states on the Atlantic seaboard with the exception of New York and the southern states expanded family responsibility to include the legal responsibility of grandchildren to provide for their grandparents. Stipulations were later added in many states beyond the "consanguinal line to the collateral line to make brothers and sisters liable" (Coll, 1973, p. 21).

The first colonial almshouses and workhouses were established during the middle of the eighteenth century in urban areas such as Boston, New York, and Philadelphia. By the middle of the nineteenth century, all major seaboard cities had almshouses. And yet, even with the proliferation of these institutions, it has been estimated that only 9% of families unable to care for themselves were in them. The majority were either contracted out to another family for a lump sum fixed as low as possible, auctioned or sold to another family, or in some instances provided "outdoor relief" in their homes.

The picture of self-sufficient families living in supportive communities had disappeared in the urban areas of the eastern seaboard by the eighteenth century, and in all urbanized areas by the middle of the nineteenth century. We now return to the question raised earlier. How realistic is the current administration's proposal that families become more self-sufficient and that the care of dependents be an intrafamily or, if necessary, an interfamily responsibility? Finally, how accurate is the charge that the welfare state brought about these changes in family responsibility and willingness to care for dependent members?

The weight of historical evidence runs counter to this charge. "Deteriorating" or "weakened" families existed long before the introduction of the modern welfare state. The situation was endemic during the Poor Law era of the eighteenth and nineteenth centuries—an era that attempted, through repressive social policies, to coerce family responsibility. Even then, the pattern that emerged appears to have been a cycle of major and minor economic depressions followed by more families seeking help followed by greater expenditures for social welfare, and not the reverse.

If the cause of family change is not the introduction of the welfare state, as Sir Keith Joseph and Connie Marshner charge, how reasonable is it to think of a return to family self-sufficiency? Is this notion of community feasible or is it an anachronism—a form of social life viable in an agrarian society but impossible in an industrialized and urbanized one?

If the latter is true, and the evidence apppears to support this, self-sufficiency and community, defined as a clustering of supportive families, would require a radical transformation of society and not an exhortation to return to an earlier way of life. Unfortunately, nostalgia and, to some extent, myth, have become the basis for current policy formulation.

Those supporting continued State intervention argue that most western Europeans countries have had some form of public social welfare since the Reformation. While the specific system may have contracted and expanded over time, and while the form and level of provision may have changed, governments have made some provisions to meet basic human needs. By definition this does not mean that the State has been generous; that it has been proactive or that it always operates with the recipients of the services first and foremost in mind. The welfare state, whether that of the nineteenth or twentieth century, was a necessary creation as we moved from simple to more complex forms of society–specifically, from an agrarian to an industrial society, a society in the western world that is founded on the belief in a free market economy. As this system matured, the simple market economy gave way to a form of capitalism that we call state capitalism or welfare capitalism. The State has two responsibilities. The first is to support the economic system (this function falls under the term "political economy"). The second is to humanize this system, i.e., to develop a mechanism that will protect individuals and families from the inevitable negative aspect of the economic system (this function falls under the term "social welfare").

The modern welfare state, unlike the welfare state of the Poor Law, is based on the premise that as a result of significant social change, families experience considerable stress. However, there is no acceptance of the notion that the family has deteriorated and that in its weakened state it is unable to carry out those functions that have traditionally been viewed as family functions, especially as they relate to the care of dependent members. That family structure, family size, and role relationships have changed is not questioned (see Chapter 3). The argument that these changes are indications of family deterioration has little empirical support. In fact, the evidence suggests that during any period of rapid social change families have borne the brunt of the transition process, since it is more capable of adapting its structure and functions.

So much for philosophical rationales. If the purpose of the modern welfare state is to buffer the stresses that accompany social change, how successful has it been? More importantly, how is success to be measured? Willis (1978) offers a reasoned defense of bureaucrats and professionals as necessary agents for dealing with a maddeningly complex world. Featherstone (1979) expands the argument by suggesting that:

> The problematic, sometimes sinister, and often tragic role that professionals play in dispensing services in a multi ethnic and profoundly unequal society is one thing. The assumption that we can water down and dispense with these services we now have is something else. . . . There are two things generally missing from current policy perspectives. One is that many people do in fact need help. The second point is that public policy ought to be about helping to provide contexts in which people could help each other. . . . The challenge is to frame contexts which offer families more choices about the kinds of help they receive. Help should augment family life rather than diminish it. (pp. 46–47)

This position is an interesting one. As discussed above, the New Right and the current administration are arguing that families should reassume their traditional responsibilities. Featherstone appears to be in agreement, at least in terms of the desired end. Featherstone, however, rejects the notion that a drastic retrenchment of the welfare state is the solution. He does question the thrust and emphases of current social policies, and his position supports the arguments introduced in Chapter 1, including the need for supportive policies based on the belief in shared responsibility. The fundamental issue, then, is to develop mechanisms that will "provide contexts in which people can help each other." Is it possible to establish artificial means (in the sense that the social services are artifacts of the welfare state) to augment natural social arrangements?

In the context of this inquiry, dependent families will not be discussed, i.e., those situations when the total family becomes dependent on other families (the thrust of the Poor Law during the eighteenth and nineteenth centuries), only families in which there are dependent members. This dependency can be physical, emotional, social, or economic. It can be intra- or intergenerational. The dependency, finally, revolves around those family functions further identified in Chapter 3.

To what extent, then, can family members interact with providers of social services and social service professionals in complementary roles? Can parents interact as equals with teachers, physicians, social workers? Even though professionals by definition bring expertise that family members do not have, is the idea of partnership viable in the sharing of vital family functions?

To address this question, the nature of these social relationships needs to be explored in some detail and at a level beyond the somewhat simplistic and nostalgic descriptions that have shaped the position of those opposing the welfare state. One key is the notion of reciprocity.

RECIPROCITY AND SOCIAL EXCHANGE

Pinker (1973) has provided a systematic and extremely useful analysis of this issue. He begins with the position that "all social services are systems of social exchange" in which it is possible to distinguish between a "category of givers" and a "category of receivers." This exchange, however, tends to be unequal.

In general, if someone gives us something, we can never reciprocate completely, even if we give something equivalent in return. Why? While the giver gave voluntarily, the receiver gives under a sense of moral or psychological duress or coercion. The initial giver experiences a sense of generosity, the receiver a sense of gratitude accompanied by feelings of obligation. While most people prefer a measure of equivalency in social exchanges, "the relationship between a giver and receiver is always unstable and unequal."

Pinker extends the argument by distinguishing between nonsocial service and social service transactions. Using the example of borrowing money, he suggests that the borrower experiences dependency toward the lender, but that the dependency is temporary and ends with the repayment of the loan and interest due on it. He then argues that when one receives social services, the dependency is permanent in that it can not be repaid with interest.

Moreover, in attempting to be responsive to individual family differences and needs by providing highly personalized social services, the exchange risks making the receiver "acutely aware of his dependency." While more generalized and anonymous services might reduce this feeling of dependency, they risk being unresponsive to need.

Pinker reviews the works of anthropologists to see whether there are examples of preindustrial or "simple" societies where other forms of social exchanges or transactions were the norm. His conclusion: yes and no. A sense of obligation and reciprocity along kinship lines also appears to permeate these relationships. However, the issue of dependency does not seem to be as critical, in that interdependency was a total way of life. In fact, Pinker concludes that in these relatively simple societies, "systems of exchange are more likely to be based on norms of reciprocity between equals."

Pinker continues by stating that in industrial, modern societies kinship obligations begin and end within the privatized nuclear family, or at times and under certain circumstances, within the modified extended family unit. However, such societies are characterized by the belief that money is the basis of whether one perceives he or she is dependent upon another. The key is that simpler societies tended to be more egalitarian, since resources were usually not concentrated in a small number of families; more complex societies are characterized by social inequalities and class distinctions.

Where, then, does Pinker's thesis take us? First, the issue does not seem to be one of dependency, since it existed in all societies, preindustrial and industrial, simple and complex. Within the former, family members were dependent upon each other and families were dependent upon other families. This interdependency operated at times along kinship lines and at other times among neighbors. Within more complex societies, families no longer functioned within extensive kinship networks and found that mutual aid among neighbors was limited.

If the issue is not dependency, what is it? Pinker suggests that it is the nature of the dependency, the extent to which the exchange is among people who perceive themselves to be equal or unequal; the degree to which receivers are able to reciprocate. In simple societies, receivers were more likely to believe that they would be able to reciprocate, and givers gave with this understanding. Thus help extended to a neighbor in crisis was based on the understanding that the neighbor would reciprocate if necessary. The bond was a moral bond grounded in a sense of trust.

In complex societies, this reciprocity appears to be more elusive. While neighboring continues to exist (as documented by researchers such as Litwak (1965), neighbors do not have the requisite resources, including goods, services, specialized knowledge, and time that most families require. Given this, modern societies created social institutions (e.g., schools to share with the family the education of children; hospitals; to share in the care of the sick; social services, to share in meeting the social and economic needs of families).

Dependency still exists, but no longer is it only within and between families; it is also within and among primary social institutions. Is it possible for these new social arrangements to be based on the notion of reciprocity, i.e., a sense of perceived equality between the giver and receiver? Do the new givers, the professionals, operate on the assumption of mutual aid, and do the receivers believe that they can eventually meet the obligations they have incurred?

SUPPORT SYSTEMS: FORMAL AND INFORMAL

To explore the issue of reciprocity and mutual aid, we now turn to the issue of social support. The kinship and neighbor driven exchanges can best be understood within the notion of "informal" support systems; those social transactions involving social welfare institutions can be thought of as "formal" support systems.

Bronfenbrenner (1977) discusses support systems as the immediate ecology or environment within which an individual or family lives. This ecology incorporates people who influence and sometimes determine what happens to the individual or family. In general, the support system is made up of extended family members, friends, and neighbors; it may also include persons affiliated with more formal agencies, such as churches, schools, social organizations, and social welfare agencies.

More than by its membership, however, the support system is identified by what it does for the individual or family (Cobb, 1976; Kaplan, Cassell and Gore, 1977). At the most basic level, the support system is the primary source of love, care, affection, concern, and emotional support for its members. The support system also serves as a primary source of esteem and identity for its members; the person is valued as a unique and singularly important individual. The support system is also the locus of primary mutual commitment and personal sharing, which involves a shared history, a sharing of goods and material assistance, a sharing of responsibility and security.

Thus, while support systems frequently provide material and task-oriented assistance, they often extend beyond such specific forms of help. This distinction is important, for while help in the forms of goods and services may foster dependency in the individual, support also includes access to information which tends to encourage independence and growth in the individual (Cobb, 1976).

A major function of support systems is to help the family or individual deal with stress. At a most basic level, individuals without adequate support from their environments have been found to experience at some point in time "psychologic and physiologic strain" (Kaplan et al., 1977). Weak or inadequate support systems, in conjunction with stress, have been associated with higher incidences of depression, neurosis, and various other psychiatric disorders (Cobb, 1976).

Individuals who have inadequate support systems experience more frequent occurrence and more rapid onset of some diseases, and conversely, those with better support systems frequently recover from illness more quickly. A similar pattern has been reported with women attempting to adjust to the death of a spouse (Raphael, 1977). Moreover, Nuckolls, Cassell, and Kaplan (1972) found that pregnant women who experienced high levels of stress combined with low levels of support from family, friends, neighbors, and community were three times more likely to develop complications during pregnancy than women with low levels of stress or women with high levels of stress and high levels of social support. Finally, in a study of men who had been terminated from their jobs, Gore (1973) found that men who perceived that they had little emotional support from their wives, friends, relatives, and neighbors experienced significantly more psychological and physiological strain than their better supported counterparts, saw themselves as economically deprived, were more likely to engage in self-blame, and complained more frequently of illness.

The support system acts as a buffer to protect the individual from the most deleterious consequences of stress and stimulates the individual's development of strategies for coping with stress (Dean and Lin, 1977).

Another major function of support systems is to improve the fit between the person and the environment, to help the individual adapt to change in that environment (Cobb, 1979; Kaplan et al., 1977). The specific activities that persons in the support system carry out may involve the transfer of money or goods, and helping with tasks and responsibilities. The support system also sets out and communicates expectations for the individual; it rewards or improves appropriate performance, and may impose negative sanctions or comfort the individual when expectations are not met. Underlying these specific activities is the constant transmission of information to the individual that he or she is a valued and respected person.

What role does the welfare state play in creating or enhancing informal support systems? Can formal support systems intermesh with informal support systems such that the latter are not weakened?

SOCIAL SERVICES AND SOCIAL SUPPORT

One perspective on social services would argue that this is not only possible, but should be the primary purpose of the social services in a modern welfare state. This section builds on the above by recasting the theoretical and empirical research findings into a social service framework. Kamermann and Kahn (1976) suggest that social services can be thought of as those services that attempt to "facilitate or enhance daily living, to enable individuals, families and other groups to develop, to cope, to function, to contribute. . . . Still others offer substitute or safe or protected living arrangements. . . ."

Given this as a focus, social services have two primary functions: social development/nurturance and social control. These functions are concerned with improving the social skills of individuals (who may or may not be living in a family setting); enlarging the resource base of each individual's social network; enhancing the prosocial orientation of the network by linking the individual and family to mainstream community values and institutions; and providing positive control when necessary.

The social development/nurturance function closely mirrors the activities of the informal support system discussed above as they relate to family functioning. First, families can be viewed as moving through developmental phases, from childlessness through several phases defined by the presence of children of varying ages and finally to aging families. Each phase requires family tasks to be mastered, such as physical maintenance, protection, socialization, and the development of independent behavior.

Second, families are also viewed as small systems operating in relationship to other societal institutions such as the extended family, the neighborhood, schools and other service bureaucracies, the community, the world of work, and the marketplace.

Third, research has underscored the importance of linkages between families in need of help or support and available social supports. Supporting families, therefore, requires the development of liaison functions to identify and mobilize these resources.

Within this framework, then, social services are those services that in part (a) improve the capacity of families to master a broad range of developmental tasks, (b) improve the quality of intrafamily systems and family relations with external systems, (c) minimize potentially harmful stresses affecting the family, and (d) improve the operation of liaison or linkage functions related to social resources and supports needed by families.

In practice, the social development function begins to blur with the social control function when a family's capacity to meet the needs of individual family members becomes impaired. Social services, then, are introduced to restore the family to some level of adequate functioning or, in some cases, to provide services that, in part or wholly, take over family functions.

The initial framework introduced in Chapter 1 is now expanded. In that chapter we raised a number of questions to guide the policy analysis. They included the need to differentiate between services that support and those that substitute for families in the care of dependent members; the importance of identifying whether families were the explicit targets of the policies and if so, what types of families; and finally, whether the State, through the social welfare system, values the caregiving role of the family.

This chapter has attempted to expand on the initial framework by identifying the needs of families; the stresses they experience in carrying out their responsibilities for dependent members; and those areas of family life where formal support systems might effectively complement informal support systems. Finally, we suggested that the notion of reciprocity between the giver and the receiver is critical.

Pinker argues that receivers of social services have been placed in a position where they do not feel they are able to reciprocate—that the exchange is unilateral rather than bilateral. This, he suggests, has produced not only a feeling of dependency (which has characterized all societies), but a form of dependency that instills and encourages a profound sense of stigma which in turn results in the receiver questioning his or her self-worth. The issue then revolves not around dependency, but dependency without the opportunity to reciprocate.

The next four chapters explore these concerns in some detail. After identifying demographic changes that affect the ability of the American family to be effective caregivers, we focus on two examples: (1) families who have mentally retarded children and (2) families who have frail elderly members.

3 FAMILIES IN PERSPECTIVE

Attempts to identify policies facilitating the family's function as a social service are seriously hampered because many of the terms are unclear. Furthermore, there is little interest in systematically exploring these terms. On one level, the speaker or writer assumes that the terms are understood, that they are self-defining. On another level, as many definitions are offered as there are disciplines, and, while each is useful in a particular context, the policy process suffers in the absence of some meaningful synthesis.

In Chapter 1, the emergence of an ideologically divergent coalition concerned with strengthening American families was discussed. But what is meant by saying that families need to be strengthened or that families in their weakened condition can no longer discharge those functions that have traditionally been theirs? Such statements must be based on some notion of strength and weakness that goes beyond rhetoric, if they are to be useful for policy. A perception or belief is implied—that families were stronger during some earlier period and that policies should actively seek to restore them to their former position. But when were families strong, social-caring units? All families or only some? In the past, were the poor able to carry out these functions effectively, or was it a function primarily of the wealthier classes who had greater resources? Is the current debate concerned with reshaping family life in general or with rehabilitating that percentage of families which does not meet certain expectations or conform to some socially desirable model? The idea of strong versus weak is all but ignored in the public forum. If mentioned, the level of the discussion is either so abstract or so ambiguous that it offers policymakers little direction.

Most participants tend to agree that there has been a deterioration of family life and offer any number of descriptions of weak families. In the preceding chapters, social indicators were listed to demonstrate these negative social changes, e.g., divorce rates, child abuse, delinquency, and teenage pregnancies. Furthermore, additional indicators, such as increased geographic mobility and employment of mothers, are seen as contributing to these developments. Weak family units, then, come to be defined as those on public welfare; those in which parents abuse their children or each other; those in which there is a single parent—the "broken family"; those lacking in nurturance, etc. These approaches offer definitions or descriptions that are based on some concept of pathology or deviance. With this underlying assumption, it is easier to understand why so many existing or proposed policies are concerned with restoration—rehabilitation through treatment and cure. This approach, however, raises some serious questions. Are these appropriate indicators on which to base public policy? Possibly not. Bane (1978:10) questions whether divorce and the work status of women are problems. "The assumption behind this categorization (i.e., nonproblems) is that the ways in which men and women choose to marry, split, have children, or work are not in themselves problems. There are, of course, circumstances under which their choices cause problems for others, particularly for children." Furthermore, the relevance of the indicators aside, how are they to be used? Indicators are merely descriptions. They do not, nor can they, explain why the conditions exist nor suggest what should be done. Within the pathological model, these indicators are used to justify policies that attempt to rehabilitate or reshape those families with these characteristics—to make them more like "nonweak families." It is implied that they are the cause of their own problems, that they are failures. Such a view deemphasizes the need to examine systems external to the family and to develop policies and services that either reverse or minimize their impact on these family units.

Even with these caveats, what useful information do such definitions offer in attempting to describe strong families? It is not too helpful to be told that strong families are those that are independent, self-reliant, and capable of meeting the needs of their members. There are no families that can completely meet these criteria. While most families are not receiving public assistance, many are benefiting from various tax and housing policies. Few families are independent to the point where they have the resources to educate their children within the family unit.

Virtually all rely on the education system, whether private or public. While this reliance may be an oversimplification, strong or weak families are more likely than not to be end points on a continuum, and each individual, or for that matter, each society, perceives a desirable point above which independence is good and dependence unacceptable. Not only does that point shift over time, but the continuum itself is really a set of continua, and strength is defined differently on each, e.g., physical care, education, and economic maintenance.

While all would agree that spouses should respect and support each other, there is less agreement as to the balance between the identity of each individual as an individual and the individual as a member of a group. There are tradeoffs involved, and few guidelines are available. Furthermore, all would agree that children should grow up in a caring environment where their social, physical, and emotional needs are met, but few agree as to the specifics of such an environment. When "solutions" are offered, they often are simplistic or, in some cases, impractical. They range from recommendations that the welfare state be gradually dismantled to suggestions that working mothers resume on a full-time basis the more "crucial" functions of child rearing. Although simplistic in their analysis of causation, the recommendations appeal to large numbers of people who seem to need uncomplicated statements of why problems exist and what can be done about them. And yet, both of these popular solutions have little basis in fact. Retrenchment in social welfare assumes that intervention has become a disincentive. Families no longer are willing to provide social care but can be forced to become more responsible. In the words of Sir Keith Joseph (1974:5), a leading British Conservative and former Minister of Health and Social Services, "when you take responsibility away from people, you make them irresponsible." Carried to its extreme, this position argues that the State should be guided by principles of Social Darwinism as evolved in the nineteenth century. The problem with this solution is that similar analyses suggesting that families had deteriorated can be found in the nineteenth and eighteenth centuries, long before the emergence of the modern welfare state (Moroney, 1976). The argument for returning mothers to their parenting/homemaking roles is equally spurious. The same problems of concern today existed before women entered the labor force in great numbers. Furthermore, most mothers work because they have to, and if policies were developed to reverse current trends without changes in economic and welfare policies, the quality of family life would be seriously altered.

It is understandable that definitional issues are set aside and the debate confined to the abstract. Each American has a definition for the

terms "family" and "strong families." Unlike other areas of policy development, most of which demand some technical knowledge, each
individual, professional or not, considers himself or herself an expert
because everyone has or at least has had a family. Those who feel that
their own experiences were good define strong families in terms re-
flecting their own. Even those with negative experiences tend to idealize
the type of family they would like to have had.

For all these reasons, the public debate is often nothing more than
rhetoric that produces lofty idealized statements and slogans. As long
as the term "family" remains vague, disagreement is minimized. A move
beyond this level of abstraction proves disquieting for many. The apparent consensus evaporates, especially if specific objectives are debated. In one way or another, the concept of family and the notion of
developing policies to affect family life inevitably raise fundamental
questions about the nature and form of society in general, including
an evaluation of what it is and what it might be.

AMERICAN FAMILIES: CONCEPTS AND APPROACHES

Families have been examined in a variety of ways from a number of
different disciplines, including demography, sociology, anthropology,
psychology, and social psychology, history, and economics. Hill and
Hansen (1960) in an early review article identified at least five major
conceptual approaches, each generating its own set of definitions.

The *interactional* approach viewed the family as a "unit of interacting
persons, each occuping a position(s) within the family to which a number of roles are assigned" (p. 300). Within this framework, the family
is defined as a relatively closed unit, and emphasis is on internal relationships. Primary attention is given to role analysis, problems of status
and conflict, processes of communication, problem solving, and decision making.

The *structure-function* approach, on the other hand, sees the family
as one of many components in the complete social system. Within this
framework, attention is given to "the interaction of the individual family
member with other individuals and subsystems in the family and with
the full family system; the interplay of subsystems with other subsystems and with the full family system; and the transactions of the family
with outside agencies and other systems in society and with society
itself."

The *situational* approach views the family as a social situation for
behavior and focuses on the individual's behavior in response to the
situation. "The family, then, is seen as a unit of stimuli acting toward

a focal point (e.g., child)" (p. 301). Within the *institutional* approach, the family is defined as a social unit in which individual and cultural values are of major concern. "Continuity is assured for the individual's values and learned needs are transmitted from generation to generation within the individual family systems which make up the institution and from the more general cultural milieu in which the family exists." Based on this perspective, the family is often described as the most important social institution in spite of loss of functions in contemporary society.

The final framework, the *developmental*, is offered by Hill and Hansen as one in which the others are integrated. It is based on the concept of stages of family life cycles from rural sociology and the concepts of developmental needs and tastes from child psychologists and human development specialists. "Using these concepts, a number of well-defined stages of the family life cycle can be identified, each with its own peculiar sources of conflict and solidarity" (p. 304). These include developmental tasks and role expectations of children, the parents, and the family as a family.

This section examines these approaches and attempts to provide a foundation for examining the capability of families to provide social services to their members. Additional terms also are introduced to identify the existing conceptual problems. The first definitions discussed are those used by the Census Bureau. The federal government has been reporting on families since 1790 (Glick, p. 162, 1957). Prior to the 1950 census, a family was defined as a unit with a "head of a household and all other members of the household related to the head." Under this definition, the head of a household living alone was counted as a family, but a mutually related group of lodgers was not. In 1947, the bureau responded to criticism that the term "family" should be used only to refer to a group of mutually related persons living together and that every group of mutually related individuals living together be regarded as a family. Since then, a family has been defined as " a group of two or more persons who live together and who are related by blood, marriage or adoption." All such persons are regarded as family members, even though they include a subfamily. A subfamily may be a married man and his wife, with or without children, or one parent and one or more children under 18 years of age, sharing a dwelling unit of a relative who is the household head. Families are further classified by the bureau as primary or secondary according to their living arrangements. A primary family contains the head of a household among its members, while a secondary family is a unit without a head of household.

These technical definitions are introduced for a number of reasons. Census data are the best available source for establishing trends in families (it is critical to note the definitional changes mentioned above), trends related to family size, composition, employment, economic status, and so forth. They are, however, less than useful for other areas of research related to the family; they were not intended for such a purpose.

First, the unit of analysis is the dwelling unit and the household living in it. As Bane (1978:21) argues, "the Census Bureau definition of family does not encompass the relationships of people who do not live together but who may think of themselves as members of the same family, maintaining emotional, social, and often financial bonds across households. Nor does it encompass unrelated people who live together and who think of their household as a family." As structured, the census definition is not able to arrive at the prevalence of three and four generation families. Furthermore, by focusing on dwelling units, the census data have been used by some researchers to show that the nuclear conjugal family is the dominant form in this society. As Glick warned over 20 years ago, "the status of the family changes in so many respects from its inception to its dissolution that it is largely an abstraction to speak of 'the average family' in the United States as of one point in time" (Glick, 1957; Norton, 1974; Glick, 1976b). Yet this is done repeatedly by those who rely heavily on census data, since these are collected in a cross-sectional survey and cannot deal directly with family formation, expansion, and dissolution. The fault is not with the Census Bureau but with the researchers. While the concept of life stages is dealt with later, it is worth stressing that census data do demonstrate the dominance of nuclear households but in no way support the position that the nuclear family is the dominant form today.

The issue of nuclear versus some form of extended family form needs examination at two levels. The first questions the appropriateness of fit between family form and those institutions that have evolved in the industrial era as well as those emerging in what has been termed the postindustrial period. This is the question of adaptation and tends to assume that one form is superior to others. The second issue, less valuative in its beginning point, is concerned with empirical reality. Is there a dominant form or a variety of forms including, but not limited to, nuclear and extended? Depending on the evidence, what are the implications for public policy? This position tends to be more neutral than the first in that it does not favor one form over another, nor does it search for policies that directly or indirectly attempt to shape family form. To do so, to work toward a form of "idealized family type," is a form of social engineering that is both presumptuous and dangerous. To see public policy moving in this direction is to accept the notion that families basically exist to meet the needs of other social institutions, that they are means or instruments to achieve extrafamilial objectives, e.g., economic growth or social control. The counter position to this, the empirical approach, begins with the search for what is, assesses the intended and unintended consequences of policies on variant forms, and identifies policies that may support these forms. Within this framework, families are not means but ends, and other institutions attempt to meet their needs.

While both dimensions, appropriateness and acceptance, are really independent, to explore either requires examining both. Existing public policies are not neutral toward families. Within a policy, the family is defined to establish eligibility, to determine what types of services or benefits will be made available, and, as importantly, how the eligible family is expected to behave.

For example, the public welfare system deals almost exclusively with female-headed families, and its operational definition of a family is a "broken family." The educational system focuses on the student and defines the family as a unit supportive to the educational system's objectives. Families are implicitly evaluated on the performance of their children. If the child does not do well, the family, not the system, is held accountable. In the health care system, especially the part concerned with rehabilitation, the focus is on the needs of the individual patient, and in many cases rehabilitation personnel define the family in terms of the patient's needs. Home care programs for the chronically ill and disabled tend to view families as responsible or irresponsible, depending on the willingness and capacity of family members to assume the management of the patient. Furthermore, family members are often seen as necessary nuisances in the therapeutic process. An example of this is strong professional bias against the father in the process of childbirth, despite the increase of literature suggesting his value.

Sussman (1976) suggests that "definitions are made on the principle of utility as defined by bureaucracies with some references to canons of statutory and common law. Implementation of programs involve establishing guidelines for eligibility. Once a definition is established, bureaucratic norms require rigid adherence to that definition." In another paper, he argues that "perceptions and descriptions of families are determined by those who control human service systems, the overwhelming majority of institutions and organizations with which families have to deal" (Sussman, 1973).

The problem is further compounded by the fact that most policies and programs are not family oriented but are developed for specific individuals, e.g., the elderly, the handicapped, children, expectant mothers, mothers without husbands, the unemployed, and so on. Services are provided to individuals on the implicit assumption that if an individual family member is provided with a service, the entire family will benefit. While these services do affect families, the nature of the impact is unknown, since the assumption has not really been tested.

THE CASE FOR THE NUCLEAR FAMILY

Social scientists interested in the family have tended to operate on the assumption that societies (at least in theory) have organized their kinship systems along either conjugal or consanguinal lines (Linton, 1936; Parsons, 1943). From this starting position, it was suggested that these patterns are associated with existing economic systems, a stable agrarian economy being characterized as consanguinal and the more industrial as conjugal (Murdock, 1949; Nimkoff and Middleton, 1960; Osmond, 1969). Furthermore, the industrial society was likely to emphasize a nucleated system, with family units consisting of husband, wife, and offspring independent from other kin, while nonindustrial societies favored the extended family in which the conjugal units were integrated into a set of kinship ties (Kerckhoff, 1972). Finally, those who accept this position imply that the history of the family should be seen as the gradual decline of the large patriarchal family and the rise of the nuclear family through a natural evolutionary process (Parsons and Bales, 1955; Burgess and Locke, 1945; Ogburn and Nimkoff, 1955). According to this interpretation, the smaller, more independent family unit is ideally adapted to the requirements of industrial society, even though a number of more traditional family functions have been transferred to other social institutions in whole or in part.

For some social scientists, the family is no longer a fully self-sustaining social unit and has had to relinguish its economic (or at least has shifted from a production to a consumption unit), educational, and protective functions, leaving it with the responsibilities of socialization and emotional support of its members (Ogburn, 1933; Nimkoff, 1965). For others, however, even these remaining functions are no longer the sole responsibility of the family; they have been taken over gradually by the health care system, formal education institutions, organized religion, and, in terms of recreation, the commercial sector (Hauser, 1976).

Primary or shared responsibility aside, proponents of this evolutionary view stress the appropriateness of certain functions still under the control of the family. Socialization of children without doubt emerges as the major family function. Socialization is defined as "the

process by which persons acquire the knowledge, skills, and dispo-
sitions that make them more or less able members of their society"
(Brim, 1968:361). "The function of socialization is to transform the human raw material of society into good working members; the content
can be considered analytically to include an understanding of the society's status structure and the role prescriptions and behavior associated with the different positions in this structure" (Brim, 1968). He
and others argue that while the literature tends to emphasize the socialization of the child, socialization continues throughout the life cycle
as adults take on new roles (Cogswell, 1968; Sewell, 1963). Lasch, in a
review of the literature, states:

> As the chief agency of "socialization," the family reproduces cultural pat-
> terns in the individual. It not only imparts ethical norms, providing the
> child with his first instruction in the prevailing social roles, it profoundly
> shapes his character, in ways of which he is not even aware. The family
> instills modes of thought that become habitual. Because of its enormous
> emotional influence it colors all of a child's subsequent behavior . . . If
> reproducing culture were simply a matter of formal instruction and dis-
> cipline, it could be left to the schools. But it also requires that culture be
> embedded in personality. Socialization makes the individual want to do
> what he has to do; and the family is the agency to which society entrusts
> this complex and delicate task (Lasch, 1975).

Socialization, then, beginning in childhood and continuing through-
adult life, is concerned with knowledge, ability, motivation of individuals, and the transmission of norms and values across generations.
Furthermore, in the view of many social and behavioral scientists,
this process is best carried out in the nuclear family (Parsons, 1968;
Weinstein and Platt, 1977; Burgess and Locke, 1945).

A second function still retained by the family is the provision of social
and psychological support (Parsons and Bales, 1955; Berger and Kellner,
1970). The modern family, in losing some of its earlier functions, has
emerged as an agency specializing in emotional services for its members. It provides adults with an escape from the competitive pressures
of the market and at the same time equips the young with the necessary
resources to master those pressures. It is within the nuclear, conjugal
unit that intimate and meaningful relationships are possible and that
alienation can be countered (Carroll, 1973).

A third function is that of providing a stabilizing environment, one
that benefits individual members as well as society as a whole (Mercer,
1967). Segre (1975), moreover, argues that the nuclear family is ideally
suited for this, while only the "less privileged" need an extended family
for survival. Hauser (1976); building on Parsons' notion of social sys-

tems, hypothesizes that "the more rapid the rate of change, the greater becomes the probability that sectors of the social order will be characterized by anachronistic relationships and dissonance which may be represented in the attitudes, values, and behavior of the individual." According to this view, the reorganization of the individual, the family, and the social order is preceded by family disorganization (Sorokin, 1941). Hauser (1976:80) concludes that the nuclear family, unlike the extended family, can best adapt to these changes. While not agreeing that the nuclear family is superior, Vincent (1967:37) discusses the adaptive function of modern families. Given the pervasive changes noted above, he suggests that society needs a family system that is highly adaptive to the demands of other social institutions as well as to the needs of its own members. The family facilitates social change by adapting its structure and functions to these external changes.

> A major reason is that the family's strategic socialization function, that of preparing its members for adult roles in the larger society, is inseparable from its mediation function, whereby the changing requirements (demands, goals) of that society and its other social institutions are translated and incorporated into the ongoing socialization of all members of the family, both children and adults.

Social scientists who agree with the thesis that the family has gradually evolved to a nuclear form see this transfer of functions as desirable. The extended family retarded industrialization by discouraging individual initiative. Because this new form is more adaptive, more stable, and more mobile than the traditional family, greater advances in economic growth are possible. Moreover, the conjugal family encourages more intimate and supportive relationships for its individual members. Finally, by transferring or sharing functions with other social institutions, the family is able to concentrate its efforts in the critical areas of socialization and emotional support.

THE CASE FOR THE EXTENDED FAMILY

As defined above, the traditional or extended family was organized along consanguinal rather than conjugal lines, tended to be large, was both a production as well as a consumption unit, and was composed of a number of subfamilies whose needs were met through as interdependent extended kin system. Recently, two major arguments that run counter to the position discussed in the previous section have emerged. The first is that the extended family never was the dominant family form of the pre-twentieth century period, and the second is that most individuals today live in families characterized by extensive kinship interaction—a modified form of the extended family.

Historians and demographers are seriously questioning the traditional concept of the existence of an inverse relationship between the growth of urbanization, on the one hand, and the decline of the extended family, on the other (Hareven, 1974). Levy has argued that there is far greater similarity in average size and composition of households from one society to another, and even where the extended family represents the social ideal, it does not constitute the statistical norm because high infant mortality and short life expectancy limited the extension of the family either vertically or horizontally (Coale, 1965). In examining preindustrial England, Laslett (1965) demonstrates that only the more prosperous lived in large households and that a great number of one- and two-person households existed, the product of high death rates and poverty. Moreover, the hypothesis that the nuclear family is the functional consequence of industrialism, that the nuclear family is isolated from the larger kinship system, and that members of nuclear families are more receptive to change has been challenged (Rao, 1973). On this last point, Van den Ban (1967) argues that there is no empirical evidence to show that persons living in extended families or in families with a high degree of kin interaction are slow to adopt innovations. Finally, there is evidence that while the "ideal" form of the extended family was nonfunctional in the industrial period, the isolated nuclear family was probably as ineffective. Anderson (1971:198) suggests that a form of the extended family actually became viable in this century.

> . . . it was probably only after the introduction of the old age pension had transferred much of the economic burden of old age from kin . . . that a really strong effective and non-calculative commitment to the kinship net could develop and "traditional" community solidarity become possible.

Rosenheim (1965) agrees when examining the American experience. Where there were three-generational families in the last century, the living conditions for most of the elderly were substandard. Care was provided but probably not freely and often without affection. Given the lack of alternatives under the Poor Law, care for the handicapped was often perceived as something that had to be done. Conceivably, the early developments of the modern welfare state had a positive effect on the family, and, contrary to the arguments of some social scientists, actually strengthened family life. In removing the economic strain and establishing an income-maintenance floor, family members were for the first time capable of providing other forms of social support.

Why then this widespread acceptance of the theoretical belief that the nuclear family not only had emerged as the dominant family form, but also that it was superior to earlier forms? There are at least three possible explanations, each of which offers partial answers. Earlier it was suggested that, because of the manner in which the Census Bureau collects data, some social scientists have equated the nuclear household with the ascendency of the nuclear family. However, to equate families with households is spurious. Further, Sussman (1965b) suggests that many of the earlier sociologists viewed the world in dichotomies. Families were characterized as either extended or nuclear units, and theories were developed when the prevalence of three-generational familes was low. Lasch (1975) goes even further and argues that many of these sociologists posited the dominance of the nuclear family because it fit their theoretical perspective. In the sociologist's view of evolving society, the extended family was conceptually disfunctional. Its emphasis on cross-sectional analysis ignores fluidity, changes, and transitions as individuals move through a variety of family patterns. Most families go through extended and nuclear phases, a fact that is hidden when social scientists rely exclusively on periodic cross-sectional samples. Family types are confused with phases in the developmental cycle of a single family organization. As Glick (1957) has pointed out, families go through a series of characteristic stages between formation and dissolution. He identifies six such stages: marriage, establishment of households, bearing and rearing of children, marriage of children, later years without children, and dissolution through death. These stages have led him to conclude that the average family as of one point in time is an abstraction. Those who argue for the dominance of the nuclear family do so because it makes theoretical sense, while those who argue for the existence of the extended family are more empirically grounded.

The argument that the dominant form of family structure is not the nuclear family but a modified extended family is based on a number of facts: the existence of three-generational families, the amount of vertical and horizontal communication between family subunits, and the extent to which family members offer assistance to each other. While it is difficult to draw conclusions about the quality of these interactions from quantitative data, interaction is a necessary condition for emotional closeness and support. Sussman (1965b:56) almost 20 years ago argued:

> The theoretical position assumed . . . is that there exists in modern urban industrial societies . . . an extended kin family system, highly integrated within a network of social relationships and mutual assistance, that operates along bilateral kin lines and vertically over several generations. The validity

of this position is established by the accumulation of empirical evidence on the structure and functioning of urban kin networks . . . (evidence) so convincing that we find it unnecessary to continue further descriptive work in order to establish . . . (its) existence.

While Sussman reported on urban areas, Rosencranz et al. (1968) found the same supportive network in rural areas. However, in spite of Sussman's position that it is unnecessary to document this further, the evidence is not an integral part of our policy development. The evidence shows not only that families of all social classes tended to function in extended kin networks, but that the support included physical care, financial support, assistance in household tasks, and counseling. Furthermore, the support was not confined to adult children supporting their aged parents. Rather, it took the form of a bilateral exchange across generational lines (Lowenthal and Robinson, 1976; Sussman, 1965. Although it might be argued that these data are old and the studies preceded the social upheavals of the late 1960's and early 1970's, two recent surveys suggest that the same patterns are operating. Cantor (1975b) reports that two out of three inner-city elderly have at least one living child. The majority of children live relatively near their parents, and the two generations have frequent face-to-face and telephone contact with each other. Parents see half their children at least once a week and two-thirds at least monthly. Intergenerational support includes assistance in carrying out chores of daily living; advice giving; intervention in a crisis, principally at times of illness; and the giving of gifts and money. Remarkably, this survey was carried out in New York City, and the findings reflect the experiences of elderly from all social classes and ethnic groups. The second piece of evidence is offered by Harris (1975) and is reported in his national survey of the elderly (Table 3.1).

Table 3.1. Amount of Contact by Elderly with Children and Grandchildren (Percentages)[a]

	Children	Grandchildren
Within last day or so, incl. living with	55	45
Last week	26	28
A month ago	8	10
2–3 months ago	3	5
Longer	8	11
Not sure		
Total	100	100

[a] Source: Adapted from Harris, L. *The Myth and Reality of Aging in America.* Washington, D.C.: National Council on Aging, April 1975, p. 73.

Table 3.2. Ways in Which Elderly Help Children and Grandchildren (Percentages)[a]

	Do	Do not	Not applicable
Gift giving	90	8	2
Help when someone is ill	68	19	13
Care of grandchildren	54	28	18
Help financially	45	44	11
Give advice	39	52	9
Shop/run errands	34	54	12
Fix things around the house	26	60	14
Take grandchildren, nieces, and nephews into home	16	64	20

[a]Source: Adapted from Harris, L. *The Myth and Reality of Aging in America.* Washington, D.C.: National Council on Aging, April 1975, p. 74.

Over half the elderly saw their children with the last day, and slightly over eight in ten within the last week. An extremely small percentage can be said to be isolated from their children. The reality of intergenerational contact is further strengthened if grandparent-grandchildren interaction is included. Moreover, the patterns of support and exchange continue to be bilateral. More than four in five elderly persons help their children or grandchildren in times of illness; three in four care for their grandchildren; and more than half offer financial assistance. While the survey does not report on the amount of help given, nor the frequency, it does show the presence of an extended-kin network. Given that the type of interaction is similar to that reported earlier (in these studies the intensity is reported on), it is reasonable to suppose that the amount and frequency are significant (Shanas et al., 1968). (See Table 3.2.)

The discussion to this point has focused on intergenerational communication. Harris (1975) also reports the extent of horizontal interaction. Of the elderly with living brothers and sisters, 44% see at least one of them weekly, while 62% of adults between 18 and 64 years of age see one of their siblings weekly.

Data such as these have led a growing number of social scientists to argue that the isolated nuclear family rather than the extended family is the rarity. Most people are housed in nuclear units, but most people live in extended networks. Litwak (1965:189) has concluded that:

> In terms of the problem of maximizing available resources, the author would hypothesize that the modified extended family would be a more efficient unit than the nuclear family—all things being equal. This results because the modified extended family, confronted with a problem, has a greater pool of resources to draw on than the nuclear family.

The argument, of course, can be extended beyond the benefits derived by individuals. Earlier it was pointed out that most social policies are oriented to individuals and not to families. Furthermore, when the object of the policy is the family, it invariably defines the family as nuclear. To shift policy development so that the modified extended family is explicitly included would require a major reorientation and tremendous creativity, but would benefit the State in the long run. If successful, such a reorientation could result in policies that set out to maximize available resources, the natural resources of the family, and the resources of the social welfare system. Such an approach begins with a search for ways to support families by complementing what they are already doing—intervening directly and indirectly, but not interfering. To identify possible strategies, it is necessary to review the characteristics of families and the external stressors they are experiencing. It is one matter to define the family as a social service, a primary caregiver for dependent members; it is another to ignore the real issue to its capacity to function in this area.

CHARACTERISTICS OF AMERICAN FAMILIES

Families today differ significantly from those of the nineteenth century, and a number of these differences potentially affect a family's capability and willingness to provide effective social care for their dependent members—to function as a viable social service. This section examines some of the more critical changes. Given the focus of this analysis, we do not attempt to review all changes related to families, but focus on family size, women and employment, and marital status.

Perhaps the most notable change is the size of the family (see Table 3.3). Toward the end of the eighteenth century, the average household size was almost six persons, and over one in three households had seven or more persons. By the end of the nineteenth century, the average household size decreased to under five members, with sizable increases in two- and three-person households. Today, the average size of a household is three. Almost half of all households are now one- and two-person units, while only one in six are households with five or more members, compared to one in two 100 years ago.

These data are, however, on households and not families. As mentioned earlier, the Census Bureau changed the definition of the family, making trend analysis difficult if not impossible. These larger households of the past included servants and boarders as well as related members.

The information on family size, although of shorter duration, shows similar trends (see Table 3.4). Fifty years ago, one in three families had

Table 3.3. Number of Households and Percentage Distribution of Households by Size[a]

	1790	1890	1900	1940	1950	1960	1970	1980
All households (000)	558	12,690	16,188	34,855	42,826	52,799	63,401	83,500
1 persons	3.7	3.6	5.1	7.7	9.3	13.1	17.1	19.4
2 persons	7.8	13.2	15.0	24.8	28.1	27.8	28.9	26.5
3 persons	11.7	16.7	17.6	22.4	22.8	18.9	17.3	14.6
4 persons	13.8	16.8	16.9	18.1	18.4	17.6	15.8	12.9
5 persons	13.0	15.1	14.2	11.5	10.4	11.5	10.3	6.1
6 persons	13.2	11.6	10.9	6.8	5.3	5.7	5.6	2.5
7 or more persons	35.9	23.0	20.3	8.7	5.7	5.4	5.0	1.6
	100.00	100.00	100.00	100.00	100.00	100.00	100.00	100.00
Mean	5.74	4.83	4.60	3.67	3.39	3.30	3.15	3.00

[a]Sources: 1790–1940—Glick, P. American Families. New York: Wiley, 1957, p. 22. 1950–1970—U.S. Bureau of the Census. Current Population Reports, Series P-20, No. 291, Household and Family Characteristics, March 1975. Washington, D.C.: Superintendent of Documents, U.S. Government Printing Office, 1976, p. 3; 1980—U.S. Bureau of the Census, 1984, pp. 22–23.

Table 3.4. Number of Families and Percentage Distribution by Size[a]

	1930	1940	1950	1975	1982
All families (000)	27,980	32,166	39,303	55,712	61,109
2 persons	26.1	29.3	32.8	37.4	39.9
3 persons	22.5	24.2	25.2	21.8	23.0
4 persons	18.8	19.3	19.8	19.7	20.6
5 persons	12.8	11.7	11.1	11.3	9.7
6 persons	8.1	6.8	5.6	5.4	3.9
7 or more persons	11.7	8.7	5.5	4.4	2.5
	100.00	100.00	100.00	100.00	100.00
Mean	4.04	3.76	3.54	3.42	3.25

[a]Sources: 1790–1940—Glick, P. American Families. New York: Wiley, 1957, p. 22. 1950–1970—U.S. Bureau of the Census. Current Population Reports, Series P-20, No. 291, Household and Family Characteristics, March 1975. Washington, D.C.: Superintendent of Documents, U.S. Government Printing Office, 1976, p. 3; 1980—U.S. Bureau of the Census, 1984, pp. 22–23.

five or more persons, compared to one in six in 1980. A significant shift occurred in the percentage of two-person families. Even though women were marrying earlier in each successive generation since the turn of the century and theoretically were likely to have more children, the birth rate dropped significantly. Although it did swing upward between 1950 and 1960, it has begun to drop again in the 1970's. The average number of children per family 75 years ago was 2.9, and today it has dropped to 2.2 (Glick, 1957). (See Table 3.5.) This trend in fertility and its effect on family structure has had a significant impact on family life. In the middle of the last century, the average mother was still bearing children well into her thirties; by 1900, she had completed her child-bearing functions at 33, and by 1970, at 29 years of age. Unlike her predecessor, the present-day mother is likely to have completed her child-rearing function in her forties, although a growing number are postponing childbearing until their thirties and are raising their children in their forties. It is interesting to note that the birth rate per 1,000 women aged 35–39 in 1920 was 86, and by 1975 it had dropped to 19.4. For ages 40–44, the birth rate per 1,000 women was 35 in this earlier period and 4.6 in 1975 (U.S. Bureau of Census, 1960; U.S. Bureau of the Census, 1977).

One argument for these changes is that as a society becomes more industrialized it develops some form of Social Security or social insur-

Table 3.5. Birth, Infant Mortality, and Maternal Mortality Rates, 1840–1980[a,b]

Year	Birth rates	Infant mortality rates	Maternal mortality rates
1840	51.8		
1880	39.8		
1900	32.3		
1920	27.7	85.8	79.9
1940	19.4	47.0	37.6
1960	23.7	26.0	3.7
1970	18.4	20.0	2.1
1976	14.7	16.1	1.3
1980	16.0	12.6	.092

[a]Source: 1840–1940—Adapted from U.S. Bureau of the Census. *Historical Statistics of the United States, Colonial Times to 1957.* Washington, D.C., 1960, pp. 23, 25. 1960–1976—U.S. Bureau of the Census, *Statistical Abstracts of the United States.* Washington, D.C., 1977, pp. 55, 70. 1980—Adapted from the U.S. Bureau of the Census, 1984, pp. 34, 35.
[b]Birth rates are per 1,000 population; infant mortality rates are per 1,000 live births; maternal mortality rates are per 10,000 live births.

ance system. Without this, many parents, however erroneously, viewed their children as their insurance for old age, and the greater the number of children, the greater the insurance (Schottland, 1963). With collective Social Security mechanisms available, the need for large families diminished. Related to this was the dramatic reduction in infant mortality rates. Over the past 50 years, this rate has dropped from 86 to 16 per 1,000 live births. (See Table 3.5.) While data for the nineteenth century are sketchy, 100 years ago (1870–1874) in Massachusetts, the infant mortality rate was as high as 170 per 1,000 births (U.S. Bureau of the Census, 1960). One can only speculate what the rates were in the frontier states. The norm was to have a large family on the assumption that only a few children would survive. Another reason was the nonavailability and/or nonreliabilty of fertility control methods. The final factor is related to changing expectations and roles of women over the past 50 years. In the past, women had few opportunities for careers outside the home. Furthermore, prior to World War II, mothers were under heavy societal pressure not to work. Since then, not only has this sanction disappeared, but women have been encouraged for economic reasons to limit the size of their families. Large families are now viewed as a barrier to social mobility and to a high standard of living.

Mothers, having completed their childbearing function by 30, had the time and opportunity to begin or resume other careers, many with paid employment (Table 3.6).

In 1900, 20% of women were employed. Over the next 40 years, this figure gradually rose to 26%. The figures for married women rose from slightly under 5 to 15% during this same period. Older women (45-64

Table 3.6. Female Labor Force Participation Rates, 1950–1990[a,b]

Age	1950	1960	1970	1975	1980	1985	1990[c]
16–19	41.0	39.4	44.0	49.1	51.8	53.6	55.2
20–24	46.1	46.2	57.8	64.0	68.4	72.5	75.2
25–34	34.0	36.0	45.0	54.5	57.4	61.2	63.5
35–44	39.1	43.5	51.1	55.9	58.3	61.1	63.0
45–54	38.0	49.8	54.4	54.6	57.1	59.1	60.3
55–64	27.0	37.2	43.0	41.0	41.9	42.2	42.3
Total	33.9	37.8	43.4	46.3	48.4	50.3	51.4

[a]Data in percentage.

[b]Source: Bureau of the Census. *Current Population Reports. A Statistical Portrait of Women in the United States.* Special Studies Series P-23 No. 58, April 1976, Table 7-2, p. 28; Bureau of Labor Statistics. *U.S. Working Women: A Datalook.* U.S. Department of Labor, 1977, Table 61, p. 65.

[c]Projected data.

Families in Perspective

Table 3.7. Labor Force Participation Rates (Married Females),
          Spouse Present[a]

	1960	1970	1980	Change (%)
With children 6–17	39.0	49.2	63.2	62
With children under 6	18.6	30.3	48.7	162
Total married	30.5	40.8	51.2	68

[a]Source: U.S. Bureau of the Census. *Current Population Reports. A Statistical Portrait of Women in the United States.* Special Studies Series P-23, No. 58, April 1976, Table 7-2, p. 28.

years of age) were less likely to be in the labor force—14% in 1900 and 20% in 1940 (U.S. Bureau of Census, 1960). (See Table 3.7.)

These trends accelerated over the past 25 years, until 46% of all women between the ages of 16 and 64 are now employed. Further, it is estimated that by 1991, one in two women will be working (U.S. Bureau of Census, 1977). Even now, married women living with their husbands make up 57% of the female labor force, and the ratio of married to single women is over two to one. The reasons for this are multiple and have been reported extensively (Kanter, 1978; Ridley, 1968). While the specific reasons may differ by social class, they can be grouped under three major headings: (1) the need for income, either to supplement a husband's earnings or, in the case of families where the women is the main provider, to survive; (2) the need for self-fulfillment; and (3) increased opportunity.

Not only have the stigma previously attached to working mothers and exclusionary labor practices diminished, but women are not tied down by large families and extended periods of child rearing. The number of women in the workforce increased by 28% over the past 20 years; it has increased by 68% for married women and by 162% for mothers with children under the age of 6.

And yet, this freedom may be only temporary. Although child-rearing years have been reduced, the overall dependency ratio has increased during this century. Also, the composition of dependents has changed dramatically. In earlier decades children were likely to be our largest group of dependents. The elderly made up only 4.5% of the population, and for every older person, there were 12 children. By 1950, this ratio had dropped to one elderly person for every six children. In the past, children were making the major demands on the family; today they are sharing them with their grandparents. Furthermore, this ratio will soon drop to one in three. (See Table 3.8.)

These shifts in the dependency ratio are creating new pressures for

Table 3.8. Dependency Ratio 1910–2000[a,b]

Year	0–14 (%)	Over 64 (%)	Ratio of elderly to children	Dependency ratio
1910	31.5	4.5	1:12	45.4
1920	31.5	4.8		57.0
1930	29.0	5.7	1:6	53.1
1940	24.4	7.1		46.0
1950	26.3	8.4		53.1
1960	31.1	9.2	1:4	67.6
1970	28.5	9.9		62.2
1980	23.0	11.0		51.5
1990[c]	23.0	11.8	1:3	55.1
2000[c]	23.0	11.7		51.4

[a]Source: Adapted from *Social Indicators, 1976*. Washington, D.C.: U.S. Bureau of the Census, Department of Commerce. December, 1977. Tables 1/2 and 1/3, p. 22–23.

[b]The dependency ratio is the number of persons under 15 years of age plus the number 65 years and over per 100 persons aged 15 to 64 years. Projectives for 1980–2000 are drawn from Series II, which assumes a fertility of 2.1 children born per woman.

[c]Projected data.

families. In most families today, there is a significant gap in years between completing the child-care period and taking on the care of elderly parents. In earlier periods, as mentioned above, mothers often began caring for their elderly parents shortly after their children no longer needed them. Few mothers worked and the transition was simpler. Not only did fewer women work, but often families had unmarried daughters or other relatives living with them. This group, especially those between the ages of 45 and 54, was a considerable resource for providing necessary social care; they were expected to assume this function. This pool of potential caregivers has shrunk over the past 80 years. As noted above (Tables 3.6 and 3.7), over half the women in this age category are working, and almost half of mothers with children are employed. Moreover, 86% of married women between the ages of 45 and 64 are working (U.S. Bureau of Census, 1977). These women, once a major source of caregiving, are either unavailable or working and caring.

The caretaker ratio (see Table 3.9) has historically assumed two potential sources of care; married and single women between the ages of 45 and 54. In 1900, there were almost 97 women in this age category for each 100 elderly persons. Fifty years later, this ratio had dropped sharply, and by 1980, had reached the level of 46 for every 100 elderly

Table 3.9. Caretaker Ratio[a,b]

Year	Total elderly population (%)	Women 45–54 (%)	Rate/1000 elderly	Single women 45–54/1000 elderly
1900	4.07	3.83	966	76
1910	4.31	4.20	974	83
1920	4.63	4.55	983	94
1930	5.45	5.10	937	84
1940	6.81	5.72	837	72
1950	8.14	5.73	708	55
1960	9.23	5.78	625	44
1970	9.80	5.88	600	29
1976	10.50	5.73	561	25
1980	11.6	5.16	456	22

[a]Rates per 1000.
[b]Source: 1900–1950—U.S. Bureau of the Census. *Historical Statistics of the United States, Colonial Times to 1957*. Washington, D.C., 1960. Series A71-85, p. 10. 1960–1970—Adapted from U.S. Bureau of the Census, 1976. 1980—Adapted from U.S. Bureau of the Census, 1984.

persons. Shifts among single women in this age group are even more striking. Whereas there were eight single women for every 100 elderly persons in 1910, today there are only two. This caregiver pool, then, has been effectively reduced by demographic changes (shifts in age structure and marital status) as well as competing demands on time and greater opportunity for paid employment.

Another characteristic of the modern family with implications related to its capacity to provide social care is the growing divorce rate. Although this trend is used as one of the major indicators of family deterioration, such an interpretation is simplistic. There is no question that divorce is becoming a common occurrence. It is further projected that between three and four of every ten marriages of women born between 1940 and 1944 will eventually end in divorce (Norton and Glick, 1976). However, this trend has been accompanied by a sharp increase in the remarriage rate. In fact, it is estimated that four of every five divorced persons will eventually remarry (Norton and Glick, 1976). Furthermore, in 1973, 60% of divorces involved families without children, an increase of 5% since 1953 (Norton and Glick, 1976; Glick, 1957).

This increase in divorce (Table 3.10) can, in part, be attributed to changing attitudes and the liberalization of the divorce laws (Goode, 1975). For example, in 1973, 23 states adopted some form of no-fault divorces, 16 since 1971, and the Office of Economic Opportunity has provided funds for free legal services to a population that had little previous access to these services (Norton and Glick, 1976). In 1974,

Table 3.10. Marriage and Divorce Rates, 1921–1974[a,b]

	First marriages		Divorces		Remarriages	
Period	Thousands	Rate	Thousands	Rate	Thousands	Rate
1921–1923	990	99	158	10	186	98
1924–1926	992	95	177	11	200	99
1927–1929	1025	94	201	12	181	84
1930–1932	919	81	183	10	138	61
1933–1935	1081	92	196	11	162	69
1936–1938	1183	98	243	13	201	83
1939–1941	1312	106	269	14	254	103
1942–1944	1247	108	360	17	354	139
1945–1947	1540	143	526	24	425	163
1947–1950	1326	134	397	17	360	135
1951–1953	1190	122	388	16	370	136
1954–1956	1182	120	379	15	353	129
1957–1959	1128	112	381	15	359	129
1960–1962	1205	112	407	16	345	119
1963–1965	1311	109	452	17	415	143
1966–1968	1440	107	535	20	511	166
1969–1971	1649	109	702	26	515	152
1972–1974	1662	103	907	32	601	151

[a]Source: Norton, A., and Glick, P. Marital instability: Past, present and future. *Journal of Social Issues,* 32: 8–12, 1976.

[b]First marriages are per 1000 single women 14–44; divorces are per 1000 married women 14–44; remarriages are per 1000 divorced and widowed women 14–54.

33.6% of a national sample felt that divorce should be easier; 21.9% felt that the current system was adequate; and 44.4% would like to make divorce more difficult (Office of Management and Budget, Social Indicators 1977). Yankelovich reports that 63% of adults disagree, and 6% were not sure that parents should stay together for the sake of the children when the marriage is an unhappy one (Yankelovich, Skelly, and White, 1977).

Whereas most Americans feel that divorce is preferable to an un- happy marriage, that people who experience divorce should remarry, and that society stigmatizes the divorced less than it has in the past, it cannot be concluded that divorce does not cause stress (Hetherington, Cox, and Cox, 1977; Schorr and Moen, 1977). Divorce clearly hinders the capacity of family members to function as a social service. Of di- vorced women (including those with children under age 6) 85% are employed (U.S. Bureau of the Census, 1977). Not all persons remarry, and, from a cross-sectional perspective, even those women who do spend a considerable amount of time as the head of a single-parent family. Furthermore, it is predicted that one in two children born during the 1970's will see their parents divorce or have one of their parents die. However, few children are in single-parent families for their entire childhood; the average period is about 5 or 6 years (Bane, 1978).

Families headed by women who have no husband represent a growing proportion of all families (Table 3.11). In 1975, over 7 million families were female-headed families, double the number in 1950. Seven of ten had children, and one in four had children under 6 years of age. Twenty-five years ago less than half such families had children. Female-headed families represent 11% of all white families and 36% of all black families. Also, whereas in 1970 39% of the family heads were divorced or separated, 6 years later this percentage increased to 50%. Finally, these 7 million families include over 10 million children.

Although most of these women work, the average income of single mothers in 1973 was $6,000 (Sawhill, 1976; Pearce, 1978). Because women are viewed as marginal workers, they are holding jobs that are low paying, have low status, and are insecure. To compound this problem, 40% of absent fathers do not contribute to child support; when there is child support, the average payment is less than $2,000 per year (The Urban Institute, 1976).

Table 3.11. Characteristics of Families Headed by Females (Percentages)[a]

	1950	1955	1960	1965	1970	1975
Total (thousands)	3,637	4,225	4,494	5,006	5,580	7,242
Race						
White	83.1	81.5	78.9	77.5	75.0	72.0
Nonwhite	16.9	18.5	21.1	22.5	24.2	28.0
Size of family						
2 persons	46.4	44.5	47.1	46.0	45.3	44.5
3 persons	26.5	24.4	24.0	23.6	23.9	25.5
4 persons	13.0	14.8	13.5	12.0	13.7	13.9
5 persons	7.1	8.0	6.9	8.5	7.9	7.7
6 persons	3.3	3.7	4.3	4.4	4.5	4.4
7 or more persons	3.8	4.5	4.2	5.6	4.7	4.0
With related children under 18	48.0	55.8	56.6	57.8	60.5	68.0
With own children under 18	34.9	44.2	46.6	49.5	52.4	60.8
With own children under 6	10.4	17.3	16.6	17.8	20.0	24.5
With own children under 3	NA	NA	NA	NA	10.7	11.2

[a]Sources: U.S. Bureau of the Census, *Census of Population: 1950, 1960, 1970* and *Current Population Reports*, 1976.

The final trend affecting the family's capacity to provide social care is the change in expectations that people have toward family life and marriage. It was pointed out earlier that industrialization did bring about a change in the social order. Furthermore, this revolution, according to Goode (1975), continues to bring "pain, bitterness, and frustration" to many until the transition is completed. One area important to the topic of this monograph is the relationship between spouses. Bott (1955:15) offers two existing polar types; the joint and segregated conjugal-role relationship.

> A joint conjugal-role relationship is one in which husband and wife carry out many activities together, with a minimum of task differentiation and separation of interests; in such cases husband and wife not only plan the affairs of the family together, but also exchange many household tasks and spend much of their leisure time together. A segregated conjugal-role relationship is one in which husband and wife have a clear differentiation of tasks and a considerable number of separate interests and activities; in such cases, husband and wife have a clearly defined division of labor into male tasks and female tasks; they expect to have different leisure pursuits; the husband has his friends outside the home and the wife hers.

These are, of course, ideal types (in the sociological sense) of family patterns, and they highlight two important points. The first is the nature of division of the labor between the spouses, and the second is the nature of interpersonal relationships. In the joint conjugal relationships, decisions are based on mutual affection and agreement rather than on a notion of obligation and a belief that certain roles and functions are more appropriate for one spouse rather than for both. This emphasis on task sharing, a belief in the equality of the spouses, and an emphasis on mutual interests tends to be found in middle-class families, while lower-class families are more likely to be characterized by segregated role relationships (Kerckhoff, 1972).

Carisse (1972) touches on this same theme in an interesting study of what she calls "innovative women." She first suggests that three "ideal" types of society exist—traditional, industrial, and postindustrial—and that family life in general and marriage in particular will be defined differently relative to an individual's basic orientation. Carisse interviewed 150 working women and explored four major topics: the family as an institution, marriage as an institution, ideal parent-child relationships, and ideal man-woman relationships.

In traditional societies, the family tends to be viewed as the basic unit of social life, essential for procreation and best suited for socialization of children. Logically, the family is the major production unit. In industrial societies, the family is seen more as a refuge from the competitive world and a source of effective mutual support for its members. In postindustrial societies, the family provides an environment in which the individual can develop as an individual, can form significant relationships, and can invent a personal life-style. In this perspective, the emphasis shifts from the family as a social organization, with meaning and value in its own right, to the individual. A content analysis of the focused but open-ended interviews showed that 38% of the responses fit the traditional definition of family, 42% the industrial, and 20% the postindustrial.

In traditional societies, marriage is seen as necessary for stability and social order, important for the transmission of cultural values between the generations. Although in the industrial view marriage is accepted as a necessary social institution, divorce is also accepted. In postindustrial societies, marriage is seen as a free and mature act, preferably after a trial period, and should allow each person to search for and develop significant other relationships (including sexual). The responses were almost equally divided in this area.

Children in traditional societies are adults in preparation, and the adult's function is to provide a role model. Moreover, in shaping children for their future lives, it is important for women to devote themselves full time to child rearing and not to work outside the home. In industrial societies the child is also seen as a potential adult, but parents respect individual tendencies and are less authoritative. Creativity, progressive authority, and shared activities are emphasized. Furthermore, parents are to provide emotional security through an expression of affection. In the postindustrial society, each generation is expected to develop a new adult model; intergenerational differences are to be accepted; and parents themselves are not to live just for their children. It is here that differences emerge. Of the response, 44% were traditional, only 13% industrial, and 43% postindustrial.

In the last area, man–woman relationships, the traditional view is that women need protection and security, the male is naturally superior, and the female should be self-effacing in love. In industrial societies, the emphasis is on the equality of the individuals and complementary roles. Finally, in the postindustrial view, weight is given to communication built on shared values, meaningful exchanges, equality within and outside the family, individual development, and self-actualization through relations with others. Of the responses 16% were categorized as traditional, 44% as industrial, and 40% as postindustrial.

Of the total 740 responses (it should be underscored that percentages are not of individuals but of responses), 20% were classified as traditional, 40% as industrial, and 40% as postindustrial. It is these latter that

Carisse points to as emerging forms and new roles. However, the women interviewed did not neatly fall into one of the three types. An individual could, in fact, be traditional in her beliefs about the family or child rearing, industrial in another area, and postindustrial in yet another. This study was discussed in considerable detail, however, because it clearly shows the current ambiguity as well as aspirations most families are experiencing. It is also useful in understanding the stresses most families face, stresses that have implications when discussing the family's capacity and/or willingness to function as a social service. Moreover, Carisse's in-depth study of a small number of women has been supported by a recent national survey of families with children under 13 years of age (Yankelovich, Skelly, and White, 1977). In exploring many of these same areas, it was found that 57% could be classified as traditionalists and 43% as the "new breed."

In the first section of this chapter it was suggested that while the current debate assumes that many families have become weakened, that deterioration of the family is taking place, and that social policies should be developed to restore families to their previous position of strength, much of the discussion is abstract and has not generated meaningful directions for State intervention. Furthermore, when definitions are used, they tend implicitly to describe "non-strong" families in pathological terms. Consistent with much of the ideological underpinning of our social welfare system, this pathology or weakness is more often than not seen as the fault of the individual family unit. Such families are weak because they are deficient; something is wrong with them. Moreover, policies are often punitive insofar as they seek to rehabilitate these families—to make them behave or act in accordance with some idea of a normal family.

The argument was made that this definitional problem had to be addressed if policies were to effectively support families as basic social institutions. The literature reviewed showed that families have been defined descriptively/demographically (e.g., the Census Bureau) by function (socialization, physical care, mediation, etc.) and in terms of relationships (e.g., conjugal or consanguinal, nuclear or extended). Furthermore, it was suggested that these definitions have been generated to fit the needs of the definer (e.g., the bureaucrat and the professional) or to meet the conceptual needs of a specific discipline. Although valid and useful, they have not necessarily been relevant to the development of social policies. In spite of this, most if not all of our policies are shaped by the belief that the normal family is nuclear and that this family is made up of a husband and wife with children, the father working and the mother remaining home to raise the children. Most policies begin with this as the norm and define variants as deviant forms. These definitions, furthermore, are used to include or exclude families from services, to penalize or benefit certain families.

To extend the analysis, several trends or changes in family life and structure were examined. The analysis was shaped by two questions. Are present-day families capable of functioning as social services? Is it possible to derive a definition of family useful for policy development?

Although family structure has changed considerably over time, and socialization and supportive functions appear to have survived and, in the opinion of some social scientists, to have been strengthened in the twentieth century. In spite of earlier theoretical conclusions that the extended family has been replaced by the nuclear family, evidence indicates that the nuclear family is not the dominant family type. While there are nuclear households, these households function in an extended family network characterized by a high degree of vertical and horizontal interaction and mutual support

Families today are smaller than they were. When coupled with changing fertility patterns and significant increases of working women and especially working mothers, it is logical to conclude that families should be deterred from carrying out certain caring functions for their dependent members, especially the frail elderly and the handicapped, and yet there is some evidence that families are willing to, and even capable of, carrying major responsibility for these members.

Families are, however, experiencing considerable stress. For whatever reason, women in the work force are the norm. Whether they work for financial reasons or to achieve self-fulfillment, they are often penalized. In some sectors of society, they are told that in working they are not being good mothers, not providing their children with the necessary environment for growth and development. Despite research on maternal employment suggesting that children of working mothers are neither emotionally neglected nor unsupervised, and that in some areas maternal employment has positive effects—e.g., greater independence, scholastic achievement, and aspirations (Hoffman and Nye, 1974)—working mothers are often made to feel guilty. Moreover, this trend has not resulted in the blurring of the more traditional male/female roles in the household. In her study of professional women, Poloma (1970:87) found that:

> . . . the assumption of a professional role by the wife does not mean a drastic change in family roles. . . . The wife was responsible for the traditional feminine tasks.

Gordon (1972:93), in reviewing the literature, suggests this pattern to be universal and not limited to the United States:

> . . .women in socialist and welfare nations which indicate that while more women may work and have better jobs than do American women . . . their domestic responsibilities are not lightened to any degree . . . and thus are doubly burdened. They work full time and take care of their homes as well.

In a sense, divorce for many is a solution to an existing problem. This "solution," however, brings with it a number of stresses. In their review article, Schorr and Moen (1977) graphically describe the economic strain (44% of female-headed families have income below the poverty line) and difficulties in parenting (no one to share the responsibility). They argue, however, that much of this stress is externally caused in that these families are defined as deviant, discussed in pathological terms, in spite of the fact that the literature is inconclusive.

The final trend is the apparent change in values about marriage and family as an institution. Expectations are shifting, especially in the area of husband–wife and parent–child relationships. A significant number of women express a desire for a more egalitarian set of relationships and yet find themselves anchored in more traditional value sets. Furthermore, in most cases, other social institutions have not supported but have, in fact, impeded this development.

On a number of levels, then, families are neither in a position to be caregivers nor are they expected to be. Those families who do care for handicapped children or elderly parents are not part of the mainstream of American life. Values appear to run counter to this function, and, to some degree, these families can be seen as more "deviant" than the single-parent family or the dual-career family.

Deviant, however, is an abused term and connotes pathology. As discussed previously, these trends in family life cannot be equated with problems. A dual-career family, a single-parent family, a childless family cannot be defined as problem families. Some might be at risk in terms of having problems or undergoing stress because they are a certain family type. A working mother heading a family may have problems in her interaction with external social service agencies and the educational system because of their hours of operation. She may have a problem, but, if so, it often is with the system which tends to be rigid. Furthermore, what is the solution to the problem? Change the family or change the external institution? Similarly, what about families providing care to handicapped members? They have problems, but more often than not it is because the social welfare system does not support them. This is covered in the next three chapters.

Finally, the issue of defining family and families for policy is addressed. There is no one dominant family type. There are nuclear isolated families—units with few or no contacts with other family units; extended families—units which are residentially near other kin and high in functionality; and modified extended families—although the families are spatially dispersed, they are characterized by considerable interactions and exchange. There are families in which both spouses work; families in which only the husband works and the mother stays home to care for the children; there are single-parent families where the head works; and others where he or she stays home; there are families with and without children. As valid as these family types are in a descriptive sense, it is simplistic and somewhat counterproductive for policy development to divide America's 50 million families into these categories. Since most data are a cross-sectional snap-shot of families, families are assumed to be static. A more realistic (though much more difficult) approach is to recognize and analyze the fluidity, change, and transitions as individuals live in a variety of family patterns. There are periods in the life cycle when an individual family may be one in which the father works and the mother stays home with the children. This stage is relatively short lived when the total family life course is analyzed. There are periods, also, when women (and men) find themselves raising a family without a spouse present, but again, for many this is a transition period. None of these types or stages, however, should be viewed as the dominant or "ideal" family type. No one family type is superior to another or to be favored over others. Effective policies and services should be sensitive to the needs and stresses of certain types of families and recognize that some families are at greater risk (statistically) than others. Policies, however, should not begin with the assumption of individual pathology and deviance, but should explore ways to support these families. In a sense, the premise of this book is that to define a "family" in concrete terms tends to exclude many families and to favor implicitly certain types of families. If this were to happen, it would be counterproductive. A more useful approach is to recognize variant forms of families and to work toward strengthening these forms.

4 FAMILIES WITH HANDICAPPED MEMBERS

While the general concern of this study is the nature of the relationship between the family and the social welfare system in the provision of social care to dependent members, it was decided to limit the focus to one type of dependency—that caused by a handicapping condition. Dependency as such is too broad a concept to deal with in a way meaningful for policy development. It becomes unmanageable in that it could include almost 40% of the population (see the dependency ratio in Table 3.8) who are designated as dependent solely on the criterion of age, or it could include those members who for any number of reasons cannot carry out necessary functions and need assistance, e.g., the poor, alcoholics or drug abusers, those with mental or physical problems. Even the emphasis on handicapped members proved too broad, and the study focus was narrowed to two subgroups: families with frail elderly members and families with severely mentally retarded children.

A number of reasons can be offered to justify this decision. First, the size of these "at risk populations" and the pressures and problems faced by these families have serious implications for future resource allocations. Second, it can be argued that any shifts in the relationship between caregivers or changes in attitudes about who should provide social care will be first seen in these families. Over the past 25 years, and especially since 1960, the State has made a commitment to the elderly and the mentally retarded, and relative to other groups of dependents, they have been identified as groups to be given high priority in the development of social programs. Again, relative to other groups, there is now less stigma attached to aging and mental retardation. The former is a natural process, one which most individuals will experience, while the latter handicapping condition, especially severe mental retardation, is no longer viewed as the fault of the individual or family. In the terminology of the Poor Law, they are "worthy" of support. Given these factors, increased commitment of resources and decreased stigmatization, if there were a transfer of the caring responsibility from families to the social welfare system, it would likely be observed with these two groups of families. The final reason for this choice was the possibility of providing some cross-national data by building on a previous study carried out in the United Kingdom (Moroney, 1976).

This chapter begins with a discussion of handicapping conditions and then moves to a more detailed analysis of the two specific groups. It is estimated that almost 7% of the adult population has some impairment, and as many as 2.5% are handicapped.

Impairment and handicap can be defined in a number of ways, and, depending on the definition used, various estimates of incidence and prevalence can be derived. This study chose to use a functional definition rather than a diagnostic one. In Table 4.1, impairment is defined as lacking part or all of a limb or having a defective organ, which may be associated with difficulty in mobility, work, or self-care. Handicap is the disadvantage due to the loss or reduction of functional ability. Within this definition, not all impairments are handicaps. This approach is similar to the one used by the National Center for Health Statistics in its Health Interview Survey. Riley and Nagi (1970), in their introduction to a review of these data, distinguish between impairment (anatomical and physiological abnormality that may or may not involve active pathology) and disability (the pattern of behavior that evolves in situations of long-term or continued impairments which are associated with functional limitations).

Table 4.1. Prevalence of Impairment and Handicap, 1980 (in Thousands)[a]

Age	Impaired	Very severely handi- capped	Severely handi- capped	Appreciably handi- capped	Totally handi- capped
16–29	554	28	25	63	116
30–49	1,511	47	124	227	398
50–64	2,842	88	320	550	358
65–74	3,431	129	374	789	1,292
Over 74	3,714	338	527	746	1,611
Total	12,052	630	1,370	2,375	4,375
Rates per 1,000	67.99	3.47	7.68	13.37	24.52

[a]Source: Age specific rates from Table 4.2. U.S. Bureau of the Census. *Statistical Abstracts of the United States*. Washington, D.C., 1983.

Although the prevalence figures in Table 4.1 are derived from the rates found in a national survey carried out in Great Britain, it seemed more useful to use these rates than those from the Health Interview Survey, since they provide a much more detailed description of various levels of handicap compared to the United States survey. Moreover, this survey tested functional ability, whereas the other asked the respondents whether they were able to carry out various functions. Finally, when they are comparable, the two surveys appear to support each other. For example, the United Kingdom survey estimated that 2.5% of the adult population were handicapped, and the American survey estimated that 2.1% were unable to carry out major functions of daily living. The British survey reports that 11.3% of the aged population were handicapped, while the American percentage for the same group was 13.5%.

As mentioned above, almost 7% of the adult American population, or almost 12 million people, have some impairment. Over 600,000 persons are *very severely handicapped*. This grouping includes those who are mentally impaired or senile, unable to understand questions or give rational answers; those who are permanently bedridden; those who are confined to a chair, unable to get in and out without aid, unable to feed themselves; or those who are double incontinent or cannot be left alone since they might harm themselves. An additional 1,370,000 are *severely handicapped*. These include persons who experience difficulty doing everything or find most things difficult and some impossible. The *appreciably handicapped* (about 2,300,000 persons) can do a fair amount for themselves but have difficulty with some functions and require assistance. Overall, it is estimated that over 4 million persons are handicapped to some degree.

Given current population projections, the impaired population by the year 2000 will have increased by 40% (an addition of almost 5 million); the very severely handicapped by 250,000; the severely handicapped by 548,000; and the appreciably handicapped by almost one million.

Neither impairment nor handicapping conditions are evenly distributed across the population (Table 4.2). Sixty-four percent of all handicapped persons are elderly; 72% of these are very seriously handicapped. Furthermore, the elderly over 74 years of age are two and a half times more likely to be very severely handicapped compared to those between 65 and 74 years of age.

Data on children and youth are more difficult to come by. Riley and Nagi (1970) state that 2 per 1,000 under the age of 17 are handicapped. This seems a reasonable estimate, given the estimate of 1.9 per 1,000

Table 4.2. Impairment and Handicap by Age (Rates per 1,000)[a]

Age	Impaired	Very severely handicapped	Severely handicapped	Appreciably handicapped	Totally handicapped
16–29	8.94	0.46	0.41	1.02	1.89
30–49	27.84	0.86	2.28	4.18	7.32
50–64	85.08	2.65	9.59	16.47	28.71
65–74	220.24	8.28	23.99	50.67	82.94
75 and Over	372.60	33.91	52.92	74.90	161.73
Total	67.99	3.47	7.68	13.37	24.52

[a]Sources: Adapted from Harris, A. *Handicapped and Impaired in Great Britain.* OPCS, Social Survey Division, HMSO, 1971, pp. 5, 236.

for those aged 16 to 29. Again, it should be emphasized that, by definition, handicapped is related to functional ability and not the presence of an impairment. Most data reporting on children tend to report on conditions or diagnoses. For example, the Bureau of Education for the Handicapped has estimated that 6% of preschool children (0–5) and 12% of school-age children (6–19) have handicapping conditions (Office of Human Development, 1978). Three and a half percent of all children are speech impaired; 2.3% are mentally retarded; 3.0% have a learning disability; and 2.0% are emotionally disturbed. These children have, of course, an impairment, but not all are handicapped or disabled.

Taking the rate reported by Riley and Nagi (2 per 1,000 under 17 years of age), the total handicapped population is estimated at 3.7 million children and adults. This is a significant number of people overall; a population that is at risk has a need for considerable services and is potentially a high user of the social welfare system. In light of the discussion in Chapter 3, this group also makes demands on families, possibly heightens stress on family life, and, at a minimum, forces families with handicapped members to function differently from most families. Are families providing social care? Are families transferring the caring function to other institutions?

Since 1950, slightly over 1% of the population has been institutionalized (Table 4.3). These institutions, moreover, include nonhandicapped as well as handicapped. While there have been shifts in the rates of institutionalization within categories of facilities—e.g., mental hospitals and facilities for the elderly—the overall rate has been remarkably constant. Between 1950 and 1970, the institutional rate has dropped for each grouping below 70, with the largest decreases in the population under 15 years of age (Table 4.4). Although the data in Table 4.4 do not present rates of institutionalization in the same age categories

Table 4.3. Institutional Population (Rates Per 1,000)[a]

	1950	1960	1970	1980
Mental hospitals	4.06	3.43	2.13	1.00
Homes for aged/nursing homes	1.96	2.56	4.56	6.30
Mental handicap	.89	.95	.99	3.6
TB/chronic disability	.50	.35	.08	3.6
Homes for neglected	.64	.40	.23	3.6
Physical handicap	.14	.13	.11	3.6
Other	2.17	2.48	2.40	3.6
Total	10.36	10.30	10.50	10.97

[a]Adapted from U.S. Bureau of the Census, *Census of Population* 1953, 1963, 1973, 1984.

as the prevalent rates of handicaps (Table 4.2), it is clear that in all age groupings rates of institutionalization are significantly lower than rates of handicapped persons.

Institutionalization, then, is not the norm. Most handicapped persons, regardless of age, are living in the community. Some live in community facilities such as shelters or small group homes; others live by themselves; and still others live with their parents or adult children. It is this latter group that is important for the purposes of this study. The elderly will be dealt with in the next section, followed by a discussion of families with mentally retarded children.

Table 4.4. Institutional Population[a,b]

Age	1950	1960	1970	Percentage change 1950–1970
Under 5	1.0	0.7	0.5	−50
5–9	3.5	2.3	1.7	−51
10–14	7.1	5.3	4.4	−38
15–19	9.2	9.8	8.5	−8
20–59	10.3	9.9	7.8	−24
60–64	16.3	15.2	11.6	−29
65–69	17.8	17.7	16.7	−6
70–74	25.5	26.4	26.8	+5
75–79 ⎫		43.4	51.9 ⎫	
⎬	47.3		⎬	+49
80–84 ⎭		77.8	102.1⎭	
Over 84	94.1	126.3	179.8	+191
Total	10.4	10.3	10.5	

[a]Rates per 1,000 by age.
[b]Source: Adapted from U.S. Bureau of the Census, *Census of Populations*, 1953, 1963, 1973.

CHARACTERISTICS OF THE ELDERLY

Since 1900, the elderly population has increased at a rate far in excess of the general population. Although the rate of increase was greater over the first half of the century, the second 50 years will be characterized by significant increases in the older elderly population, especially those 85 years of age and older. While these trends reflect advances in medical technology and environmental and social conditions, the shift in the population has also brought with it the need to develop services and commit resources to guarantee the quality of life of this population. The greater the successes in overcoming the problems of infant mortality, in controlling the infectious diseases, in discovering and applying cures, drugs, and techniques that have saved lives and increased longevity, the greater the spread of long-term disability. The achievements and the problems are the reverse side of the same coin— the paradox of progress.

At the turn of the century (Table 4.5), the elderly numbered slightly over 3.5 million people, about 4% of the total population. Approximately one of every four elderly was 75 or older, and only three of every one hundred elderly were 85 or older. Over the next 50 years (1900–1950), the percentage of the population over 65 doubled, but the age structure of the elderly remained the same. Since 1950, there have been significant shifts in the age composition. By 1970, almost 4 of every 10 elderly were 75 years or older, a ratio that will be reached by 1990. At the end of the century, 1 of every 10 elderly will be 85 or older (Table 4.6). In 20 years' time, there will be almost 14 million people over 74 (an absolute increase of 6 million over 1970) and over 3 million people over 84 (an increase of approximately 1.8 million). These increases, especially in the older elderly, will create considerable demands on the social welfare system, since the elderly have historically been the heaviest consumers of health and social services.

Another demographic shift is in the sex composition of the elderly population (Table 4.7). From 1910 until 1930, 50% of the aged were

Table 4.5. Percentage Increase in the Elderly Population[a]

Population	1900–1950	1950–2000	1900–2000
Total	100	85	270
65 and Over	247	165	820
75 and Over	334	275	1529
85 and Over	387	473	2690

[a]Source: Adapted from U.S. Bureau of the Census *Demographic Aspects of Aging and the Older Population in the U.S.* Current Population Reports: Special Studies, Series P-23, No. 59, May 1976, Tables 2-1 and 2-4.

Table 4.6. Elderly Population as a Percentage of the Total Population[a]

Year	Total population (000)	Elderly over 65 (%)	Elderly over 75 (%)	Elderly over 85 (%)
1900	76,094	4.1	25.1	3.9
1910	92,407	4.3	30.7	4.2
1920	106,466	4.6	29.4	4.3
1930	123,077	5.4	29.3	4.1
1940	132,594	6.8	29.5	4.1
1950	152,271	8.1	31.4	4.7
1960	180,671	9.2	33.6	5.6
1970	204,878	9.8	37.7	7.1
1980	222,943	11.0	37.3	8.4
1990	246,106	11.8	39.9	8.6
2000	264,866	11.7	44.4	10.5
2010	281,288	11.9	42.0	11.6

[a]Source: Adapted from U.S. Bureau of the Census *Demographic Aspects of Aging and the Older Population in the United States. Current Population Reports.* Special Studies, Series P-23, No. 59, May 1976. Tables 2-1 and 2-4.

female. Even among the elderly over 74, there were approximately 92 males for each 100 females. By 1960, the ratio of males to females had dropped to 83 (75 for those over 74), and by the turn of the century the ratio will have decreased to 65 and 52, respectively (U.S. Bureau of the Census, *Demographic Aspects of the Aging and the Older Population in the United States,* 1976). Not only will there be more elderly women, but they are likely to be older than elderly men. The more

Table 4.7. Age and Sex Distribution of the Elderly Population, 1910–1995 (Percentages)[a]

	1910	1975	1985	1995
Total elderly population				
Males	50.3	41.0	40.1	39.6
Females	49.7	59.0	59.9	60.4
Males				
65–74	71.8	65.9	66.0	64.1
75–84	} 28.2	27.6	27.8	29.2
Over 84		6.5	6.2	6.7
Females				
65–74	} 69.7	59.6	58.4	55.6
75–84		31.1	31.6	33.1
Over 84	30.3	9.3	10.0	11.3

[a]Sources: Adapted from *Social Indicators 1976.* U.S. Department of Commerce, Washington, D.C., December 1977. p. 22; and *Current Population Reports,* P-25, No. 60, *Projections of the Population of the United States: 1975–2050.* Bureau of the Census, October 1975, Table 8. pp. 67, 77, 87.

significant differences are found in the over-84 group. By the year 2000, not only will there be over 3 million people this old, but 7 of every 10 will be female.

Over the past 25 years, there has been a consistent shift in the marital status of the elderly (Table 4.8). The proportion of elderly men who are married has increased significantly (U.S. Bureau of the Census, *Demographic Aspects of the Aged and the Older Population in the United States*, 1976). Even within the 1960–1975 period, the elderly, both male and female, were more likely to be married than they were previously. This pattern holds for both sexes. However, marital status differs sharply between the sexes. Almost twice as many men as women in the age group 65 to 74 were married, and three times as many in the older group were married. In 1970, 7 of every 10 men over 74 were married (an increase of 18% since 1960), compared to only 1 in 4 of women of the same age. If these ratios were to remain constant, by the year 2000 there will be almost 6.8 million women over the age of 74 without a spouse (single, widowed, and divorced). When the unmarried men are added, the number exceeds 8 million people.

While it is generally agreed that the elderly are more likely to be disabled and have higher rates of handicapping conditions than the general population, it is difficult to locate comparable time series data to measure historical patterns. The data reported here are based on the figures in Table 4.1. In 1980, a total of almost 2.3 million elderly were handicapped, 700,000 severely handicapped, and 360,000 very severely handicapped. Two of every three impaired elderly were female, and over half were 75 years of age or older.

Table 4.8. Marital Status of the Elderly Population (Percentages)[a,b]

	1960		1975		2000	
	65–74	≥75	65–74	≥75	65–74	≥75
Males						
Married	78.9	59.1	83.9	70.0	6,199	3,256
Single	6.7	7.8	4.3	5.5	318	256
Widowed/Divorced	14.4	33.1	11.8	24.5	872	1,140
Females						
Married	45.6	21.8	49.0	23.4	4,748	2,075
Single	8.4	8.6	5.8	5.8	562	514
Widowed/Divorced	46.0	69.6	45.2	70.8	4,380	6,279

[a]The figures for the year 2000 are estimated numbers (000's) for each category and are based on 1975 patterns. While these estimates are tenuous, they are included to show what the situation might be at that time.
[b]Sources: Adapted from U.S. Bureau of the Census, *Current Population Reports*, P-23, No. 59, p. 46; and *Social Indicators 1976*, U.S. Department of Commerce, Washington, D.C., December 1977, p. 22.

Table 4.9 presents estimates of the number of very severely and severely handicapped elderly for the period 1970 to 2000. They are straight-line projections, based on age-specific prevalence rates for men and women applied to population projections. By the year 2000, this group will have increased by 65%, or an additional 700,000 persons, of whom 550,000 will be women. Within 20 years, there will be over 600,000 very severely handicapped elderly. Three of every four will be female and over 74 years of age. Or, by the year 2000, there will be more than 230,000 persons who are either bedridden or confined to a chair, over 170,000 of whom will be women over 74, and 75% will be widowed, divorced, or single.

Over the past 25 years, between 5 and 6% of the elderly population have been residents in institutions at the time of the decennial census. Most of these people are in nursing homes, homes for the aged, and mental hospitals. The data in Table 4.10 include these three types of facilities rather than just nursing homes. While rates of institutionalization for nursing homes have increased significantly (from 19.6 per 1,000 in 1950 to 45.6 per 1,000 in 1970), this increase on face value is misleading. During the 1960's, many elderly patients in mental hospitals were transferred to nursing homes with the inception of Medicaid. These massive relocations were due in great part to financial reimbursement incentives, since the federal government shared the costs of nursing home care, while states bore most of the cost of mental hospital care.

Table 4.9. Number of Very Severely and Severely Handicapped Elderly by Sex and Age, 1970–2000 (in Thousands)[a]

Sex and age	1970	2000	Percentage increase
Males			
65–74	118	161	36.4
75 and over	176	272	54.5
Total	294	433	47.3
Females			
65–74	283	392	38.5
75 and over	489	932	91.2
Total	772	1,324	71.5
Both Sexes			
65–74	401	553	37.9
75 and over	665	1,204	81.0
Total	1,066	1,757	64.8

[a]Sources: Age- and sex-specific rates based on Harris, A. *Handicapped and Impaired in Great Britain*. OPCS, Social Survey Division, HMSO, 1971. pp. 5, 236. *Social Indicators 1976*. U.S. Department of Commerce, Washington, D.C., 1977. p. 22.

Table 4.10. Nursing Homes, Homes for the Aged, Mental Hospitals[a,b]

	1950	1960	1970
Males			
65–69	17.71	16.27	14.88
70–74	23.72	22.41	22.00
75–79	34.94	34.36	37.96
80–84	51.89	58.36	70.49
85+	79.97	95.20	122.98
Females			
65–69	14.25	14.40	14.55
70–74	23.55	25.13	27.03
75–79	39.93	45.33	56.35
80–84	65.40	84.51	114.22
85+	97.71	136.47	200.15
Total			
65–69	15.70	15.28	14.69
70–74	23.64	23.87	24.83
75–79	37.30	40.45	48.86
80–84	59.39	73.72	97.45
85+	90.59	120.38	172.45

[a]Rates per 1,000.
[b]Source: Adapted from U.S. Bureau of the Census, *Census of Populations*, 1953, 1963, 1973.

Institutionalization is clearly related to age and sex. Since 1950, the rates for the younger elderly have actually decreased, while the major increases have been in the population 80 years of age and older. In 1970, about half (52.2%) were over 80 and one in four (28%) over 85. Less than 2% of the population between 65 and 74 were institutionalized, but more than 17% of those over 85 were. Seventy-one percent of the elderly in nursing homes and 60% of the elderly in mental hospitals are women, differences that increase with age (National Center for Health Statistics, 1973).

The major reason for institutionalization is that the elderly (by and large the frail elderly) are unable to look after themselves or anticipate that they will not be able to in the near future. Admission is often preceded by an illness or death of the family member who provided care for the elderly person, or the elderly person has no family and is unable to care for him or herself (Townsend and Wedderburn, 1965; Brody, 1966; Gottesman and Hutchinson, 1974). Gottesman and Brody conclude that:

> Among those in institutions who have families, there is no widespread dumping or abandonment of their disabled members. The notion has been thoroughly refuted by the clinical and research literature. Prior to admission

of retarded, the mentally ill and the disabled, families are likely to have extended themselves over a long period of time to provide care, to have tried alternatives, and to have endured severe personal, economic, and social stress in the process. (p. 128)

These rates of institutionalization need to be compared to the rates of handicapping conditions (see Table 4.2). Twenty-one of every 1,000 elderly between 65 and 74 years of age are in institutions, while 83 of every 1,000 in this age group are handicapped. Ninety-two of every 1,000 of the elderly over 74 are institutionalized, but 162 per 1,000 are handicapped. These differences are significant, especially since it is unlikely that all elderly residents in long-term care institutions are physically handicapped (U.S. Government Accounting Office, 1971; National Center for Health Statistics, 1969). Based on current rates of utilization, which have to be viewed as conservative, and the projected age structure of the elderly population by the year 2000, it is likely that an additional 600,000 aged will be in institutional settings, assuming there are no shifts in social policy nor changing patterns of family care. Of these, over half a million will be over 74 years of age.

These numbers, however, must be put in perspective (Table 4.11). Between 1950 and 1970, 94 to 95% of the elderly population lived in noninstitutional settings. Almost all elderly persons lived in households, the majority in primary families. In 1976, slightly more than 28% lived alone, a percentage close to that of 1970 but significantly higher than that of 1950 (U.S. Government Accounting Office, 1971; National Center for Health Statistics, 1969). Women were 2½ times more likely to be living alone than men. For example, of the more than 6½ million elderly living alone in 1976, 80% were female. Those living alone are also likely

Table 4.11. Living Status of the Elderly (Percentages)[a]

	1950	1960	1970
In households	94	95	94
In primary families	76	73	67
Head or wife of head	69	56	54
Parent of head	15	12	9
Other relative of head	6	6	3
Living alone	18	23	27
In institutions/group quarters	6	5	6
Total	12,244,380	16,197,834	20,091,825

[a]Source: Adapted from U.S. Bureau of the Census, *Census of Populations,* 1953, 1963, 1973.

to be older; almost one in two are over 74 years of age (U.S. Bureau of the Census, 1973).

A large number of the elderly are living with their children or other relatives as their dependents. In 1970, this represented almost 2½ million elderly, of whom 1.8 million were living with their adult children. Although this percentage has been decreasing since 1950 (from 21 to 12% in 1970), the absolute numbers have remained constant.

While these data might be used to support the thesis that families are less willing to provide care, this conclusion is not warranted, since the age composition of the two groups differs considerably. In 1950, of those elderly living with their children or other relatives, 46% were 75 or older, and 71% were women. By 1970, 57% were in the older age category, and 78% were women. The 1976 data show that 62% are the older aged, and 80% are women. What seems to have happened is not that families are giving up the caring function for their parents who are handicapped (note the constant institutional rates over these same years), but that many of the elderly who are physically and mentally capable of caring for themselves are living alone or with just a spouse. Thirty years ago there was a housing shortage, especially housing for the elderly. Many elderly persons were forced to live with relatives. Today, those living as dependents are just that, while those living alone are likely to be capable of independent living.

The elderly do live alone, but usually by choice. Their preference has been and continues to be to live near their families but not with them. The elderly do want contact with their children and other relatives, and, as pointed out in Chapter 3, there is considerable interaction between the generations. By and large, the increase in the percentage of the elderly living alone can be interpreted as a positive social trend. As pointed out, the elderly are more likely to be impaired or handicapped, isolated, and have lower incomes than the general population. Fortunately, however, most of the elderly are not in these positions. Almost 75% are not impaired; 90% are not handicapped. Furthermore, a recent survey on the attitudes of the elderly provides strong evidence that, for most, old age is a positive experience (Harris, 1975). Older people today are more independent than in the past, possibly because of better health status, more adequate housing, increased levels of income maintenance, and expanding community support services.

Regardless of their living status (whether they live alone, with their spouses, or with their children), when the elderly person becomes ill or disabled, it is the family who is likely to provide care. Under each category of tasks reported by Shanas and her colleagues, children were the major source of help in one third of the situations. With the exception of heavy housework, the patient's spouse was the primary provider of care. It should also be noted that with the exception of help in bathing, one third of the care was given by children or others who did not live in the patient's household. When the elderly person was permanently bedridden, children were even more likely to be the primary caregivers (Shanas et al., 1968). In approximately 40% of these situations, help in housework, shopping, and preparation of meals was provided by children living in the same household, and in 10% of the cases by children living elsewhere. In very few cases were social services involved (Table 4.12).

Those who live with their children or other relatives are more likely to be older, female, and widows. They are also more likely to be disabled and need considerable amounts of physical, emotional, and financial support (Table 4.13). Whereas 12% of all elderly lived with their children or other relatives, 46% of the handicapped elderly did. Where the elderly lived was also correlated with the severity of the handicapping condition. Harris (1971) found that the percentage of the elderly living alone decreased with the degree of incapacity, and those with the greatest level of handicap were most likely to be living with their children. Men who are handicapped tend to be cared for by their wives, mainly because most elderly men are married (78%). Two of every three women, however, are widowed, divorced, or single and rely on children or other relatives. It must be remembered, moreover, that three of every four severely handicapped are women and three of every four are over 74 years of age.

To appreciate the pressures these frail elderly bring to their families,

Table 4.12. Percentage of Elderly Who Were Unable to Carry Out Various Functions and Received Help[a,b]

Major source of help	Housework[c]	Heavy housework	Bathing	Care of feet
Spouse	37	25	42	32
Child in household	18	19	18	22
Child outside household	15	12	13	12
Others in household	7	9	10	6
Others outside household	12	21	13	25
Social services	—	—	—	—
None	12	14	4	2
Percentage unable to do task or have difficulty	26	44	3	9

[a]Percentages relate only to those elderly who were assessed as needing assistance in carrying out these functions.
[b]Source: Adapted from Shanas, E., et al., Old People in Three Industrial Societies. New York: Atherton Press, 1968, pp. 113–120.
[c]Applies only to people ill in bed.

Table 4.13. Living Arrangements of Noninstitutional Elderly With
        Marked Incapacity (Percentages)[a,b]

Living status	Male	Female	Total
With spouse only	56	19	29
With spouse and children	19	5	10
With children only	6	37	28
With relatives/others	8	8	8
Living alone	11	31	25
Total	100	100	100

[a]Marked incapacity as defined includes those elderly who can perform the
following tasks with difficulty or are unable to do some at all. The six tasks
are: (1) go out of doors, (2) walk up and down stairs, (3) get about the house,
(4) wash and bathe self, (5) dress and put on shoes, (6) cut own toenails.
    [b]Adapted from Shanas, E., et al., *Old People in Three Industrial Societies*.
New York: Atherton Press, 1968, p. 217.

it is useful to restate what handicap means. The definitions used in this
analysis are related to functional ability, those basic tasks that people
can or cannot do for themselves. A handicapped person is one who
cannot do tasks that are taken for granted for normal living. A number
of frail elderly have difficulty and need assistance; others, the severely
handicapped, often need someone to take over completely.

One in six handicapped, an estimated 360,000 elderly persons, are
very severely handicapped (Harris, 1971). This group was defined as
those who were:

> . . . permanently bedfast or confined to a chair, unable to get in and out
> without the aid of a person; or are senile or mentally impaired, unable to
> understand questions or give rational answers; or are not able to care for
> themselves as far as normal everyday functions are concerned and need
> assistance. An estimated 85 percent of the very severely handicapped are
> in this category or slightly over 300,000 elderly.
> . . . need help in going to or using the toilet practically every night; need
> to be fed, dressed or washed; high percentage of those who are doubly
> incontinent. An estimated 15 percent of the very severely handicapped are
> in this category, or more than 50,000 non-institutionalized elderly.

Three in 10 handicapped, over 700,000 elderly persons, are severely
handicapped. This group includes those who:

> . . . have difficulty doing everything or find most things difficult and some
> impossible. Twenty percent, or an estimated 140,000 of the severely hand-
> icapped, come under this category.
> . . . find most things difficult, or three or four items difficult and some
> impossible. Eighty percent, an estimated 560,000 elderly persons, can be
> so classified.

The appreciably handicapped, numbering over 1,200,000 elderly persons, are those who can do a fair amount for themselves but have difficulty with some items. Given that these are rates for the noninstitutional population, and that the evidence supports the fact that many of the handicapped elderly and most of the severely handicapped are living with their children or other relatives, it is not difficult to imagine the kinds of pressures they create. The amount and kind of care may vary among families, but most behave responsibly and often heroically.

Sainsbury and Grad de Alarcon (1971) report on the degree to which families will tolerate severe burdens in caring for the aged. In a series of interviews with families who had been referred to a community health service, they found that 80% of these families were experiencing problems; 40% had severe problems. Two of every three elderly members of these families needed nursing care, and one in two needed it constantly. The stress on the family was evidenced by restrictions of their social life (50% of the families), decline in the physical well-being of the caregiver (60% of the families), and a disruption in domestic routine (36% of the families). Given these strains, the authors found it remarkable that the precipitating factor in seeking help was not the burden on the family as much as a fear that the patient's behavior was dangerous to himself. Moreover, more than one third of the families had endured the situation for over 2 years without seeking professional help.

Other research confirms the willingness of family members to care for their handicapped members. Morris et al. (1976b) found that 63 percent of families with severely disabled aged parents were willing to take the patient into their home and continue care after their initial hospitalization, a finding consistent with that of Beggs and Blekner (1970) as well as Lowther and Williamson (1966). This willingness is, moreover, long term and not crisis assistance. Maddox (1975) reports that among the elderly who receive care at home, one in four has received care for over 5 years, and 73% of those 75 years of age and older have required care for over 1 year.

Newman (1976), in a national study of older parents living with their adult children, has been able to document the specific types of stresses and strains associated with family care. Her findings are significant, since the sample covers a range of families, from those with severely handicapped elderly parents to those families whose parents are in reasonable health. In one third of the families there had been a net increase in the amount of housework and chores after the elderly parent moved in. Forty percent of daughters housing parents who required care devoted the equivalent of full-time work hours to that care. Almost 6 of every 10 families reported that they were spending more time at home and less in social activities outside the home. Twenty-two percent reported that their financial situation was more difficult since the elderly parent moved in, and 30% of all families expected it to get worse in the future. Forty percent made physical changes in the home, ranging from someone giving up a bedroom to adding or renovating rooms (e.g., ramps or handrails). An additional one in three families wanted to make changes but could not afford them. Forty percent of the families reported increases in stress, including interpersonal conflicts, and felt restricted, anxious, tense, and physically rundown. These stresses were associated with the functional ability of the aged parent: The more the child had to wash, dress, feed, etc., the more likely the stress. A re-markable finding, however, was that 90% of the adult children were mostly satisfied with these living arrangements, and only 7% were dis-satisfied.

This book began with the assumption that both the State and the family had responsibilities in the care of the dependent and especially the handicapped. In terms of the frail elderly, the family is clearly car-rying its share. Large numbers of handicapped elderly persons are living with and being cared for by their children and other relatives—far more than are in institutions. Evidence is available to show that the social, emotional, financial, and physical costs are considerable, and yet fam-ilies want to bear them. The State's function or contribution to the sharing of responsibility through the social welfare system is examined in Chapter 5.

FAMILIES WITH SEVERELY RETARDED CHILDREN

Families providing care to severely retarded children are different from those with frail elderly in a number of ways. Although the intensity of the stress and the nature of the demands are often the same (e.g., financial, physical, emotional), the differences warrant a separate anal-ysis.

The aging process is perceived as normal, one which most people will experience. Furthermore, even though a number of elderly become dependent upon their children or spend their last days in an institution, they were independent for most of their lives. Even the relatives pro-viding care for the 2½ million elderly living in families as dependents know that this will end in a matter of years and they can pick up their lives after their parent dies. In most cases, also, these families have led normal lives before these demands were made.

Given the medical and technological advances of the past few dec-ades, the severely mentally retarded child can be expected to survive childhood, and the majority will live an adult life. Parents are confronted with the possibility of providing care for the rest of their lives, unless they decide to place the child in an institution. For these families, a "normal life" has to be redefined.

As argued earlier, an analysis of these two different, but in other ways similar, types of families should provide some insight into the kinds of social policies that might be developed. Additionally, their experiences should be generalizable to most families caring for handicapped members. Services that support families caring for a frail elderly parent or severely retarded child should not be too different in principle from those that support a family with, for example, a child with cystic fibrosis or a young adult who is a quadriplegic. While the handicapped individual requires specialized services, the family is likely to need more generic services.

Unlike the issue of elderly and family care, there is little systematic data available for analysis regarding the retarded. An historical data base does not exist, and even current data often cannot be synthesized. Researchers use different categories and even different definitions in their work. Since 1973, the World Health Organization's classification has been used in this country. Four categories are currently used: profound (IQ less than 20); severe (IQ 20–35); moderate (IQ 35–50); and mild (IQ 50–70). A profoundly retarded individual requires constant care and supervision; while adults may achieve limited self-care, they need nursing care. Severe retardation is associated with limitations in motor and language development. While the individual may not be completely dependent, he or she will need complete supervision to develop self-maintenance and self-protection skills. Moderately retarded individuals are slow in their development but are able to learn to care for themselves. As adults they are capable of a degree of self-maintenance under supervision (Office of Human Development, 1975; Grossman, 1973).

While criticisms are made of a classification system based on intelligence testing, Tizard (1974:5) has argued that:

> For epidemiological purposes the value of assessing grade or severity of mental handicap in terms of IQ is very great. . . . Moreover, well established epidemiological findings indicate that the traditional distinction between idiots and imbeciles or severely retarded persons, on the one hand, and morons, feebleminded or mildly retarded persons, on the other, is a meaningful one biologically and socially.

The emphasis in this study is on families with severely retarded children, defined as those with IQs 0–50. Abramowicz and Richardson

(1970), in reviewing 20 of the more "reliable" epidemiological surveys, have concluded that the prevalence of severe retardation is somewhere between 3 and 5 per 1,000 population. Conley (1973) has offered age-specific prevalence rates which show slightly higher rates for children than adults.

The prevalence of severe mental retardation shown in Table 4.14 is drawn from the studies of Tizard (1974) and Kushlick (1964). Although they are slightly more conservative than Conley's estimates, they have the advantage of being replicated a number of times. The peak prevalence rate is estimated at 3.6 per 1,000 persons aged 15 to 19. This prevalence rate is probably close to the true prevalence rate for all age groups up to 15, insofar as severe retardation is almost always present from birth or early infancy (Tizard, 1974).

Given these rates, it can be estimated that there will be 620,000 severely retarded persons in the United States by 1990. Over 200,000 will be severely retarded children.

The projections for the next 15 years are based on extremely conservative assumptions. They begin with the position that the prevalence among children will not increase substantially (Tizard, 1972), and that the possibilities of preventing severe retardation are limited, given current knowledge (Department of Health and Social Services, Better Services for the Mentally Handicapped, 1971). The projections further assume that the ratio of children to adults will remain the same, 1:2, although, as many more severely retarded children now are surviving

Table 4.14. Estimated Prevalence of Severe Mental Retardation (in Thousands)[a,b]

Year	Under 15	15 and over	Total
1950	146	243	389
1960	200	271	471
1970	208	320	528
1980	184	377	561
1990	209	411	620
2000	211	449	660

[a]The rates used were: For the population under 15 years of age, 3.6 per 1,000; for the population over 14, 2.2 per 1,000, giving a total prevalence rate of 2.5 per 1,000.

[b]Sources: Population figures for 1950–2000 were derived from Social Indicators 1976. Office of Management and Budget, Washington, D.C., December 1977. p. 22.

to adult life, the number of adult retardates is increasing (Tizard, 1972). Therefore, the rate of 2.2 per 1,000 for the population over 14 years of age will possibly be higher. Regardless, the figures are useful, especially for the younger age group, and offer reasonable estimates for planning future services.

Severe retardation usually brings with it a range of physical disorders such as epilepsy, and visual, hearing, and speech defects. Abramowicz and Richardson (1970) found that approximately half of all severely retarded persons have at least one additional handicap, and that one in four have multiple associated handicaps. Their findings are supported by other studies (Conroy and Derr, 1971; Tizard and Grad de Alarcon, 1961; Moncrieff, 1966; Bayley, 1973). Table 4.15 gives estimates of type and degree of physical and behavioral difficulties associated with severe retardation. The Kushlick rates are used in this study, since Kushlick reports on functional disability, is specific to severe mental retardation, and documents the differences between children and adults. The Abramowicz and Richardson or Conroy and Derr studies were not used, since these researchers reported on diagnostic categories and did not distinguish between levels of retardation.

One in five of all severely retarded persons needs assistance in personal care functions; one in eight has severe behavioral problems, and one in fourteen is incontinent. With the exception of behavior problems, those under 15 years of age are more likely to have associated handicaps. Children are twice as likely to be incontinent and need assistance in personal care functions and four times more likely to be nonambulant. Of the severely mentally retarded children 80% are likely to have a physical or behavioral problem, compared to 40% of the severely retarded adults.

Based on the prevalence rate of 3.6 per 1,000 for this age group,

Table 4.15. Incapacity Associated with Severe Mental Retardation[a]

Incapacity	Under 15	15 and over	Total
Nonambulatory	24.06	6.23	11.45
Behavior difficulties requiring constant supervision	14.06	11.23	12.06
Severely incontinent	12.55	5.20	7.34
Needing assistance to feed, wash, and dress	28.33	15.29	19.25
No physical handicap or severe behavior difficulties	21.00	61.85	49.90
Total	100.00	100.00	100.00

[a]Source: Adapted from Better Services for the Mentally Handicapped. Cmnd 4683, HMSO, 1971. Table 1, p. 6.

over 44,000 severely mentally retarded children are nonambulant; 52,000 need assistance in feeding, washing, and dressing; 23,000 are severely incontinent; and almost 26,000 have severe behavioral problems.

Severe mental retardation is not, then, just a measurement of the intelligence level of an individual. For children it means that someone has to provide care and supervision over and above what "normal" children require. This decision to maintain the child in the family setting seriously affects the family life of the other members.

One of the more critical areas affected is the physical health of the primary caregiver. Hewett (1972) and Tizard and Grad de Alarcon (1961) found that 14% of mothers with severely retarded children were in poor health, 12% were run down, and 60% experienced periods of depression. Holt (1958) found almost one in five mothers exhausted at the time of her survey. The presence of a severely retarded child means additional household chores (Aldrich et al., 1971, report that 44% of mothers interviewed felt these additional chores were excessive) and considerable demands on the parents' time in general (Dunlap, 1976).

These demands, coupled with other sources of stress, often result in high degrees of social isolation. Holt (1958) found that 66% of families were noticeably isolated. Furthermore, 74% of parents of severely retarded children felt that their neighbors objected to the handicapped child associating with their children. What is even more telling is that in 40% of these families, the parents were never able to go out together. These findings were supported by other researchers who report that normal social contacts were limited in 50% of families with severely retarded children, and in 15%, social contacts were severely limited (Tizard and Grad de Alarcon, 1961). In their survey conducted in Washington State, Aldrich et al. (1971) found that the presence of a retarded child adversely affected vacations (36% of the families), geographic mobility (33%), recreation (38%), social activities (32%), and ease of obtaining babysitters (28%). These findings are supported by a large number of other studies. The parents felt isolated and stigmatized. Whether they were actually rejected by the community or had chosen isolation themselves is not clear (Schonell and Watts, 1956; Kershaw, 1965; Peck and Stephens, 1960; Gottlieb, 1975; Justice, Bradley, and O'Connor, 1971).

A third area of stress is financial. Handicapped children obviously cost more to raise and care for than nonhandicapped children. How much the additional costs are, however, remains unknown. Aldrich et al. (1971) found in 44% of families that financial problems associated with the care of a retarded child adversely affected the family's lifestyle. In their studies, Holt (1958) reports that 29% were faced with additional expenses, and Dunlap (1976), 27%.

It is also known that the severity of the retardation is correlated with levels of personal expenditures. Although the data as presented are difficult to use, Aldrich demonstrates that parents with children who are profoundly or severely retarded are much more likely to spend over $5,000 (the categories used are $1–$100, $101–$1,000, $1,001–$5,000, and over $5,000) for services, while those with mildly retarded children are likely to spend significantly lower amounts (Aldrich et al., 1971). The study, however, is severely limited in that age is not controlled for and these cost figures on lifetime expenditures have not been standardized. One study, restricted to medical care expenditures, is significant. Although the data include a range of chronic illnesses and levels of severity. Sultz and his colleagues provide the type of detail useful for analysis (Sultz et al., 1972). They found, for example, that these families spent, on the average, 6.6% of their mean gross income for medical care for the chronically ill child, and 16% reported medical expenses exceeding 15% of their annual income. At the time of the survey, mean out-of-pocket expenses for American families (care for all members) amounted to only 5.5%.

Sultz was also able to show that reported medical costs varied little by level of family income but that out-of-pocket expenses as a percentage of family income were significantly higher for low-income families. Families in the lowest income bracket were expending 16.5% of family income for medical care, compared to only 4.1% for those in the highest bracket. Furthermore, those with higher family incomes benefit from income tax policies. (See Table 4.16.)

Finally, the presence of a handicapped child creates stress in family relationships. Wolfensberger (1967:34) suggests that the family of a retarded child is faced with three types of crises. The first crisis is that which is most likely to occur when the diagnosis is made to an unsuspecting parent.

Table 4.16. Mean Costs for Total and Out-of-Pocket Medical Expenses, 1970[a]

Expenses	Gross family income							
	<$3,500		$3,500–$4,999		$5,000–$7,499		$7,500 and Over	
	$	Income (%)	$	Income (%)	$	Income (%)	$	Income (%)
Total	1,141	46.8	1,134	26.5	1,026	17,2	896	8.9
Out-of-Pocket	405	16.5	404	9.6	477	7.9	404	4.1

[a]Source: Adapted from Sultz, H., et al., *Long-Term Childhood Illness*. Pittsburgh: University of Pittsburgh, 1972, Table 6.4.

At a point of great vulnerability, an unexpected event disorganizes the parents' adjustment as when they are told that their baby is a "mongolian idiot." The parents realize that the event is rare and that their expectations have to be radically revised, but they know virtually nothing about what the realistic expectancies now are. The crucial element here is not retardation at all; it is the demolition of expectancies.

The second crisis is described as a value crisis.

Retardation and its manifestations are unacceptable to many persons for a number of reasons. . . . Fear of social and abhorrence of physical stigma, censure by inlaws, feelings of guilt or failure, and other essentially subjectively determined anguish may contribute to the value crisis. (p.35)

The third is the reality crisis.

Forces external to and only partially controllable by the parents result in situations that make it impossible, exceedingly difficult, or inadvisable for the retardate to remain integrated into the family or the community.(p. 35)

Some researchers have argued that parents of a handicapped child experience severe strains, often resulting in marital breakdown (Bone, Spain, and Martin, 1972; Farber, 1975; Farber and Ryckman, 1965; Farber, Jenne, and Toigo, 1960; Farber, 1960). Parents have been described as both angry and guilty—angry that it has happened to them and guilty that they might be responsible (Cohen, 1962; Reid, 1958). Another speaks of the "chronic sorrow" parents live with (Olshansky, 1962). The trauma that brings on bitterness, guilt, and shame in turn contributes to serious emotional problems, quarreling, and, in a number of cases, disintegration of family relationships. These strains are felt by more than the handicapped child's parents. A number of parents felt that their normal children were experiencing problems, including role tensions (Fowle, 1968; Tew and Laurence, 1973a). Holt (1958) found that some siblings resent their parents paying too much attention to the handicapped child, and often they are embarrassed when interacting with their peers.

It is a gross understatement to say that these families are "at risk." The problems and demands that they are experiencing are staggering. For two sets of reasons, it is reasonable to expect that most families with severely retarded children would seek to institutionalize them. The first is that throughout this century, especially the first 60 years, official policy and professional practice have supported institutionalization as the most desirable alternative. Families who did decide on institutionalization were not likely to be stigmatized. In fact, the evidence seems to suggest the opposite. Families who decided to care for the retarded child felt isolated from the rest of the community. The second is related to the changing expectations and aspirations of women—historically the primary caregivers in this society. In Chapter 3, Carisse's study of "innovative women" was discussed. Within her framework of three basic value orientations, only women with traditional values toward marriage, family, and child care can be expected to willingly provide care for their severely retarded children. Women with traditional or preindustrial orientations accept their dependency on their spouses, believe the male should be the primary wage earner, and, most importantly, feel that women should devote full time to child rearing. In a postindustrial society, these values are nonexistent or at least deemphasized. As mentioned above, the family provides an environment for individual growth and development. The family as a social organization is secondary to the individual. Parents as individuals are not expected to live for their children, and tasks or functions are not sexually determined. Moreover, self-development is best achieved through extrafamilial relationships and, in most instances, through paid employment.

Caring for a retarded child is contrary to these values. Parents, especially mothers, live for their handicapped children. Extrafamilial activities, whether social or recreational, are curtailed. Individual life-styles and self-fulfillment (postindustrial) are difficult if not impossible, since so much time and attention are given to the handicapped member of the family. The wife and mother is especially penalized since it is she who most often becomes the caregiver.

Given these shifts in values and the probability of a high degree of ambivalence among adults during this period of transition and social upheaval, it can be argued that decisions to maintain a severely retarded child in the home and not to seek institutionalization are not to be expected. Furthermore, it would seem reasonable to find growing rates of institutionalization. What has been the experience?

Over a 20-year period (1950–1970), there was a 50% increase in the number of persons residing in institutions for the mentally retarded (Table 4.17). This growth, however, was uneven. Sixty percent of the increase occurred between 1950 and 1960. The decade of the 1960's shows a slight slowdown. The institutional rates have increased from 89 to 99 per 100,000 population (11%), but this cannot be interpreted on face value as evidence of recent unwillingness on the part of families to provide care. As was pointed out above, up until the mid-1960's, the prevailing professional practice was to recommend early institution-

Table 4.17. Mentally Retarded Patients in Mental Retardation
            Institutions[a]

	1950	1960	1970
Public institutions	125,650	160,225	176,103
Private institutions	8,539	14,502	25,889
Total	134,189	174,727	201,992
Rates per 100,000 population	89	95	99

[a]Source: Adapted afrom U.S. Bureau of Census, *Census of Populations,* 1953,
1963, 1973.

alization, and families more often than not complied. Earlier institutional
rates show even higher increases. In 1920, for example, the rate was
under 40 per 100,000; 20 years later it had doubled (Baumeister, 1970).

Conley (1973) reports that the total institutional population was closer
to 269,000 in 1970. These additional 67,000 persons included those retarded persons in schools for the blind, deaf, mental hospitals, residential treatment centers, chronic disease hospitals, federal and state
prisons, and general hospitals with psychiatric in-patient services. This
larger number would give an overall rate of 132 per 100,000. However,
proportionately, as many if not more retardates would have been residents in these institutions in the earlier decades. It should also be
noted that these figures include the mildly retarded as well as the more
severely handicapped.

Age-specific rates of institutionalization do show significant shifts
over the past 20 years. While the overall increase between 1950 and
1970 was 11% (Table 4.17), much higher increases are found in the
younger age groups. Although the rates for those under 5 years of age
are considerably lower than the other age categories, the rate of increase for this group was the highest (76%), compared to 35% for those
between 5 and 9 years of age and 15% for those between 10 and 14
years of age. The data show a slight decrease for those between 15 and
19 years of age. These shifts are directly related to the overall age composition of these public institutions. In 1950, one in three residents
was under age 20. In 1960, two of every five were under 20, and by
1970, one in two. (See Table 4.18.)

Admission rates increased slightly between 1950 and 1965, from 7.3
to 7.8 per 100,000 population. The highest rates are found among children between 5 and 14 years of age. However, all age groups with the
exception of 5 through 9 years of age show decreases. Those admitted
are likely to be younger than previously. In 1950, 79% of all admissions
were for persons under 20. By 1970, this group accounted for 85% of
all admissions. (See Table 4.19.)

The final part of the equation is discharges. In 1967, the median

Table 4.18. Mentally Retarded Patients in Public Institutions for the Mentally Retarded (Per 100,000 Population)[a]

Age	1950	1955	1960	1965	1970
0–4	11.9	19.8	17.1	19.2	21.0
5–9	53.7	67.9	77.2	85.1	72.9
10–14	124.9	130.6	139.8	151.9	143.6
15–19	181.6	185.7	197.9	194.1	178.6
20–24	151.6	167.3	177.1	178.8	
25–34	118.8	118.4	123.6	132.8	
35+	64.1	67.2	66.2	66.0	

[a]Source: Office of Mental Retardation Coordinator, 1973.

length of stay in public mental retardation institutions was 16.4 years (Office of Research and Statistics, 1971). This was considerably higher than other long-term care institutions (psychiatric hospital—8.1 years; chronic disease facilities—1.6 years). Two of every three adults had remained in these institutions for 10 or more years; one in three for 20 years or more. (See Table 4.20.)

Although it is impossible to obtain accurate information on exact length of stay for different age groups, estimates can be derived. The Census Bureau reports on those individuals who were in the same residence 5 years before the census was taken. Overall, there seems to be some decrease in the length of stay. Whereas 78% of all residents in 1960 had been there for at least 5 years, the percentage had dropped to 67% in 1970. This decrease is, however, accounted for by the adult population. Among those aged 5 to 13, the percentage had increased markedly. Length of stay is obviously affected by the characteristics of the retarded person, especially the degree of their handicap. Tarjan et

Table 4.19. Admission Rates to Public Institutions for the Mentally Retarded[a,b]

Age	1950	1960	1965
0–4	10.7	11.1	9.9
5–9	17.6	19.9	21.9
10–14	22.9	20.8	21.9
15–19	19.4	17.8	15.9
20–24	6.6	5.0	5.1
25–34	3.3	2.0	2.0
35+	1.2	1.0	0.7
Total	7.3	7.6	7.8

[a]Rate per 10,000 population, age at admission.
[b]Source: Office of Mental Retardation Coordinator, 1973.

Table 4.20. Percentage of Persons at the
Same Institution for the Mentally
Retarded[a,b]

Age	1960	1970
5–13	32	42
14–24	61	66
25–44	83	80
45–64	87	78
65 and Over	90	61
Total over 5 Years of Age	78	67

[a]Data for 5 years before the 1960 Census, 5 years
before the 1970 Census and still there at the time
of the Census.
[b]Source: U.S. Bureau of the Census, 1978.

al. (1958), in an early study of one institutional population, found that
residents between ages 14 and 17 had the highest rates of discharge 4
years after being admitted, and those between 0 and 9 the lowest. One
in three young children (0–4) died within 4 years of admission. Those
discharged were likely to have IQs over 50 (over 60% of those with IQs
50–69, and over 70% of those with IQs 70 or greater). Slightly more
than 5% of those with IQs under 20 were discharged, and one in five
died. These data suggest that when very young children are admitted
they are likely to be severely retarded and have multiple handicaps. A
significant percentage die within a few years of admission, and those

Table 4.21. Median IQ of First
Admissions to Pacific
State Hospital[a]

Age (years)	Median IQ
Under 5	19.0
5–9	21.9
10–13	49.5
14–15	57.2
16–17	57.5
18–24	54.3
25–34	39.2
35 and Over	40.0
All Ages	42.9

[a]Source: Adapted from Tarjan, G., et
al. The natural history of mental deficiency in a State hospital: Probabilities
of release and death by age, intelligence
quotients, and diagnosis. Journal of Diseases of Children, July 1958, pp. 64–70.

who survive tend to remain in the institution for long periods. (See Table 4.21.)

More recent data on California's institutional population show that almost half (49%) of the residents were profoundly retarded and an additional 25% severely retarded. Ninety-three percent of the residents had IQs below 50 (California Department of Mental Hygiene, 1975). A national survey reports that 44% of residents in public residential facilities have IQs of less than 20, and 30% have IQs between 20 and 35 (Scheerenberger, 1976).

The institutional population is also younger than it was 20–30 years ago. In 1950, 32% of this population was 35 years of age or older; by 1970, the percentage was 24.6%. During this same period, the percentage of those under 5 years of age increased from 1.5 to 3.9%, and for those between 5 and 9 years of age, from 5.6 to 11.5% (Office of Mental Retardation Coordinator, 1973).

The last piece of information needed before concluding that shifts in patterns of care provided by families are occurring is related to the percentage of severely retarded persons in institutions. The trend may be toward younger admissions and fewer admissions of the less severely handicapped, but how many of the severely retarded are in institutions and how many are in the community?

Table 4.22. Institutional and Noninstitutional Severely Mentally Retarded[a]

Year	Estimated number of severely mentally retarded	Resident population in mental retardation institutions	Estimated number of severely mentally retarded in institutions	Percentage not in mental retardation institutions
1950				
Under 15	146,000	25,845	23,260	84,07
15 and over	243,000	108,408	97,567	59.85
				(68.94)
1960				
Under 15	200,000	46,269	41,642	79.18
15 and over	271,000	128,458	115,612	57.34
				(66.61)
1970				
Under 15	208,000	48,141	43,327	79.17
15 and over	320,000	153,851	138,466	56.73
				(65.57)

[a]Estimated number of Severely Mentally Retarded drawn from Table 4.14; Resident population in Mental Retardation Institutions drawn from Table 4.17; Estimated number of severely mentally retarded in institutions drawn from Scheerenberger, 1976

The data in Table 4.22 assume that 90% of the institutional resident population are severely retarded (IQ below 50). Eight of every ten severely retarded children and slightly more than two of every three of all ages are not in institutions, ratios that have remained fairly constant since 1950. Not all of these are being cared for by their families. A number may be in foster care, nursing homes, boarding homes, hostels, or other facilities. While it is impossible to determine the numbers involved, it is fair to estimate that, at least for children, most live with their family if they are not institutional residents. This suggests that more than 188,000 severely retarded children will be living with their parents or other relatives in 1990.

Earlier, the problems and strains associated with the presence of a severely handicapped child were discussed. Despite these, most families either do not seek or delay institutionalization. The majority appear to develop a number of coping mechanisms (Hewitt, 1972). Although as noted in Table 4.15, the incapacities associated with severe mental retardation are considerable, those who are institutionalized are likely to be even more handicapped. In a Social Security survey of 75,000 caregivers who had institutionalized their retarded relative, the following reasons shown in Table 4.23 were given.

In studies of families who had decided on institutionalization and families who kept their children home, significant differences were identified. Hobbs (1964) reported that the institutional group had a higher incidence of antisocial behavior and were more likely to be from broken homes. Graliker et al. (1965) found that the institutionalized child had more severe and multiple handicaps and that 68% of their parents showed significant emotional problems requiring professional help. In yet another survey, Wolf and Whitehead (1975) found that 92% of the families choosing institutionalization mentioned disruption of family life as a major contributing factor. Unfortunately, none of these studies has identified how long even these families provided care. Still, long-term or permanent institutionalization among children does not appear to be the norm. When a child is placed, he or she is likely to

Table 4.23. Reasons for Institutionalization[a]

Reason	Percentage
Needed permanent care	49.8
Had to be watched and looked after more carefully	42.8
Needed special training	36.5
Too hard to handle at home	27.5
No one to look after at home	13.1

[a]Source: Office of Mental Retardation Coordinator, 1972.

be severely handicapped, causing problems associated with behavior or management, leading one researcher to suggest that "in spite of the obvious hardships which many families had to bear in caring for a mentally handicapped child at home, the proportion who wished for institutional care was small" (Tizard, 1974).

The overriding issue in this study is the nature of the relationship between families and the State in the provision of care to handicapped individuals. A basic assumption is that the caring function should be shared by both social institutions—that each has a responsibility and each a contribution to make. Furthermore, it is argued that neither has the resources to function as the sole caregiver. This chapter has examined the first part of the equation—the family as provider.

The chapter first examined the nature and extent of handicapping conditions. It was pointed out that almost 10 million persons have some impairment. Of these, approximately 2.7 million are handicapped insofar as they are functionally disabled, and over 1½ million are severely handicapped. And yet, the total institutional population in this country (including prisons) was only 2.1 million persons, or 1% of the population. Given this, it can be argued that significantly more of the handicapped are living in noninstitutional settings and that a considerable number are living with their families.

The analysis then shifted to two groups of handicapped persons—the frail elderly and the severely mentally retarded children. It was felt that a more detailed discussion of these two groups would be useful in determining the extent to which families are providing care and the impact the caregiving function has on family well-being.

Two and three-tenths million elderly are handicapped, 1 million severely handicapped. Although the elderly account for 63% of all handicapped persons, they represent less than 10% of the total population. More than one in ten elderly persons (11.3%) are handicapped, and, one in twenty severely handicapped (5.3%). However, the percentage of the elderly institutional population has remained fairly constant—between 5 and 6%. Twelve percent of the elderly, or 2.5 million persons, are living as dependents with their adult children or other relatives. Both the institutional population and those living with relatives tend to be older, female, widowed, and handicapped. Based on population projections, this at-risk population is expected to increase at a much faster rate than the population as a whole. This should, in turn, result in greater demands on the institutions and on families for the provision of physical and social care.

By 1980, there were an estimated 561,000 severely mentally retarded persons in this country. Of these, 180,000 are children. Despite the fact that severe retardation is associated with multiple handicaps, 80% of the children are not residents in institutions. Most, in fact, are living with their parents.

Recent surveys of values and beliefs associated with family life, marriage, expectations, and roles of adults would argue against family care. It is demanding, disruptive, and requires family members, especially the mother, to make major adjustments to family life. Although there are alternatives (e.g., nursing homes and institutions for the mentally retarded), most families apparently choose to provide care, often for long periods.

However, there have been slight shifts in institutional trends. While the data are inconclusive at this time and the long-term pattern is still unknown, it is clear that once a placement is made, it usually means long-term care. There is also some evidence to suggest that families who are not provided support are less willing to take handicapped members back into their homes after an admission to an acute-care facility.

This chapter identified the pressures and strains both sets of families (those caring for handicapped elderly and those caring for severely retarded children) are experiencing. Not all families are experiencing all of these stresses, but all of these families are "at risk" in that statistically they are more likely than families without handicapped members to have these problems. There are significant commonalities in the types of strains among both groups of families. In fact, they are probably common to families providing care to all of the physically handicapped. In turn, these pressures can be translated into the services that families could benefit from. These pressures include: additional financial costs; stigma; time consumed in personal care, e.g., feeding, washing, dressing; difficulty with physical management, e.g., lifting, ambulation; interruptions of family sleep; social isolation, negative attitudes of neighbors and kin; limitations in recreational activities; behavioral problems; difficulty in shopping and other normal household routines; limited prospects for the future.

The next two chapters examine the other part of the relationship, the social welfare response. First, the organizational response is analyzed, followed by a discussion of how the major resource—the human service professional—interacts with families providing care. Is there a shared responsibility, one in which support services are made available to families retaining the primary caregiving function?

5 THE SOCIAL WELFARE RESPONSE: RESOURCES

What is the most desirable, effective, and feasible division of responsibility between the family and extrafamilial institutions in meeting the
needs of individuals, and in what ways can these institutions relate to
each other to maximize benefits? As introduced in Chapter 1, the question has provided the framework for this study. The question evolved
from the fact that the structure of the welfare state depends on a set
of assumptions concerning the responsibilities which families are expected to carry in providing care to the handicapped and other dependent persons and a set of conditions under which this responsibility
is to be shared or taken over by society. Later, this statement was expanded, and it was argued that both institutions, the family and the
State, had roles to play, that each shared this responsibility, and that
neither could function effectively without the other. This relationship
is best understood by analyzing whether social welfare measures support the family as a primary social service or whether they take over
the caring function. The notion as formulated, however, requires some
elaboration. The State can substitute partially by assuming certain
functions and leaving others with the family. An example of this is the
development of social insurance programs through which the State assumes responsibility for providing financial support to the elderly. In
principle, this program is a major break from the earlier Poor Law tradition that required children to support their parents. In a sense, then,
the State, in assuming this function, has substituted in part for the family. Homemaker services are another example of partial substitution.
These services make it possible for elderly persons to maintain independent living by carrying out various domestic functions children

might have done in the past. Both of these services support the individual elderly person by partially substituting for the family. If the
handicapped person is institutionalized, on the other hand, the social
welfare system takes over the caring function.

This total transfer of the caring function can be either permanent or
temporary. If temporary short-term care is provided in an institution
so that the caregivers are given some relief, the purpose of the transfer
is to support the family. If, on the other hand, the transfer is permanent,
the purpose becomes one of replacement. Given this distinction (the
purpose rather than the service itself), it is important not to conclude
that institutional care always implies substitution for the family, just as
community services do not always support the family. Community care
cannot be equated with family support. More often than not it has
come to mean the provision of care to certain groups of dependent
people in community settings as alternatives to care in the larger institutions. If the handicapped person receives services while living
alone, with his or her spouse (elderly), or in a hostel, these services
support the individual but substitute for the family.

The preceding chapter discussed the characteristics of two at-risk
groups, the frail elderly and severely retarded children. The extent to
which families are providing care and the strains associated with caregiving were identified. This chapter examines the social welfare response, beginning with an analysis of social expenditures in general
and moving on to the specific implications of those expenditures for
the retarded and the elderly. An attempt will be made to determine
whether responses are organized and provided to support families or
whether they emphasize taking over the caring function when families
are unable or unwilling to continue as caregivers. To extend the analysis,
it is important to identify whether the object of the policy or service
is the individual or the family unit.

Unfortunately, the analysis has to be more exploratory than defin-
itive, in that there are several gray areas. Policies often have multiple
objectives. On the other hand, the analysis can identify themes that
give an indication of past and current priorities, especially as they relate
to families. It is clear that services supporting families do exist, but it
is not clear whether sufficient resources are being made available. The
notion of sufficient, of course, cannot be defined in absolute terms,
nor can any discussion assume that resources are limitless; the major
task is only to determine what is needed. This analysis is more concerned with the share that support services are given relative to social
welfare expenditures and, in particular, relative to services that sub-

stitute for the family. It becomes more a question of balance based on the idea of a more equitable distribution of resources.

A major problem encountered throughout the analysis was the lack of a coherent data base on community services. As the President's Committee on Mental Retardation (1976) noted:

> In a discussion of service, one fact is paramount. There is a serious dearth of valid and reliable information through which to present an accurate picture of the state of services for mentally retarded people. . . . Perhaps most critical among these problems is the fact that current statistics are rarely available on a national, regional or even statewide basis. In Fiscal Year 1975 many agencies are still analyzing information from 1971 or before, if they keep information at all.

This situation is found in almost all areas of community services and is not unique to services for the retarded. The analysis, then, must be limited to a discussion of pieces of fragmented information and cannot establish clear trends. Still, the identification of emphases is useful in addressing the issue of shared responsibility through the provision of support services.

Two concepts, normalization and least restrictive environment, are being used more and more as the basis for developing community services and are directly related to the notion of support. While the concepts are discussed primarily in terms of the needs the mentally retarded have, they apply to all handicapped populations.

The first, normalization, argues that with appropriate support services the mentally retarded person will be able to live as normal a life as others within the constraints of the level of functional disability (Nirje, 1970; Wolfensberger, 1972). Nirje describes this supportive environment as one which provides the individual the opportunity to "share a normal rhythm of the day, with privacy, activities and mutual responsibilities; a normal rhythm of the week, with a home to live in, a school or work to go to, and leisure time with a modicum of social interaction; a normal rhythm of the year, with the changing modes and ways of life, of family and community customs. . . ." The second concept is that services should be provided in the least restrictive environment. If mentally retarded persons cannot or should not live any longer with their families or in their own homes, they should be able to live in facilities of normal size located in residential areas. These principles have been supported in a number of recent court decisions.

Horejsi (1975) suggests that this approach requires five types of services: (1) family support, including genetic counseling, diagnostic services, respite care, homemakers, parent/child training, recreation, and financial assistance; (2) child development services; (3) residential services for those who cannot remain in their own homes or for those at an age when it is normal to leave home; (4) vocational training and employment opportunities; and (5) coordinating services. Other services often mentioned are leisure time and recreational programs, transportation, and health care services (Thurlow, Bruininks, Williams, and Morreau, 1978). Underlying these concepts is the belief that wherever the mentally retarded person lives, he or she should be supported. Building on this approach, when the handicapped person lives within a family setting, both the handicapped person and the family require supportive services.

As mentioned above, these concepts are applicable to all handicapped persons, including the frail elderly. Normalization and least restrictive environment mean that since most elderly want to live independently, alone or with their spouse, appropriate support should be made available. Various income maintenance programs, especially retirement benefits, appear to make this possible for most. If the elderly person becomes partially disabled and finds it difficult to carry out some homemaking or personal care functions, he or she often can remain at home if services are provided. If the elderly person experiences greater difficulty in maintaining independent living, a range of alternatives, only one of which is the nursing home, should then be available. These include living with adult children, special housing for the elderly, sheltered housing, and other forms of congregate living. The nursing home or long-term care hospital is seen as the last choice, only to be used when other less dependent arrangements are not viable. Such a system, found in many European countries, is built on the idea that the individual can progress through a number of stages, from complete independence to totally dependent living, and should be able to remain at each level as long as possible through the provision of support services.

A least restrictive environment or progressive stages of care are viable concepts only when real choices or options exist. Without a community system offering a wide range of services, the choice is often limited to institutional care. Without such a community system, there is no meaningful choice at all.

Choice, of course, is not a simple concept and has to be examined closely, if it is to become a criterion for policy development. In suggesting that families should be able to decide whether they want to assume, maintain, or transfer the caring function, it does not follow that either family care or institutional care is equally desirable in all situations or that both serve the same function.

Data in Chapter 3 showed that significant numbers of families are providing care to handicapped relatives. Insofar as they are, it might be argued that they choose to do so. But was this a conscious, rational choice based on an assessment of available alternatives? Were there appropriate options—a requirement for real choice—or was the only option institutional care? If the family and individual chose care in the home, were they provided with necessary services? If the choice was for substitute care in an institutional environment, were these facilities offering the highest level of care possible? If all of these services were available, the choice was meaningful. If, on the other hand, a family caring for an 85-year-old incontinent, bedridden parent finds that they are ineligible for supportive services in their home, but that their parent would be eligible for nursing home care, do they have a real choice?

If the essence of a caring society involves the development and pro-vision of a wide range of services so that families can choose what is most appropriate, emphasis must be placed on policies and programs that are supportive. Support, unlike substitution, requires sharing. The issue of whose responsibility it is to care for the handicapped cannot be reduced to either the family or the State. Nor is it a matter of the family providing care without external assistance, until this care be-comes impossible, and then transferring the function to the State. Most families need the social welfare system to carry some responsibility while they maintain their role as the primary caregiver. For these fam-ilies, sharing may mean financial assistance to offset the economic strains associated with the handicapping condition; practical help and advice related to the physical care of the child or elderly parent; physical adaptations to the home; and short-term relief for vacations, shopping, or recreation. On another level, sharing may mean giving the family some assurance that when and if the burden becomes intolerable, when they can no longer maintain the handicapped person in their home, appropriate residential care will be available. On still another level, sharing may mean that even after institutionalization, the family visits their child or parent frequently and occasionally takes him or her home for short holidays.

These elements, the choice to maintain the relative at home or to seek institutionalization, and the provision of services in such a way that families share the responsibility with others, require not only a range of services but services that are flexible and innovative. What has the response been?

THE SOCIAL WELFARE COMMITMENT

As a rough measure of commitment, expenditure levels show, in relative terms, the value a society places on social objectives. In this sense it can be interpreted as an indicator of social welfare effort (Wilensky, 1975). Two specific indicators are often used—welfare expenditures as a percentage of the Gross National Product (GNP) and per capita expenditures for social welfare purposes.

Social welfare expenditures as a percentage of the GNP have more than doubled since 1950 (Table 5.1). Or, whereas the GNP increased by 423% between 1950 and 1975, social expenditures grew by 1000%. By 1975, these expenditures accounted for over one quarter (26.3%) of the national income. Expenditures were divided fairly equally among health, income maintenance, and education in 1950. Spending for the social services was relatively low at this time, accounting for less than 1% of the GNP. During the following 25 years there were a number of shifts in this pattern. While total expenditures in constant dollars were increased by 427%, public sector spending was increased by 484%,

Table 5.1. Social Welfare Expenditures as Percentage of Gross National Product[a]

	1950	1960	1970	1975	1975 ($ millions)
Income maintenance					
Public	3.41	5.20	6.19	8.81	132,094
Private	0.34	0.70	1.18	1.38	20,700
Total	3.75	5.90	7.37	10.19	152,794
Health					
Public	1.07	1.26	2.57	3.33	49,947
Private	3.13	3.85	4.47	4.57	68,552
Total	4.20	5.11	7.04	7.90	118,499
Education					
Public	3.27	3.56	5.28	5.53	82,859
Private	0.54	0.73	1.00	1.03	15,500
Total	3.81	4.29	6.28	6.56	98,359
Welfare and other					
Public	0.46	0.31	0.79	1.44	21,647
Private	0.24	0.21	0.20	0.20	3,000
Total	0.70	0.52	0.99	1.66	24,647
Total					
Public	8.21	10.33	14.83	19.11	286,547
Private	4.25	5.49	6.85	7.18	107,752
					(394 billion)

[a]Source: Office of Management and Budget, *Social Indicators, 1976, 1977,* Tables 4/1 and 4/8.

compared to 324% in the private sector. This shift was reflected in the decrease of the private sector's share, from 33% of all expenditures to 27% during this period. This 25-year growth, however, was not evenly distributed. The period 1965–1970 accounted for the most significant expansion—61% over the preceding 5-year period, compared to 37% in the period 1970–1975. Until 1965, moreover, the private sector outstripped the public sector in growth rates. After this, the government assumed a greater share of expenditures, especially in the health care field, primarily through the Medicare and Medicaid programs. In relative terms, this society has made a commitment to social welfare, and this commitment continues to grow. It is becoming associated more and more with the public sector, with the government assuming direct responsibility for assuring that basic needs are being met. The private sector, while still significant, has experienced less growth, although its share of the expenditures for health care remains high.

This commitment on the part of society, in general, and the State, in particular, is also characterized by the decision to meet needs primarily through the provision of income. Total expenditures for health and education relative to income maintenance have decreased since 1950. Social services (a category that includes various housing, rehabilitation, institutional and personal social services), never large, accounted for 6% in 1975, a slight increase over the 1950 level. (See Table 5.2.)

The data in Table 5.3 measure the social welfare effort in yet another way. Between 1950 and 1975, per capita expenditures increased by $1,000 (constant dollars), or 314%. While there were increases in per

Table 5.2. Social Welfare Expenditures by Category (Percentages)[a]

	1950	1960	1970	1975
Total				
Income maintenance	30	38	34	39
Health	34	33	33	30
Education	31	28	29	25
Social services/other	5	1	4	6
	(100)	(100)	(100)	(100)
Public				
Income maintenance	41	50	42	46
Health	13	12	17	17
Education	40	34	36	29
Social services/other	6	4	5	8
	(100)	(100)	(100)	(100)

[a]Source: Office of Management and Budget, *Social Indicators, 1976, 1977,* Table 4/1.

Table 5.3. Per Capita Social Welfare Expenditures under Public Programs[a,b]

	1950	1960	1970	1975
Social insurance	67.20	175.29	352.31	567.32
Public assistance	33.95	37.37	106.68	187.13
Health	28.06	40.68	63.10	76.80
Veterans	92.23	49.12	58.08	76.23
Education	90.75	160.45	329.17	361.95
Welfare and other services	6.31	12.00	33.62	49.99

[a]Data in constant 1975 dollars.
[b]Source: Office of Management and Budget, Social Indicators, 1976, 1977, Table 4/2.

capita expenditures for health and education, these increases were less than the overall increase (174 and 299%, respectively). Welfare and other social services show a considerable increase but, given the extremely low level of 1950, the increase is not significant. For example, in 1950, per capita expenditure in this category accounted for only 2 cents of every public social welfare dollar, and only 3 cents in 1975. In general, the major increases were accounted for by the income maintenance programs. The social insurance expenditure grew by 744% and the public assistance benefits by 451%.

Based on the criterion of rates of growth, the commitment exists, and a priority has been established. The overall strategy that has evolved combines a mix of income maintenance, payment for medical care, and the provisions of social services. In placing the greatest emphasis on channeling income to individuals and families, the State tends to favor indirect involvement, a policy consistent with the value of non-interference in family life. This assumes that recipients are better off when they make their own decisions and choose how to spend these funds.

SOCIAL WELFARE EXPENDITURES FOR THE HANDICAPPED AND THEIR FAMILIES

As mentioned earlier, detailed information on expenditures and utilization is difficult to locate. A recent publication from the Family Impact Seminar (1978), George Washington University, makes a valuable addition to this data base. Although not specifically focusing on the handicapped and their families, the analysts evaluate over 1,000 federal programs in terms of their direct and indirect impact on families. In their report, programs with a "direct impact" (i.e., the provision of financial assistance, in-kind subsidies, or services to individuals and families) are differentiated from those with an "indirect impact" (i.e., provision of resources or services to state or local agencies, institutions, or organizations). In addition, a number of programs were seen as having an "explicit family impact" when the family or a unit of at least two family members were the intended beneficiaries. Although the authors view their findings as tentative and feel that further analysis may require some adjustments, they estimate that in fiscal 1976, 268 programs administered by 17 agencies and accounting for $180.6 billion in obligated funds were potentially affecting families.

One hundred and nineteen of these programs (44% of the total) were administered by the Department of Health, Education, and Welfare (Table 5.4). These programs accounted for 66% of all funds obligated by the 268 programs. It appears that 31 of these programs focus specifically on the handicapped or provide benefits and services to them as one of many eligible groups. Thirteen of these are administered by Welfare, nine by the Office of Education, seven by the Social Security Administration, and two by the Public Health Service (Table 5.5).

These 31 programs were obligated at $102.7 billion in fiscal 1976. Seventy-one percent of this total were accounted for by various income maintenance programs, 25% by programs paying for medical care services, and 4% by the providers of services. While this investment is significant, the distribution itself raises some questions. A fundamental issue in developing an improved support system for families caring for handicapped members lies in the dominance of the income approach. Federal policy in general has been primarily an income policy and, while income supports are needed, their value may be lessened in the absence of a network of support services.

Table 5.4. Inventory of Programs with Potential Impact on Families, DHEW, Fiscal Year 1976[a]

	Potential family impact programs	Total obligations ($ millions)	Explicit family impact programs	Total obligations ($ millions)
Social Security	8	99,473	2	17,761
Welfare	25	18,336	9	15,568
Education	59	5,881	2	75
Health	25	1,387	6	348
Office of the Secretary	2	151	1	124
Total	119	119,228	20	33,876

[a]Source: Adapted from Family Impact Seminar. *Toward an Inventory of Federal Programs with Direct Impact on Families*. George Washington University, February 1978, p. 17.

Table 5.5. Federal Programs Potentially Benefiting Families with Handicapped Members (DHEW)[a]

Catalog number	Agency	Title	Obligations fiscal year 1976
A. Specific services			
13.427	OE	Educationally deprived children/ handicapped	96 M
13.433	OE	Follow through	59 M
13.443	OE	Handicapped, research and demonstration	11 M
13.444	OE	Handicapped, early childhood assistance	22 M
13.446	OE	Handicapped, media services and films	16 M
13.449	OE	Handicapped, preschool and school programs	100 M
13.450	OE	Handicapped, regional resource centers	10 M
13.520	OE	Special programs for children with learning disabilities	4 M
13.568	OE	Handicapped, innovative programs, severely handicapped	3 M
13.624	OHD	Rehabilitation services and facilities	720 M
13.627	OHD	Rehabilitation, research and demonstration	24 M
13.630	OHD	Developmental disabilities, basic support	32 M
13.631	OHD	Developmental disabilities, special projects	19 M
13.635	OHD	Special programs, aging, nutrition	125 M
13.636	OHD	Special programs, aging, research and development	6 M
Total			1,247 M
B. Income maintenance			
13.761	SRS	Public assistance-maintenance	5.9 B
13.803	SSA	Retirement insurance	45.1 B
13.804	SSA	Special benefits for those over 71	185 M
13.805	SSA	Survivors insurance	16.8 B
13.806	SSA	Special benefits, disabled coal miners	961 M
13.807	SSA	Supplemental security income	4.4 B
Total			73.3 B
C. Medical care—financial			
13.800	SSA	Medicare—hospital insurance	12.2 B
13.801	SSA	Medicare—supplementary insurance	4.7 B
13.714	SRS	Medical assistance program	8.3 B
Total			25.2 B

Table 5.5. (Continued)

Catalog number	Agency	Title	Obligations fiscal year 1976
D. General social services			
13.600	OHD	Headstart	462 M
13.608	OHD	Child welfare, research and development	15 M
13.754	SRS	Public assistance, social services	16 M
13.771	SRS	Social services, low income	2.2 B
13.707	SRS	Child welfare services	53 M
13.211	PHS	Crippled children's services	77 M
13.232	PHS	Maternal and child health services	219 M
Total			3 B
Grand total			102.7 B

[a]Source: Adapted from Family Impact Seminar. *Toward An Inventory of Federal Programs with Direct Impact on Families.* George Washington University, February 1978, pp. 37ff.

As discussed in Chapter 3, most families are experiencing financial strains. Inflation has threatened the standard of living that families have come to view as normal and desirable. These expectations have, in turn, been a major factor in large numbers of women entering the labor force and in the evolution of the two-earner family as the norm. Chapter 4 showed that families caring for a handicapped child or elderly parent feel not only normal strain, but also financial pressures associated with the handicapping condition. Furthermore, when families decide to carry the responsibility, more often than not one earner, the mother or daughter, leaves the work force if she is employed, or never enters it at all. These families in a sense are penalized. If they decide on institutionalization, they will be better off financially in that all adults can work.

Are the income maintenance programs, then, organized to recognize the unique needs of families with handicapped members and to support their efforts? Unfortunately, no. Little of the $73 billion for income maintenance is for "family support." Sixty-three percent of these funds provide benefits to elderly individuals through retirement insurance. Moreover, the level of the benefit is not related to the beneficiaries' physical status, nor does it matter whether the retiree is living with children or alone. These factors are not material to the purpose of the program, which is to offer protection against the loss of earnings resulting from retirement so that the elderly person will not become a dependent. The program clearly supports the elderly but is implicitly neutral to the family. While many beneficiaries living with their children or other relatives probably contribute to their own maintenance, the object of the policy is the individual and not the family providing care to a handicapped parent.

Twenty-three percent ($16.8 billion) of the income maintenance funds were for benefits to survivors of an insured worker. This program has become a major source of financial assistance to individuals who are handicapped. For example, in 1975, over 5½ million people (of whom almost 5 million were children) were drawing benefits. Although these benefits appear to be oriented toward family support (unlike the retirement program) and some of the beneficiaries are likely to be handicapped, the presence of such a condition is immaterial. Benefit levels do not vary by the physical status of the recipient, nor is the presence of a handicap a part of the eligibility determination. The intent of the program is simply the replacement of income because of the loss of the wage earner.

Two other income maintenance programs (Public Assistance and Supplementary Security Income) account for 14% of the total, or $10.3 billion. Although these programs involve considerable funds, they are somewhat limited. The most serious is that both are income related or means tested. Aid to Families with Dependent Children (AFDC) is the major program under Public Assistance. The purpose of the program is to maintain children in their own homes by providing income when the wage earner dies, is incapacitated, is absent from the home, and, in some instances, is unemployed. As in the other income maintenance programs, the existence of a handicapping condition is not a part of eligibility determination, nor will it substantially affect the level of the benefit. One admittedly conservative estimate suggests that 4% of all children receiving AFDC benefits are mentally retarded (National Center for Social Statistics, 1970). It is unlikely that many families who have decided to care for their children would qualify for these benefits. Even if they were to meet the income criterion, they are apt to be two-parent families.

The second program, Supplementary Security Income, has recently replaced those categorical programs providing financial assistance to the elderly (OAA), the disabled (APTD), and the blind (AB). This program (as with disability insurance) explicitly recognizes a handicapping condition as a major factor in determining eligibility. In terms of the two groups emphasized in this analysis, by definition the elderly and the mentally retarded are major beneficiaries. For example, in 1970, approximately 140,000 mentally retarded individuals received support under the APTD program (National Center for Social Statistics, 1972). These represented 16% of this program's beneficiaries. A major limitation, however, is the reliance on income testing to determine eligibility. Moreover, the notion of family support is ignored insofar as the stated purpose of the program is to guarantee a minimum income to "individuals" who have insufficient resources. The emphasis is on the individual at risk because of age or disability, and formal recognition is given neither to the caregivers in the family nor to the fact that this care involves additional financial stress. In fact, the policies behind the program in some instances actually seem to penalize families. For example, SSI recipients who lived in their own household with no countable income received $157.70 per month in 1976 (Office of Research and Statistics, 1976). In order to prevent or delay institutionalization, the program allows for higher benefit levels to those recipients who are unable to live independently but are capable of functioning in a domiciliary care facility. These facilities include foster-care homes, family-type settings for fewer then five persons, and even larger group settings. As stated, "the major purpose of foster care is to enable handicapped and elderly persons to live within a family setting." At the time of the survey, 107,000 SSI recipients in 15 states were in domiciliary care facilities and other supervised care arrangements. These recipients represented approximately 2.5% of the total. Forty percent were 65 years of age and over, and 5% were children.

Federally administered payments to persons in these settings averaged $232 per month, or 43% more than for the recipient living independently. Payments to the elderly averaged $205; blind adults, $241; disabled adults, $246; and disabled children, $283. This policy makes a great deal of sense, building on the principles of normalization and least restrictive environment, and thus benefits the recipient. Alternatives to nursing home care are encouraged, potentially cutting back on expenditures, since institutional care on the average is twice as costly.

However, *the federal payment is reduced by one third if an individual is living in another person's household and receiving support and maintenance from that person.* On the one hand, the policy pays more money to stimulate the development of surrogate families on the assumption that families provide better environments than institutions. On the other hand, this policy reduces the benefit if the recipient is living with and being cared for by a relative. Natural families are penalized, while others are paid to function as families. Though difficult to understand, the policy is consistent with the basic thrust of income maintenance policies in general. Major emphasis is placed on substituting for the family, and little priority, at least in terms of income maintenance, is given to family support. Once again, this does not mean that these benefits are misplaced. It is not being argued that they be redirected and that the emphasis shift away from the individual and that families always be the object of the policy. Nor does it imply that families should resume total financial responsibility. Finally, it is not being argued that these payments are not beneficial to individuals and families. These families have identifiable financial needs, and income maintenance programs can be designed to meet these needs. In such a system the benefit would be given to the caregiver and not to the handicapped individual.

Such policies do exist in a number of European countries as part of their overall income maintenance program. Family allowances are still another example of family support policies. Benefits are paid to families in recognition of the financial strains that childrearing creates for most families. These programs tend to be universal in provision and are not means tested. This notion of financial support to families is explored in some detail in Chapter 7.

The second largest area of federal expenditure is medical care. Of the $25 billion obligated, 67% was for the Medicare program (Title XVIII of the Social Security Act, 1976). Although this program is technically not for long-term care, it does allow for the provision of services that theoretically could be supportive to the handicapped and their families. However, in 1975, 92% of the expenditures under both the Hospital Insurance and Supplementary Insurance programs were for inpatient hospital care and services provided by physicians. Home health services accounted for only 1.3% of the total (U.S. Department of Health, Education, and Welfare, 1977). The Medicaid program (Title XIX of the Social Security Act), on the other hand, can provide a much broader range of medical care services, including long-term care as well as the more traditional inpatient hospital, clinic services, and physician services. In 1975, 42% of the Medicaid expenditures went toward the provision of long-term care (Table 5.6).

Less than 0.6% of these long-term care expenditures were used to pay for services provided in the patient's home. Under this program, long-term care services have come to mean institutional care. The program will pay for skilled nursing care, home health aids, physical and occupational therapy, social services, and medical supplies delivered in a noninstitutional setting. It also allows for the provision of personal care services, such as assistance in activities of daily living, as long as they are supervised by a registered professional nurse and ordered by a physician. It is these services, the home health and personal care services, that are extremely important to those families caring for a handicapped child or parent, and yet they are the least developed.

Table 5.6. Medicaid Expenditures by Type of Service (1975)[a]

Service	Expenditure[b] ($ millions)	Percentage
Skilled nursing facility	2,200	43.75
Intermediate care facility	1,838	36.56
ICF mentally retarded	362	7.20
Psychiatric hospital	600	11.93
Home health	28	0.56
Total	5,028	100.00

[a]Source: U.S. Department of Health, Education and Welfare, 1977, p. 48.
[b]Total Medicaid expenditures $12,028.

The frail elderly are the major users of this program. For example, in Massachusetts, 40% of all vendor payments were made for the care of the elderly in licensed nursing homes and chronic hospitals. The remainder paid for inpatient care, outpatient services, physician services, and drugs for the total eligible population, i.e., children, elderly, and adults. Institutional care benefits a relatively small percentage of the elderly population and yet receives the largest share of the available funds. To complicate the situation, costs for nursing home care continue to escalate. In 1964, monthly costs averaged $211. By 1969, they had reached $356, and by 1973, $495. The latest available data show these costs to have reached $605 in nonprofit facilities and $588 in for-profit homes (U.S. Bureau of the Census, 1978). Huge investments are being made for approximately 5% of the elderly population. The Federal Council on the Aging (1977) has concluded that:

> Care for the impaired aging indicates first that such programs as available are limited to financial reimbursement mechanisms rather than the provision of direct services for frail elderly at home; and second, that we have chosen to finance long-term care on a means tested basis and offer it primarily through nursing homes. . . . (This) places a substantial burden on families caring for a frail parent where family and kin are present.

This same emphasis is found in services provided to the mentally retarded. The President's Committee (1976) has estimated that only 10% of all mentally retarded are residents in institutions. It was shown earlier (Table 4.22) that only 20% of severely retarded children and 33% of all severely retarded persons live in these institutions. And yet, over 40% of all expenditures for the retarded were for this form of care. Although Medicaid is not the only source of funding for institutional care, it seems appropriate to include patterns of care for the retarded here (Table 5.7).

Table 5.7. Total Expenditures on Mental Retardation Services
($ Millions)[a]

	1968	1970	Percentage increase
Public residential care	1,004	1,307	30.2
Federal	110	196	78.2
State/local	768	937	22.0
Other	126	174	38.1
Community care	1,391	1,868	34.3
Federal	121	192	58.7
State/local	1,207	1,580	30.9
Other	63	96	52.4

[a]Source: Adapted from Conley, R. *The Economics of Mental Retardation.*
Baltimore: Johns Hopkins, 1973, and cited in President's Committee on Mental
Retardation, *Mental Retardation. The Known and the Unknown.* Washington,
D.C., February 1, 1975, p. 96.

In 1970, $3.2 billion were spent for services to and care for the men-
tally retarded, a 32% increase over 1968 levels. These increases, however, did not emphasize a major commitment to community care insofar
as increases for institutional care were as high as for community services. It is not being suggested that institutional programs should not
receive resources sufficient to provide the highest level of care possible
to residents, nor that resources should be channeled from institutions
to community-based services. As long as mentally retarded persons
live in these facilities, every effort should be made to improve the quality
of their lives. However, as with nursing home care, institutional care
is costly, is becoming still more costly, and is touching the lives of a
small number of persons relative to the total at-risk population. (See
Table 5.8.)

Table 5.8. Average Daily Costs in Public Institutions for the
Mentally Retarded[a]

Year	Average daily cost ($)	Percentage change over previous 5 years
1960	4.20	—
1965	6.09	45.0
1970	11.64	91.1
1976	27.60	137.1

[a]Sources: 1960–1970—Office of Mental Retardation Coordinator, *Mental Retardation Sourcebook, 1973,* Table 20; 1976—U.S. Bureau of the Census, Survey
of Institutionalized Persons *1978, p. 57.*

Unlike community services, institutional costs are not easily manipulable (outside the scale factor). If resources for community services are limited, recipients living in the community can be given less than they need or be denied services totally. For example, an agency providing homemaker services may find that, although the demand for services has grown, resources have either remained constant or decreased. Faced with this problem, the agency may decide to continue accepting applicants, allow the caseload to grow, but cut back on the hours of service to each recipient. An elderly client would receive 3 instead of 5 hours each week. On the other hand, the administration may believe that certain levels of service to each recipient must be maintained if the support is to be effective. Rather than cutting down on services, new applicants are not accepted by the agency, or more rigid eligibility criteria are introduced. These often are based on notions of risk or hierarchies of need. Although either strategy may be undesirable (i.e., fewer services to more people or a freeze on the size of the caseload), both are possible. These options are not as readily available once institutionalization takes place.

Average per diem costs for the institutional care of a mentally retarded person were $4.20 in 1950. Twenty-six years later the costs were $27.60, an increase of 557 percent. These increases reflect in part the effort to improve the quality of care in such institutions and in part inflation. The costs, however, are only average costs. In one large state institution, operating expenses per resident day increased from $16.50 in 1972 to $41.00 in 1974. As costs continue to rise, even a stable institutional population requires larger investments of social welfare expenditures. Insofar as these costs are fixed, will the additional resources become available only at the expense of community resources? (President's Committee on Mental Retardation, 1976). Another concern is the direction that federal involvement seems to be taking. As seen in Table 5.7, the federal share increased from 1968 to 1970. Furthermore, federal expenditures grew by 68%, compared to 27% in state and local spending. Over half (55%) of the additional funds, however, went for institutional care. Once again, federal priorities seem to emphasize taking over from families rather than supporting them.

The third category of federal programs (Table 5.5) with potential applicability for families caring for handicapped members contains programs offering social services to the general population. Although the handicapped and their families are not specifically identified as targets, by definition many of the services may, in fact, support their effort. Seventy-three percent of the total $3 billion are for social services under the Title XX amendments to the Social Security Act. In 1974, several programs were consolidated, and each state was given discretion to develop those services it felt were needed. Within the constraints of a $2.5 billion ceiling, block grants are distributed to the states. As mentioned, the purposes of Title XX are the reduction of dependency and the protection of vulnerable populations. Services are to be organized around one or more of the program's goals: (1) to achieve or maintain economic self-support in order to prevent, reduce, or eliminate dependency; (2) to achieve or maintain self-sufficiency; (3) to prevent or remedy abuse, neglect, or exploitation of children and adults; (4) to reduce or prevent institutionalization by providing community-based or home-based care; and (5) to secure institutional care when other forms are not appropriate.

These goals, especially the fourth, are consistent with the notion of normalization through the provision of appropriate supportive services. Services allowed include homemaker and chore services, home-delivered or congregate meals, day care, respite care, and transportation. Although it is difficult to determine the actual number of people receiving services, it has been estimated that in fiscal 1975, $380 million ($284 million federal funds) were spent to deliver in-home services to two million people. However, expenditures varied widely from state to state, e.g., California spent $88 million, compared to New York, which spent $22 million. (See Table 5.9.)

Morris et al. have provided more detailed information on patterns of expenditures under this program (Table 5.10). The data suggest that even if these social services are theoretically available to families caring for a handicapped member, provision to date has been inadequate.

Table 5.9. Social Services Expenditures (Title XX) Fiscal Year 1975[a]

Service	Expenditures ($000's)	Percentages
Day care	484,718	24.7
In-home services	284,000	14.5
Foster care	264,947	13.5
Services to the mentally retarded	249,247	12.7
Drug abuse/alcoholism	92,241	4.7
Family planning	43,177	2.2
All other (protective, information, etc.)	542,243	27.7
Total federal expenditures	1,962,573	100.0
Total expenditures	2,622,364	—

[a]Source: Adapted from U.S. Department of Health, Education and Welfare, *Long-Term Care: A Challenge to Service Systems, 1977* p. 51.

Table 5.10. Title XX Services[a]

Category	No. states delivering services	Total expenditures (%)	Recipients without income regard (%)
Day care—children	50	22.0	1.1
Foster care—children	41	9.0	7.0
Protective services—children	48	8.0	59.6
Counseling services	43	7.0	8.3
Chore services	35	7.0	0.9
Education/training services	44	7.0	1.8
Homemaker services	49	5.0	1.8
Transportation	45	2.0	1.2
Day care—adults	36	2.0	1.1
Home/congregate meals	32	0.4	0.8
Recreation services	21	<0.1	0.7

[a]Source: Adapted from Morris, R.; Leschier, I.; and Withorn, A. *Analysis of Federally Supported Social Services: Options and Directions.* Waltham: Levinson Policy Institute, Heller School, Brandeis University, September 1977, pp. 6 and 8.

The authors found that some combination of 38 services was being provided by the states. Sixty percent of total expenditures, however, was being spent for only six of these services. Day care for children, potentially a major support for families, was the largest program and was found in all 50 states. Despite this coverage, almost all of the recipients (98.9%) were either recipients of income maintenance or were income eligible. Chore services, another major form of support, were also restricted in practice to low-income populations (99.1%), and coverage was limited to 35 states. Table 5.10 lists five additional services which can be viewed as those services necessary for the development of a supportive network for the handicapped and their families. And yet, they account for less than 10% of the total Title XX expenditures, coverage is not universal in terms of the states, and they are being used only by the low income or poor.

This pattern raises serious questions. Title XX has become the primary funding source for social services. Moreover, it is being used to finance a number of social services that were previously funded by other agencies, e.g., NIMH, Administration on Aging, and Child Welfare. While the notion of consolidation makes sense, it appears that in practice social services are only available to those who meet the income eligibility criteria.

Poverty can be seen as the primary criterion for receiving most federally funded social services. Even those programs which define their eligible populations in terms of handicapping conditions (e.g., Vocational Rehabilitation Services and Developmental Disabilities) or demographic vulnerability (e.g., Administration on Aging), in practice tend to attach such criteria to a consideration of income status (Morris et al., 1977).

The majority of families providing care for handicapped children or elderly parents is probably excluded from these services, not because they do not have a need for the service, but because they are not poor enough. As Title XX has evolved, those services available to the general population (not income eligible) are to meet crises or to protect individuals in danger of being abused or neglected. Whereas the federal regulations require that at least 50% of the recipients be low income, in practice, all are. Furthermore, the $2.5 billion federal ceiling will probably result in little change in defining the target population or in determining which services are to be given priority. Current emphasis would seem to be on day-care and protective services. Considerably less is being used for supportive services. For example, it has been estimated that of the 12.2 million recipients of Title XX services (1977), 100,000 were elderly persons who received services designed specifically for them. These "Services to the Aged" were allocated at $15.9 million, or 0.001 percent of the total Title XX expenditures. Although the elderly do use services available to the general population—e.g., transportation and information and referral—it is felt that their overall share of the total is low (Federal Council on the Aging, 1977).

Child welfare, another potential resource for families with severely retarded children, has two major goals: the first, to strengthen the family through the provision of preventive services (e.g., homemaker services and counseling); the second, to develop appropriate alternatives when necessary (e.g., foster care, adoption). However, a recent survey of child welfare agencies has reported that:

A significant proportion of the child welfare funds appears to be spent on out-of-home care for children such as foster family care and institutional care. . . . Furthermore, resources appear to be directed toward removing children from their own home and placing them in foster care. . . . Currently, 25 percent of children receiving child welfare services are in institutions and such care is costing about one-half of the total budget (Office of Human Development, 1976).

In half of the states, eligibility for services was based on income, and, with the exception of child abuse, outreach received a very low priority. When services are provided in the child's own home, there is some question of its purpose. For example, a homemaker is often seen as "teacher-aide" to a poorly functioning parent. Finally, almost every state reported that the multihandicapped child is the least served population group. It appears that in spite of the goal of strengthening families, the program emphasizes services that substitute for rather than support families, and only low-income families are likely to be eligible for these.

In fiscal 1976, $462 million were obligated for Headstart programs (Table 5.5). This program, within the Office of Human Development, provides comprehensive health, educational, social, and nutritional services to preschool children. The 1972 Amendments to the Economic Opportunity Act require that at least 10% of the children be handicapped. It was estimated that approximately 2,100 mentally retarded children were in Headstart programs. This number represents 7.4% of the handicapped children in the program, or less than 1% of the 287,100 enrollees (Office of Child Development, 1974). In 1976, 350,000 children participated in Headstart programs. If the same proportion of mentally retarded to all handicapped held, approximately 2,600 of the children would have been retarded. This use of a quota is not the only concern. As with other federally funded programs, income is used as a major eligibility criterion.

The final programs listed under the category of general social services (Table 5.5) are the Crippled Children Services and the Maternal and Child Health Services. A little less than $300 million were obligated for these two programs. Both aim toward children in low-income areas and use income to determine eligibility for certain services. Services that are provided include diagnostic, counseling, treatment, and follow-up. Specialized mental retardation clinics have been developed under the Maternal and Child Health programs. In 1971, approximately 61,000 children were seen in 154 clinics. However, of the new patients seen in 1971, 39 percent were found not to be retarded, 38% had IQs between 52 and 84 (borderline and mild), and 23% were severely retarded (IQ less than 52). Furthermore, although these clinics were established to reach the mentally retarded early in their lives, only one third (36.2%) of the new patients were under 5 years of age. Most children were being referred only after beginning school (Office of Mental Retardation Coordinator, 1972).

The final category in Table 5.5 contains those programs that are designed specifically for the handicapped. Nine of these programs are under the Office of Education and are to assist educationally deprived-handicapped children at the preschool and school-age levels. The National Advisory Committee on the Handicapped (1976) has estimated that 90% of all school-age retarded children are being served by the schools. The Bureau of Education for the Handicapped reported that in the school year 1971–1972, 723,747 children with IQs between 51 and 70 and 148,466 children with IQs between 36 and 50 were receiving educational services in the public school system (President's Committee on Mental Retardation, 1976). The National Association for Retarded Citizens (1974) estimated that 826,177 mentally retarded children were served by the schools in 1972–1973, and represented 1.87% of the total school population. Forty-seven states and the District of Columbia have specified ages for eligibility for school services. Fifteen states as of 1974 provided services only to children 6 years or older. Thirty-nine states required the children to be at least 3 years old, and only eight states had not set a lower age limit (Council for Exceptional Children, 1974). Even the most recent legislation dealing with the education of handicapped children (PL 94-142) requires states to provide full educational opportunities only to those children 3 years of age and above.

Although data are not readily available on utilization patterns, it appears that while utilization is growing, the shortfalls are still significant. U.S. Department of Health, Education and Welfare (1977) has estimated that some 250,000 noninstitutionalized mentally retarded persons received some service other than education in 1971. This number represents less than half of the severely retarded and many times less than the total number of all mentally retarded.

Forty-two of 46 states responding to a national survey offered day training services. However, there is a wide variation among the states in the programs offered and the numbers served. For example, one state had six centers serving 96 clients, while another had 163 centers serving 12,000 clients. Furthermore, only 31 of these states served preschool children (National Association of Coordinators of State Programs for the Mentally Retarded, 1974). As of 1970, approximately 92,000 mentally retarded persons received services in some 2,000 facilities. Seventy percent of these facilities offered training, 67% personal care services, 24% sheltered workshops, 10% treatment, and 5% diagnosis and evaluation (Office of Mental Retardation Coordination, 1972). Other services for the mentally retarded person are very spotty. In 1971, for example, an estimated 18,000 individuals were served in activity centers, and in 1974, 7,753 persons were residents in group homes (President's Committee on Mental Retardation, 1976).

While these data are sketchy and even cover different time periods, a number of conclusions are possible. First, many of the services are provided primarily to the adult population; i.e., those 18 to 64 years of age. These include the programs which are employment/training related as well as the residential care programs. Fewer services have been developed for the retarded child, and even these (e.g., education) tend to focus on children 3 years of age and older. Second, these services are usually available to all mentally retarded persons, regardless of severity of the handicapping condition. While it is not possible to determine in most instances the ratio of severely retarded recipients (IQ under 51) to all retarded recipients, it is not only possible but also likely that most recipients are less severely handicapped. Finally, while programs listed under Specific Services for the Handicapped (Table 5.5) account for roughly half of all the programs in the table, their share of the obligated funds was a little more than 1% of the total (1.2%).

This analysis of obligations, expenditures, and utilization patterns suggests the following. The nation has made a commitment to the social well-being of its citizens. Social welfare expenditures have increased significantly over the past three decades, whether measured by per capita expenditures or expenditures as a percentage of the Gross National Product. This trend is found in the three major areas of social welfare: income maintenance, health, and education. A fourth area, broadly defined as social services and housing, although relatively small, still demonstrates considerable growth since 1950.

The analysis further shows that within the Department of Health, Education, and Welfare there has been a serious commitment to develop programs that at least in principle offer services to handicapped persons and their families. Thirty-one programs falling into four clusters were identified and discussed. Approximately 4% of the total funds obligated for these programs in fiscal 1976 were for the provision of services, while the remainder provided financial support (71.4%) or paid for medical-care services (24.5%). However, of the $4.2 billion obligated for services, only 28.6% were specifically earmarked for handicapped persons, while the remainder provided services either for the general population or for a large number of groups designated as "at risk." Although the handicapped are consumers of these more general services, they are not the major users.

Within the framework of relative expenditures, it can be argued that since current levels are greater than they were in the past, more needs are being met. For example, more is being spent on community services today than in past years. Expenditures for these services increased by 34% in just 2 years, 1968–1970 (see Table 5.9). In dollars, this represented almost $500 million in additional funding (from $1.4 billion to $1.9 billion). South Carolina, over an 8-year period (1968–1975), developed 55 day-care programs, 38 adult activity centers, 12 community homes, and 60 family-care homes across the state. Prior to this, there were virtually no community-based services there. Maine spent approximately $3 million (to be matched by $2 million local funds) in 1975, compared to $70,000 in 1970. Alabama spent only $25,000 in 1969, compared to $1.5 million in 1975. The National Association of Coordinators of State Programs for the Mentally Retarded in its report points out that most states have experienced similar developments (President's Committee on Mental Retardation, 1976).

An alternative approach to examining the issue of commitment is to shift the base from past levels (growth) to the numbers at risk or with need. This frame of reference shows that even with these increases, the shortfalls are considerable. To increase use from 5 to 10% of the target population may be a doubling of effort, but it still means that 90% of the need is not being met and that current patterns of growth are inadequate. Earlier sections of this chapter identified utilization of services by the mentally retarded. These same shortfalls are found in services for the elderly. For example, in 1977 there were 28.7 home helps per 100,000 population, a ratio that almost doubled since 1973 (15 per 100,000). However, during this same period, the ratio of home helps per 100,000 population in Sweden grew from 825 to 923; in Norway from 577 to 840; in the Netherlands from 405 to 599; and in Great Britain from 138 to 265 (Little, 1978). Even if these home help services were restricted to the elderly, the 1976 ratio was only 2.6 home helpers per 1,000 elderly.

This general pattern raises a number of troublesome questions. The emphasis on income maintenance and the financing of medical care is based on the assumption that services are either less important or that individuals and families can obtain services if they have the means to pay for them. This assumption, however, has not been borne out. In some instances there has been market failure; in others, the income support has not been adequate. As developed, most services are related to income, so that only those individuals or families with low income are eligible. While many families caring for handicapped members do receive and benefit from these services, more are ineligible. Again, this seems to assume that those whose income is too high to qualify have the means to obtain services. A final problem is that, with few exceptions, benefits and services are provided to individuals and not to families.

Services and financial support are provided to handicapped persons—i.e., the elderly, the sick and disabled, the socially disadvantaged—but the family is not the object of the policy or service. Little emphasis, if any, is given to supporting families caring for mentally retarded children or frail elderly parents. While existing services and benefits may indirectly support these caregivers, they are not provided with them in mind, and it is spurious to argue that if individuals living in families receive support, the entire family is supported. Such a belief may appear logical, but practice has shown otherwise. Overall, these policies have tended to ignore the family with a handicapped member, just as they ignore families in general. This emphasis on the individual is also found in a number of government publications. A striking example of this is the President's Committee on Mental Retardation report, *Mental Retardation . . . The Known and the Unknown* (1975a). In a report of over 100 pages, the family is mentioned just three times. On page 47, the report identifies home health services and public health nursing as "two significant health measures which, in enabling families to deal with special medical or management problems, can minimize the need for residential care outside their homes." Under income maintenance for the retarded, Aid to Families with Dependent Children (AFDC) is listed and statistics on the percentage of retarded recipients reported (p. 59). The final mention of family is found in the section discussing where the mentally retarded live (p. 61). It begins with the statement that "all children cannot live with their families," and then, with one exception, deals with alternatives to family care, e.g., group homes, hostels, boarding homes, foster care, and institutions. The natural home is identified as one of many possible community residential care settings.

This committee report has not been singled out for criticism. It appears to be fairly representative of any number of reports dealing with the handicapped. It is quite useful in that it provides information on the handicapped—their characteristics, their problems, their needs, and services that would support them to live as independently as possible. With this focus, however, the needs of families tend to be deemphasized, and little attention is given to necessary and critical support services.

THE ISSUE OF RESOURCE CONSTRAINTS AND FAMILY SUPPORT

In spite of the considerable growth in social welfare expenditures, there are still significant shortages, and these shortages are continuing to be felt most heavily by the families who are carrying the major responsibility for their handicapped parents and children. While these families may be in a better position than their counterparts of the 1940's and 1950's, insofar as many of the community services either did not exist then or were in their infancy, they are more often viewed as "less needy" than other at-risk groups. Even if additional resources are not made available, most of these families will continue to manage, at least for a time. However, it is somewhat simplistic to assume that when the country enters into another expansionary period and more can be made available for social welfare purposes, the additional resources will filter down to these families. Such a rationale suggests that the needs of these families can only be met after services are provided to those in more acute situations, e.g., the elderly living alone, children in danger of being abused, the mentally retarded without families. Such a position is based on a number of questionable premises, namely, that social welfare expenditures will increase proportionately to economic growth in general; that the needs of those without families will be met eventually; and that the present system is capable of providing appropriate supportive services.

But how realistic is it to expect sufficient increases in expenditures for social welfare purposes in general and for expansion for the handicapped and their families in particular? Furthermore, even if there are increases, what is the likelihood that these families will receive a share of these additional resources? It can be argued that, given the present highly specialized social welfare system, a system made up of a large number of loosely connected public and private agencies, expansion and an emphasis on family support are unlikely. It is naive to expect significant increases in resources to provide a minimum level of income, access to medical care, and personal social services, given the anticipated higher prevalence rates of handicapping conditions, unless the system itself is restructured. If the norm continues to be fragmentation, and each categorical subsystem is allowed to expand as it pleases, priorities for resource allocation will be established primarily through competitive, rather than rational, processes. As it is now, agencies find themselves competing with other agencies for resources. In periods of retrenchment, agencies dealing with some groups of disabled find themselves at a distinct disadvantage, whether their numbers are small compared to others (e.g., the visually handicapped) or the specific disability is less attractive politically (e.g., the alcoholic). Additionally, a number of the disabled and their families are well organized for lobbying efforts, while others are not. Unchecked, it is conceivable to imagine a scenario where advocates for different groups of disabled persons vie with each other to prove that some disabilities are more important than others, that some disabled are more worthy than others. It may be argued, for example, that children should be given priority over the elderly since their lives are just beginning; that the blind and the mentally retarded should be favored over the alcoholic and the drug abuser since they themselves were not responsible for their disability; that adults should receive disproportional amounts of resources since they can contribute to overall economic growth by working, while children and the elderly are basically consumers. Although each group is sincere and rational in what it does, the enemy becomes "other" disabled, and survival is achieved only at the expense of others. Only by bringing together all disabled and professionals, by forming a unified front, does expansion become possible.

A fresh look at the organization of services would permit a more systematic consideration of alternatives, which might range from better coordination among the fragmented and incomplete specialities to a more structured and generic approach to the problem. Given our negative experiences with coordination efforts (the current policy thrust), it is suggested by some that only large-scale reorganization can be effective.

Two strategies are usually offered. The first involves restructuring agencies in terms of functional needs with emphasis on certain commonalities. All the disabled, regardless of diagnosis, have difficulty performing the major functions considered normal for their age; the severely disabled require attention from an adult for some time of the day or night; the situation will persist for many years. There are also financial difficulties, family stress, and a lack of social stimulation. In reorganizing the system along functional lines, high-quality, specialized services can be offered to all disabled regardless of the specific diagnosis. The alternative is to build on the growing trend to restructure governmental agencies into umbrella human service configurations. Although the evidence to date is not clear, the concept is appropriate. What is needed is the development of mechanisms to integrate these services at the delivery level. To date, most efforts have emphasized state-level operations, with little attention given to changing community structures.

A second concern for proponents of a generic approach is that the fragmented system has dissipated any meaningful effort on behalf of community support services that are needed by most disabled. While there are agencies, programs, and lobbies for the blind, the mentally retarded, and children with cerebral palsy, there are none for meals on wheels, home care, or transportation services, and needed expansion in this area has suffered. A restructuring along some dimension of a generic approach would highlight these deficiencies.

The issue of generic services is controversial. While specialized knowledge and skills are essential, it does not necessarily follow that they can only be developed through categorical agencies. The provision of services specifically for the handicapped or for a distinct group of handicapped persons tends to isolate them from other people and may deny them equal opportunity. In the past, for example, it has led to the provision of poorly paid jobs that were inappropriate to the potential of the handicapped worker. Furthermore, it is interesting to note the demands by parents of mentally retarded children for admission to ordinary schools and for opportunities for their children to interact with nonhandicapped children. They argue that segregation often reinforces rather than corrects negative attitudes in local communities.

The difficult question remains, however, as to how comprehensive the generic approach should be. It would be easy to destroy the effectiveness of any program by making it so comprehensive that the needs of all the handicapped are included, such as housing, income maintenance, medical care, education, rehabilitation, and socialization. There are approaches between the extremes of specialized agencies and fully generic agencies that should be examined more thoroughly. They include programs such as Triage in Connecticut, which provides comprehensive services under a single administration. These services range from acute hospital care, through intermediate nursing and home nursing services, to chore and neighborhood support services. Other examples are Personal Care Organizations, Community Care Corps, and Home Care Corps, all of which are organized on relatively generic grounds. These efforts, while building on the common needs of the handicapped, do not necessarily imply that all agencies be restructured to meet the functional needs of the disabled. Rather, they are building meaningful bridges with the specialized agencies by creating interfacing mechanisms. These efforts are also realistic attempts to reexamine the relationship between the community support system for the long-term disabled and institutional care. Despite the rhetoric of choice and preferences for the handicapped and their families, priority (resources) has been given to the latter. And yet, the evidence shows that most families favor home care over institutional care and that they are doing so with little support from the organized health and welfare system.

Much of the reluctance to address the issue of an integrated policy stance lies in the fear that in highlighting these needs and the probability that total costs will mushroom over the next few decades, government will seek ways to retrench. However, there is little evidence to support a position based on the hope that by not raising the issue, resources will be made available. The problem of financing has to be confronted head on if an adequate and effective program for handicapped persons and their families is to be achieved, and a number of alternatives should be considered and analyzed.

Insuring lifetime maintenance care for the severely disabled in much the same way that the acute aspect of catastrophic illnesses is now insured is one option. To be feasible, however, greater attention should be given to identifying populations at risk. This task is complex in that there are many technical and clinical differences related to the nature of the condition. The blind, retarded children, individuals with multiple sclerosis, the quadriplegic, the severely crippled arthritic, all have different clinical requirements. There is still a need, however, to aggregate disabling conditions across diagnostic categories, and yet there are no commonly used or accepted criteria of severe disability. Numerous scales measuring activities of daily living, such as Barthel's and Pulse's, measure not only functional status but also intellectual and emotional adaptability, but none of these permits comprehensive aggregation of data. Once these aggregations are feasible, it would then become possible to derive firmer estimates about the range of services or benefits the at-risk population is likely to require and to identify the likely utilization rate.

An approach other than full insurance would involve payment in a form comparable to the disability allowance in the United Kingdom (Constant Attendance Allowance), whereby individuals identified as needing the attention of another person are given a supplementary cash allowance so that they may secure the supportive assistance they require. This allowance is not income tested, but is given solely on the basis of disability.

Short of full insurance, the present Medicare and Medicaid programs could be expanded to encourage the provision of less costly and often more desirable home care services. If one chooses a noninsurance route, a variety of existing programs may be considered for expansion into more generic approaches, such as programs for the blind and for crippled children. The new amendments to the Social Security Act (Title XX) that provide for personal social services may be considered as a viable nucleus around which to construct such a system.

Regardless of the specific mechanism, whether it is the creation of a national health insurance program, some form of guaranteed income related to disability, or the large-scale development of various generic supportive services, it is unlikely that such comprehensive policies can be realized unless the professionals, the agencies, and the lay associations present a united front. If these organizations continue to act separately and only push for distinct categorical groups of handicapped, these policy issues will be either ignored or given low priority.

Finally, while the issues of adequate resources and more effective delivery systems are critical, there are still others as important. Increases in resources and a new organizational structure are two key dimensions, but only two. A third component is the attitude and behavior of those persons in direct contact with the recipient, the staff responsible for actually providing the services. These three—resources, structure, and professional practice—cannot be separated, and each will have an influence on the overall effect of improving the status of families with handicapped children and elderly parents. This issue is dealt with in the next chapter.

6 THE PROFESSIONAL RESPONSE: THE CAREGIVING FUNCTION

The previous chapter examined the issue of the State's responsibility to meet social need in general and, specifically, its relationship to families with handicapped members. It was suggested that if patterns of expenditure were used as an indicator of commitment, the State has demonstrated its social concern despite the fact that serious shortages still exist. But reliance on this form of analysis can be misleading and counterproductive because it assumes that solutions are known and that social needs will be met when adequate levels of resources become available. Furthermore, the analysis is based on the notion that the needs have been identified, that they are known, and that they will remain constant over time. Yet, there is every likelihood that, as the State provides more services, it will be called upon to make greater and greater provision. Increases in services may heighten expectation and trigger new demand, and need itself must be viewed as relative and fluid (Moroney, 1976).

In spite of significant expansion in the social services, families providing care to handicapped parents or severely retarded children are still receiving fewer services relative to other groups. While the State has explicitly noted in numerous pieces of social legislation that its primary function is to strengthen the capacities of families, and only when this is not possible to substitute for the family, this secondary function still consumes most of the available resources. Some of the factors associated with this pattern have been discussed, namely, inadequate resources and the way services have been organized. The conclusion, however, that the solution to this problem would be only to provide more resources and to restructure service delivery systems is incomplete without including a third and equally significant part of the equation—the attitudes of the people responsible for providing the services. These three are interdependent factors.

Services tend to be organized in such a way that emphasis is clearly on substituting for families, on taking over certain functions that families are incapable or unwilling to perform, on becoming a surrogate family either totally or partially. It is critical to determine whether professionals in these agencies merely respond to this definition of function and purpose or whether they themselves are conditioned in their training to substitute for families. The former suggests that once resources become available and services organized around support, professionals would behave differently. In this view, professionals are capable of responding to any situation, since as professional caregivers they are flexible and adaptable. The latter interpretation, that professional behavior is conditioned by training, argues that no amount of additional resources or restructuring of organizations will bring about interventions that support families caring for handicapped members, since professionals are either unwilling to function in this way or incapable of doing so because they do not know how to support.

This issue is, of course, stated in polar or dichotomous terms. Such is not the intent. As with resources, professional behavior and attitudes fall on various points of a continuum. In the previous chapter, services were classified as either supportive or substitutive; it was necessary to go beyond the simple description of the service—e.g., institutional care or community care. The purpose of the service, implicit or explicit, became the primary criterion. Why was it being delivered? What was it attempting to achieve? In recognizing that most services could not be neatly identified as either/or, the analysis looked for emphases.

It also has to be so in examining professional response. Regardless of the agency's expressed purpose, some professionals define their functions as either supportive or substitutive. Still others see their function changing from case to case, client to client, patient to patient. It should be possible to identify dominant themes related to professional attitudes, themes that describe family-professional interaction. These themes should indicate what, if anything, should be done if both sets of caregivers were to share responsibility for handicapped persons.

ATTITUDES TOWARD FAMILIES: A TYPOLOGY

Using such descriptors as family care, family support, family structure, family systems, and family services, 551 citations were produced from computer searches of *Sociological Abstracts* and *Psychological*

Abstracts. A third search, undertaken from the National Library of Medicine's National Interactive Retrieval Service, *Medlars II,* produced 238 citations. Given the type of literature covered by this system, descriptors such as family and elderly, family and handicapped, family and mentally retarded, and community support were used. The fourth and final search was provided by the Division of Special Mental Health Programs, National Institute of Mental Health, and produced 511 citations. In all, 1,300 articles, books, or reports were generated and abstracted. Of this pool, 312 specifically dealt with the issue of family care as defined in the study. An additional 213 citations were identified from the citations produced by these searches and from other sources. The total working bibliography, then, contained 525 citations, each of which came under one of the following major categories: mental retardation, mental illness, physically handicapped children (excluding the mentally retarded), or physically handicapped elderly. Each citation was then content analyzed and evaluated in terms of the following five conceptual views:

1. *Families as part of the problem.* A number of citations dealing with families with mentally or physically handicapped children and physically handicapped elderly tended to discuss the family as a barrier to the successful treatment and rehabilitation of the individual. When the desired outcomes were not achieved, the family received much of the blame. The mental health literature discussed the family as a part of the problem in a different way. These studies viewed individual illness as symptomatic of family pathology in general.

2. *Families as resources to the handicapped person.* These studies tended to view the family as caregiver to the handicapped individual. The family members are not discussed as people in their own right, but seem to exist only in terms of the handicapped child or elderly parent.

3. *Families as resources to the professional caregiver.* In this literature, the family continues to be viewed as a resource to the handicapped person but now functions as an extension of the professional. The assumption underlying this approach is that the professional maintains overall responsibility for diagnosis and treatment but also delegates certain tasks to the family. The family, of course, carries out these functions under the supervision of the professional.

4. *Professionals as resources to the family.* These studies are significantly different from the above three. Although the focus is still on the successful treatment/rehabilitation of the handicapped person, the family is recognized as the primary caregiver. Whereas in the third cat-

egory, the family is supportive to the professional and is dependent on professional direction, this literature emphasizes that family caregivers in their own right are capable diagnosticians (at least in terms of needs and services) and can carry major responsibilities for much of the treatment/rehabilitation process. The professionals become supportive to the family, and the dependency relationship has shifted to some degree.

5. *Families needing resources.* This category includes literature that for the first time shifts the focus from the individual (the object of the intervention) to the family. The family is recognized as a unit in its own right, a unit that needs support because it is providing care to a handicapped member. Because the presence of a handicapped child or frail elderly parent often brings with it physical, social, emotional, and financial stress to other family members, supportive services are made available to prevent or ameliorate any accompanying problems.

The analysis showed that the typologies had to be used more as ideal types rather than discrete categories into which each citation could be placed. For example, in many studies emphasizing that families were part of the problem, the implicit assumption was that families could be effective resources to the handicapped individual. Families were, therefore, viewed as objects of treatment, at least initially, so that they could be caregivers. Moreover, although categories 3 (families as resources to the professional caregiver) and 4 (professionals as resources to the family) are conceptually distinct and the difference in emphasis is significant, it was often impossible to determine into which category a number of citations should be placed. It was therefore decided to combine the two into a single category in which the family was viewed as a part of the caregiving team. Where possible and appropriate, the distinctions were noted. Finally, the analysis was able to determine patterns, even though many of the individual citations had to be counted in more than one category.

Following this coding process, a number of alternative ways to present and interpret these "data" were explored. One possibility was to use the professional discipline as the organizing principle. Did professionals tend to react differently to families with handicapped members? Is there a distinct pattern, for example, among psychiatrists that is significantly different from that found in social workers, nurses, counselors, therapists, physicians, etc.? A preliminary analysis showed some discipline-unique patterns but also enough deviation to cloud the results. For example, psychiatric social workers may tend to approach the family as part of the problem, while medical social workers may emphasize the family as part of a rehabilitation team or as a resource for the handicapped individual. These same patterns were found among physicians, nurses, and counselors. Although inconclusive, the first hypothesis—agencies determine how the individual professional will react to the family—seemed to be supported. However, the data were ambiguous, and the approach along discipline lines was deemphasized. A second possibility for aggregation was to organize the findings around handicapping conditions. As mentioned earlier, these included mentally retarded children, physically handicapped children, physically handicapped elderly, and the mentally ill. This approach proved to be more fruitful. First, to some extent it controlled for the agency defining functions and professional behavior; second, it produced distinct patterns; and finally, it offered the possibility for policy intervention.

It was decided that such a review should also examine these emphases on family care along a time dimension. With a 20-year review, was it possible to determine shifts in attitudes and approaches? For example, did professionals dealing with mentally retarded children see families as contributing to the problem 10 or 15 years ago? Do they now see families as team members or as needing resources in their own right? If these trends exist, they argue for an evolutionary process that will eventually result in more family support.

These five views of family should not be seen as a continuum, with one end superior to the other. Such a progression is not intended. Although the argument to this point has been for more supportive services to families providing care to handicapped children and parents (category 5), it has also emphasized the notion of shared responsibility underlying categories 3 and 4 (family as part of the caregiving team). These views of the family are compatible and not counterproductive. It is also likely that in some instances families do actually inhibit or retard the rehabilitation of the handicapped member. If they are to be effective caregivers (assuming they want to function as such), they have to be helped. The notion underlying this form of intervention is not to support family members but to treat them. The object of treatment begins with the handicapped person and expands to define other members as patients or clients. The purpose of the intervention is to bring the family to the point where they can function effectively as caregivers or providers of social services. The following analysis identified examples of the literature falling into one or more of the conceptual typologies. The listing is not offered as exhaustive in any sense. It is drawn from the general bibliography used in this study.

FAMILIES AS PART OF THE PROBLEM

While much of the literature under this heading tends to view the family as a potential barrier to successful treatment of the handicapped member rather than to emphasize the family as causing the problem, it is useful to begin with this latter position. While families are not described as causing the physical handicap or the mental retardation as is often the case in mental illness, many professionals appear to interact with family members from this perspective of pathology. How, then, are these families defined by professionals?

In their review of the literature covering the years 1920–1958, Spiegel and Bell (1959) point out that most mental health practitioners assumed that if an individual experienced problems, the entire family had a problem. Furthermore, most professionals, in their search for the etiology of the individual's illness, began with a focus on the family and the events antecedent to the development of the illness. The family was more often than not identified as contributing to the etiology, usually in one of three ways. Faulty parent-child relationships, structural aspects of the family (e.g., birth order, number of siblings), and genetic or constitutional factors were all presumed to be factors. They report, further, that in those studies in which family factors were considered to be related to the occurrence of mental illness, half attributed the problem to "one or more traits in the patient which were seen as unchanging, permanent aspects of the mother's or father's personality and behavior. . . . In the other half the investigators have viewed the pathogenesis of the child's disturbance as the result of a process of on-going events between parents and the child and in a few instances of the dynamic interrelationships throughout the family" (p. 98).

A more recent review article (Kreisman and Joy, 1974) argues that this earlier approach tends to still dominate practice. Throughout the 1960's and into the 1970's "the study of the family in relation to the mental illness of a relative has generally focused on its possible role as an etiological factor in the origin or outcome of the disorder." Appleton (1974) supports this conclusion and states that "many schools of psychiatric thought implicate the patient's family in aggravating or even generating the illness." This literature, then, emphasizes the need to focus on the family unit when attempting to identify the nature and cause of the problem—the diagnostic task (see also, Ehrlich, 1962; Meszaros and Meszaros, 1961).

Much of the literature on mental illness discusses the appropriateness of identifying the family as the treatment unit when one member is ill. Robinson (1975) explains that "in family therapy, the dominant forces in personality development are thought to be located externally in the organized behavioral characteristics of the family . . . the family is viewed as a rule governed, change resistant, transactional system with an operational program that has evolved through several generations. . . ." Numerous articles, such as those by Aponte (1974) and Gatti and Colman (1976), describe techniques to involve the family in the therapeutic process on the assumption that the entire family has contributed to the problem.

Two other variations on this theme are also found in the literature. Whereas families, especially parents, are not seen as the "cause" of the problem when a child is mentally retarded or physically handicapped, they have at times been seen as incapable caregivers or as barriers to successful treatment.

Wolfensberger (1967) and Carr (1975), in their review articles, suggest that professionals until and through the early 1960's strongly urged parents of severely retarded children to seek institutionalization as soon as possible after birth. This recommendation was related to the notion that the family could do very little for the child, that the condition was irreversible, and that if the child were to remain with his or her family, all would suffer. It was further estimated that 80% of pediatricians recommended institutionalization at birth (Werkman, Washington, and Oberman, 1961). Kramm (1963) reported that 44 of 50 families with mongoloid children were advised to institutionalize when informed of the diagnosis, and 31 were urged to do so immediately. Physicians tended to discuss this decision only with the father and before the mother had seen the child (Aldrich, 1947). Farber (1960) wrote persuasively that institutionalization was the only effective strategy to preserve the rest of the family. Most professionals believed that if families elected to keep their children at home, they did so because they were "guilt ridden, anxiety laden and overprotective" (Barsch, 1968; Wolfensberger, 1967). When families opposed professional advice, they were relegated to the role of secondary patients. The parents, furthermore, were provided counseling services or psychotherapy so that they eventually would accept institutionalization (Cohen, 1962).

Even after the professionals changed their attitudes about institutional care being superior to family care, family problems and pathology were emphasized in the literature. Pinkerton (1970) writes of parental anger and overprotection and, through the use of numerous examples, discusses how parents' attitudes are counterproductive to the child's well-being. Poznanski (1973) also discusses the reactions of parents to the birth of a handicapped child and emphasizes how they create barriers to successful rehabilitation.

This view of the family is also found in the literature dealing with the care of physically handicapped children and adults. Goldie (1966) points out that when a child is "sick, abnormal or deformed," the child psychiatrist should be aware of family adjustment problems that could stand in the way of treatment. This view is supported by Kohut (1966 p. 166), who argues for family counselling: "For the sake of the abnormal child, it is essential that parents receive guidance with identifying some of the troubled and complex feelings that exist between them and their child and other members of the family." Binger et al. (1969), in discussing childhood leukemia, found that 50% of the families in the study had one or more family members developing emotional disturbances that were severe enough to interfere with adequate social functioning and that required psychiatric help. Others, such as Perrin et al. (1972), Davis (1975), and Pless (1976), argued that long-term illness and disability in a child are usually accompanied by problems of adaptation by other family members and that the child's treatment is related to parental coping and attitudes more than to the degree of disability. Initially the purpose of Perrin's study was to determine the effectiveness of physician and social worker involvement in a comprehensive care program for handicapped children. Finding little evidence of professional input and successful outcome, the authors seem to imply that the family was somehow impeding the treatment/rehabilitation process.

Livsey (1972) argues from a perspective that includes the whole family and not just the handicapped adult. Though the stated purpose of this focus was to identify ways to help families cope, the article draws heavily on family-focused literature that diagnoses the family as the patient. Peck (1974), in discussing the family dynamics of rehabilitation, presents case studies in which the family was clearly a barrier to treatment and concludes that "it is not safe to presume a blanket of good will motivation on the family's part towards its disabled relative . . . . If the rehabilitation of one family member goes sour, it most frequently is a sign that other family members are involved in some uncooperative strategy." Another study (Moss and Kaplan-De-nour 1975) found that in renal failure and chronic hemodialysis cases, families tended to have negative accusing attitudes toward the patient, signs of empathy were missing, and any professional attempt to help in that direction was rejected.

In labeling this literature as emphasizing pathology, either from the perspective that the family is somewhat responsible for the individual member's handicapping condition or that the family is a block to successful rehabilitation or treatment, it is not being implied that this approach is misdirected. If families do have problems, it is legitimate that the family as well as the handicapped person becomes the treatment unit. But such an approach is longstanding and has great currency. It begins with the notion that, until demonstrated otherwise, family pathology exists. For example, Leavitt (1975) reports that families of patients to be discharged from mental hospitals complained that, in preparing for this, they were being treated by the professional staff as if they were patients and not as responsible caregivers. Or, even more pernicious, family members seem to be blamed for unsuccessful treatment outcomes, while professionals are responsible for the successes.

Another theme that has emerged more recently also begins with a variation of this assumption. Whereas 25 years ago, the decision to keep a severely retarded child in the home was seen as symptomatic of underlying pathology on the part of parents, today this same diagnosis of pathology is made when parents seek institutionalization. Hewett (1976) points out that the current professional attitude assumes that seeking institutional care indicates a rejecting attitude on the part of the mother. Wolfensberger (1971b:37), a leading advocate for community and family care, has argued that parents should not have the right to decide whether to keep a retarded child or to transfer the care to some other social institution. "We need to reconceptualize the parental right as being one of seeking divestiture of the child but not necessarily of implementing it. At least where public funds are involved, society through its representatives, and not the parents, must be conceptualized as making the ultimate decision on whether parental demand for divestiture should be met." Wolfensberger goes on to recommend that foster care become a major alternative to family (natural) care since many parents refrain from transferring their responsibility if they know that another family, probably in the same town, will accept the child as their own. The assumptions behind this position are clear. Home care is always superior to institutional care. It is better for the child, better for the parents, better for the other children. Any deviation from this is considered to be an indication of pathology. Furthermore, just as the present administration's initial welfare-reform proposal sought to strengthen families by forcing filial responsibility, so this approach would coerce parental responsibility on the assumption that it would be in the best interest of the family.

FAMILIES AS RESOURCES TO THE HANDICAPPED PERSON

While some of the authors cited in the above category do identify the family as a potential resource to the handicapped member, they are not discussed under this heading since they tend to define the family in pathological terms. Families are expected to have problems when a handicapped person is present. These problems retard the treatment/rehabilitation of the handicapped person. Finally, the family is viewed as a unit needing treatment if it is to become an effective resource.

The literature included in this category begins with the assumption that families can be capable caregivers. Families are seen as under stress, but stress is not equated with pathology. When a child is born with a severe handicap or an elderly parent has a stroke, family equilibrium is disturbed, a crisis exists, and adjustments are required.

As early as 1962, Cohen pointed out that parents go through a series of stages when they learn that they have a handicapped child, but that these stages are normal reactions and not indications of family breakdown. Both she and Wolfensberger (1967) argue that most parents adjust to these crises and can provide a vital caring function to the child. Neither, of course, is suggesting that families do not need support in working through these crises. They argue that parents do have strengths, and coping patterns can be developed.

Yannett (1957:169), reacting to the then current practice of recommending institutionalization for children born with severe mental retardation, argued that such actions were questionable. He stated: "It is difficult to rationalize successfully the withdrawal from what must be one of the strongest instinctual demands of parents—the care of the young." Yannett's argument is simple: Parents of handicapped children have much in common with parents of nonhandicapped children. One area is parenting or child rearing, and, although handicapped children may make greater demands and create additional stress, their parents more often than not feel they can or should carry out this function.

Hobbs (1975:116) suggests that when children are handicapped, there is a tendency for professionals to neglect or deemphasize the "vital child rearing roles of family," the "normal source of affection, security, instruction and discipline of children in our society." Others, such as MacKeith (1973), emphasize that a major function of parents with handicapped children is to provide emotional support, and that, until proved otherwise, the family setting is the best environment for this. Birenbaum (1971) argues that the family is able to help the retarded child in expressive activities, at least while the child is young. Later, as the child grows older, he needs outside help. Caplan (1976), agreeing with Hobbs, views the family as the appropriate support system for the handicapped child and identifies a number of critical parenting functions. These functions, he suggests, are not unique to parents of retarded children but are universal to all families with children. His premise is that families with handicapped children have much in common with families in general. These parenting functions include: (1) the collection and dissemination of information; (2) the provision of appropriate feedback to the child (i.e., a guidance system); (3) a source of personal ideology; (4) service as mediator and guide for problem solving; (5) a source of practical and concrete services; (6) an environment for recuperation; and (7) a source and validation of personal identity.

This position is more than just wishful thinking or undue optimism. Fowle (1968), in her comparison study of families providing care to retarded children and families who had institutionalized their children, reports that the former did experience considerable stress but were able to function as capable caregivers. Stress, however, was not defined as pathology, and these families did not exhibit more numerous problems than those who had given up the caring function. The amount of literature on this issue is large and was discussed in Chapter 4.

The mental health literature tends to deemphasize families as caregivers. Families are identified as important to treatment and successful outcome, but the weight of the argument is toward family pathology and treatment of the family. There are, of course, exceptions. Rubenstein (1972) states that families can and should share responsibility for the patient's treatment, not because they are responsible for the illness, but because they can do so and thus prevent institutionalization. Hall and Bradley (1975) and Mannino and Shore (1974) report that patients discharged to receptive families have need for fewer services than those patients without families or whose families are unwilling to assume responsibility for the caring function. What distinguishes these writers from their colleagues in mental health seems to be their approach to families. While the former assume pathology until proven otherwise, the latter tend to begin with the notion that families can support the mentally ill member. They do, of course, recognize that in some instances families may have "caused" or exacerbated the problem, and in other instances the family is a barrier to treatment. Family members are then appropriate objects of treatment. Their conclusion is simple: Assume the family can be a resource until the weight of evidence demonstrates this to be impossible.

While there are more examples of articles discussing families as resources to the physically handicapped than those found in the mental health literature, the number is considerably lower than those discussing family care and mentally retarded children. Two emphases are found: the first, the important management function of family members as well as the general socialization of the handicapped member (Mattson, 1972; Kogan and Tyler, 1973; and Battle, 1974). Critical to this is the family's acceptance of the handicap and its ability to accommodate uncertainty. The second and complementary position discusses the need for professionals to give accurate information on the diagnosis, prognosis, and treatment plan (Tymchuk, 1975; Jenkins et al., 1976). In doing so, it is felt that the caregivers can realistically anticipate difficulties, that present and future stress can be defused, and that family members will be in a position to assume an active role in the care of the handicapped member.

FAMILIES AS TEAM MEMBERS

"In reviewing the medical literature over the past twenty years, the terms 'team' and 'team approach' have become increasingly common in all fields which suggests that we have entered the 'Age of the Team' in the delivery of health care, not just for handling chronic illness and complex long-term problems, but also in providing care for short-term acute problems" (Katz et al., 1975:218). The team approach evolved initially in the field of rehabilitation, where it became apparent that the variety and complexity of patients' needs could not be met by professionals working alone. These needs were some combination of medical, psychiatric, social, and vocational. Given the fragmented nature of the human service delivery system, multidisciplinary teams were organized to diagnose and treat the "whole patient." In time, this team came to include not only physicians and nurses, but a growing number of allied health professionals such as social workers, nutritionists, physical and speech therapists, health aides, and psychologists.

Historically, the physician has been pivotal, and other team members were viewed as ancillary. Moreover, relatives of the patient were not seen as part of this team. Parsons (1951), in his article on the role of physicians, notes that the patient was expected to become dependent on the professional, since only the professionally trained could know enough to cure. The "good patient" accepted this status difference and followed orders. A patient, often defined to include family members, was a person in need of help as determined by the professional. Goffman (1961) expanded on this notion by observing that patients were required to place absolute trust in the knowledge and techniques of the professional, since only the professional could translate symptoms into diagnosis and treatment.

This practice of excluding the patient and the family from the team has been questioned over time. It has been found that when perceptions of needs differed between professionals and family members, the treatment plan tended not to be carried out (Bedard, 1967). One response has been the development of procedures to orient patients and their families so that they will understand and accept the professional's reason for whatever is recommended. While this strategy is still not based on accepting family members as equal partners, it does expand the role of nonprofessional caregivers.

The literature in this section has two distinct emphases. The first views the family as part of the team but secondary to the professionals. Family members can carry out certain functions under the supervision of others. Just as early developments in team care were dependent on the ability to divide tasks historically performed by the physician and delegating some of them to "lower level" personnel, families were brought into the team when certain tasks could be identified as nonprofessional. Magraw (1968) and Mills (1967) label these as the role of knower and the role of doer. In one context physicians are knowers (problems-solving knowledge) and ancillary professionals are doers (performing a technical function). In another context, all professionals are knowers and possibly doers, but family caregivers are never knowers. They do something under a professional's direction. The second type of literature views family members as both knowers and doers. They are fully participating team members and as such contribute to the diagnostic/assessment function as well as to the treatment phase.

As an example of the latter, Matheny and Vernick (1969) report on a study of parents with retarded children who were asked to estimate the level of the child's functional ability. These children were then assessed by professionals. The results showed little difference between professional and parental assessment. The one difference found was that parents tended to have slightly higher expectations as to the capability of the child for learning various tasks. A followup of the children showed that the parents were in fact more realistic than the professionals.

Increasingly, parents of mentally retarded children are seen by professionals as effective teachers. This trend is frequently based on learning theory or behavior modification (Dorenberg, 1972). Parents are beginning to be accepted as both correct and reasonable in their demands for information, guidance, and training techniques rather than in need of psychodynamically based counseling.

This view of parents underscores programs developing skills in parents while their children are in institutions (Bullington et al., 1976), in various out-reach programs such as the Georgia Program (Hamilton, 1975), and in the growing number of parent group programs (Jew, 1974). In these efforts the professional developed a partnership relationship with the parents and in most instances acted as resource persons. The Parent Involvement Programs, first developed in the mid-1960's, have demonstrated the effectiveness of this strategy. Wiegering et al. (1978), in their review of the literature on these projects, report that outcomes as measured by IQ and achievement were favorable and long lasting. Their review included the studies of Karnes and Zehrbach (1975), Bronfenbrenner (1974), and Lazar et al. (1977).

Some writers have ventured further. Goolsby (1976) sees professionals and the parents of mentally retarded children as interdependent and partners, interacting to identify needed services. Duff (1976:74) argues that the physician does not have the right to unilaterally decide on what should be done: ". . . at issue is how the family and other resources are used, how people live . . . since individuals have strong feelings about such things, the deliberated choices of patients and families should be considered pivotal if not paramount for they primarily must bear the consequences." Boggs (1978) is forceful in her discussion of family care of the retarded, as opposed to institutional care. She evaluates family care as successful if the care is tolerated by the family without major psychic costs to parents and siblings, and if such care is at least as beneficial to the handicapped person as some other alternative care. She continues her argument by asserting that parents are more often than not in the best position to make the decision. Neither Duff nor Boggs is eliminating the contribution that professionals make in these decisions, but they have moved away from the more dominant belief about professionals as described by Parsons.

The mental health literature that views the family as part of the team has a different emphasis. Here the concern seems to be on lessening the demand for services, especially for institutional care. Clausen and Yarrow (1955) argued almost 30 years ago that if families were to participate as caregivers, more discharges would be possible and, as importantly, readmission rates would be lowered. Their concern as stated, however, was that mental hospitals were lacking in resources and were understaffed. If families provided services, this pressure on the system would be lessened. Shea (1950) came to the same conclusion when he pointed out the value of hospital staff working with family members before discharge and then maintaining an ongoing supportive relationship with them. The primary emphasis was not on the well-being of the patient so much as on the well-being of an overly taxed mental health system. In benefiting the system it was, of course, implied that the patient would benefit. As Leavitt (1975) stated, such objectives could be achieved if families accepted their share of the care and treatment of psychiatric patients.

Examples of literature viewing family members as part of the team are numerous in the area of physical handicap. Insofar as this literature emphasizes the medical care approach, families tend to be included for two reasons. The first is simply the notion that if family members participate in the caregiving function, they are likely to carry out professional recommendations. In assuming the role of ancillary personnel, they implicitly agree to supervision. Second, just as nurses, social workers, therapists, and other members of the team work under the direction of the physician leader and become physician extenders, so also do family members become extenders. The team approach achieves coordination and service integration through a form of control. Members are coopted (in a positive sense) and work toward common goals. In this case, the goal is the successful treatment/rehabilitation of the patient, and more care is made available.

This cooptation idea is significant. It differs from the pathological position that begins by treating family members so that they will not obstruct patient care (the family as patient) and will be able to fuction as a resource to the patient. The team approach does not assume pathology. It does recognize that if family members are excluded from the treatment planning and treatment delivery process, the outcome can be negatively affected. Kanthor et al. (1974) found that patient care was uncoordinated if the professionals did not provide a clear understanding of what was happening to family caregivers, and this lack of coordination slowed the process significantly. This recommendation has been supported by the work of Kisly (1973), Schwab (1975), and Weller (1976), who argue that the successful patient outcome is as much related to family members participating with professionals in the rehabilitation process as it is to the quality of the professional care.

The extender notion (similar to the literature on mental retardation, where parents become teachers) is equally important. Goodell (1975) typifies this approach when she suggests that hospital personnel should instruct family members in proper methods of administering medical care, including procedures for physically transferring patients from bed to chair, etc., and for feeding, bathing, and dressing. The caregivers thus extend the nursing and physical therapy staff. Houghton and Martin (1976) describe a home program which emphasizes helping the family provide the patient with necessary dietetic and personal care while the professional team maintains the medical, nursing, social, and therapeutic function.

In general, this literature assumes that family members can be effective caregivers. What is of note is that only in the literature dealing with mental retardation is there an explicit commitment to family members as coequal members of the team. In the literature discussing mental illness and physical illness, professionals tend to view the family as a resource to the professional caregivers. In the former instance, the family is viewed as the primary social service, and professionals define their function as supportive. The handicapped person is treated/rehabilitated by the family, which in turn is assisted by others. In the latter case, the professionals are the primary social services, and family members support them. Under appropriate supervision, they are encouraged and trained to carry out certain nonprofessional or quasi-professional tasks. The family becomes an extension of the professional team, thus benefiting the professional caregivers.

FAMILIES NEEDING RESOURCES

Up to this point, the literature cited has focused on the handicapped individual. Here the emphasis shifts dramatically; the family becomes the object of the intervention, and services are discussed in terms of supporting the nonhandicapped members. The handicapped child or adult still retains a place of prominence, and rehabilitation or treatment services are not ignored. However, unlike the previous literature, the family is not viewed primarily as a resource to the individual or to the professional. These authors argue instead that the decision to care for a handicapped person tends to bring with it considerable demands on other family members and more often than not disrupts normal family functioning. It is further argued that unless supportive services are made available, the family's ability to function as effective caregivers is threatened and in time the handicapped person and other family members will suffer.

The pressures that families are experiencing were discussed in detail in Chapter 4. It was shown that families caring for severely retarded children and families caring for frail elderly parents faced similar stresses. It was further suggested that these stresses were probably common to families providing care to handicapped persons in general, regardless of the diagnosis. These included in a generic sense the following: financial stress associated with the care of the handicapped person; the significant amount of time required for personal care; the physical well-being of the caregiver; constant interruptions of family routines, including sleeping; the sense of social isolation and a perceived stigmatization by others; difficulties in shopping, household routines, and limitations in recreation and other social activities; the handling of behavioral problems; the sense of limited prospects for the future.

The analysis in Chapter 5 showed that, although financial assistance, medical care, and social services are available and have grown in both scope and scale, these services are designed to support the handicapped individual. Relatively speaking, services to support families are nonexistent. Family needs are not recognized.

And yet, there is a literature base that has assumed the value of supporting families. Unfortunately, it is not as well developed as the other views of family and caregiving. As early as the 1950's, the World Health Organization (WHO 1969; Wolfensberger and Kurtz, 1969) discussed the need to consider the family rather than the severely retarded child as the unit of service. Breaking away from the then traditional pathological view with its psychodynamically oriented approach, this organization suggested that economic and social conditions should be dealt with so that parents would not be penalized by keeping their children at home. Well before such notions became acceptable, it was argued that social costs should be considered in deciding on the relative merits of home or institutional care insofar as parents have little real choice if supportive services are nonexistent. Holt (1958), in her seminal work, documented the need for family support services but, like so many others, offered little in the way of specific recommendations. (Much of the literature cited in Chapter 4 falls into this category.)

Horejsi (1975) is an exception. In an important piece, he lists five types of services necessary for normalization and the development of a least restrictive environment. While four emphasize the needs of the retarded individual, the first discussed is family support, including genetic counseling, diagnostic services, respite care, homemakers, parent/child training, and financial assistance. Others, such as Dunlap (1976) and Thurlow et al. (1978), also offer specific recommendations.

In another article, Horejsi (1978) argues that in beginning with the needs of the individual, the needs of the family are deemphasized. Whereas more sophisticated diagnostic services are continuously being developed, little attention is given to the development of appropriate homemaker services. Special education teachers are provided, but babysitters are not. Wheelchairs are considered appropriate expenditures for handicapped children, but not washing machines. The handicapped child may be sent to a camp, but families are not helped to have a vacation. Finally, residential care services are provided once a retarded person leaves home, but little in the way of respite care has been developed to support family members who want to continue as primary caregivers.

Skarnulis (1978:6) supports this general thesis and comments:

> When faced with a family having a difficult time coping with a handicapped member we usually say in effect, "We realize your burden is great and getting heavier. Would you like to consider one of our group homes?" We should learn to define solutions in terms of unmet needs, not available resources.

Boggs (1978) makes a telling point in her discussion of "burnout." She argues that the closer the professional is to the handicapped person (the direct service practitioner), the more likely he or she will experience burnout. To alleviate this constant stress, human service agencies are attempting to find ways to provide other, less intense functions for professionals to perform. In balancing the professionals' work, it is hoped that they will be able to continue working with the handicapped. Boggs continues, however, by pointing out that whereas professionals can resign, most natural families cannot. If burnout is associated with the intensity and amount of personal contact, it would seem that families are at the greatest risk. A professional can seek other employment; the parent of a severely retarded child cannot. A professional employed full time still has time away from practice; the family caregiver often does not.

This notion of family support is also found in other instances of families caring for handicapped members. Teicher (1969:374) describes the stresses experienced by parents of children with cystic fibrosis. After discussing the "staggering economic drain," he continues:

> What cannot be measured are the costs of around the clock watchfulness and attention by parents and often by siblings, the demanding schedule of visits to doctors, clinics or centers, and the strain on family relationships.

These comments are similar to those offered by Bayley (1973), who speaks of "the daily grind," and Hewitt (1972), who describes "the practical aspects of day-to-day living" when parents choose not to institutionalize their handicapped child. Others, such as Kulczki (1970) and Burton (1975), in identifying the specific strains families with cystic fibrotic children experience, produce lists that are remarkably similar to the strains faced by families with members who have other handicapping conditions. Moreover, Freeston (1971) and Taft (1973) offer comparable data when discussing families who have children with spina bifida and muscular dystrophy.

A QUESTION OF EMPHASIS

This analysis shows that examples of all four approaches to the family and the care of a handicapped person are found in the literature. Moreover, examples of each can be identified in the fields of mental retardation, mental illness, physically handicapped children, and physically handicapped adults, including the elderly. What the analysis did not show was the relative emphasis of the literature. It should be underscored that the fairly large number of citations used were identified by a series of computer searches augmented by additional sources identified after reviewing the initial pool. It is not nor can it be argued that a scientific sample is really possible. Still, the analysis is probably more representative of the literature than not. Moreover, the distribution of the articles over the four components of the typology is consistent with various theoretical notions of how families are to be viewed, given certain discipline orientations.

The distribution across the four types of handicapping conditions in order of actual numbers was: (1) families as resources to individuals; (2) families as part of the problem; (3) families as team members; and (4) families needing resources. This pattern was not consistent, however, within the four categories. (See Table 6.1).

Professionals writing in the field of mental retardation tend to view the family as effective team members. Moreover, there is as much emphasis on professionals as resources to family members (primary caregivers) as there is on the family as extender to the professional team. Following this, families are discussed in terms of their needing supportive services. This position explicitly recognizes the pressures families experience when they decide to care for the child in their home. Furthermore, a number of authors have identified the pressures in extremely concrete terms. Most tend to agree that practical support— e.g., financial assistance, information, physical and behavior management training, transportation, and periodic relief—rather than coun-

Table 6.1. Relative Emphasis of How Families Are Viewed[a]

	Mental retardation	Mental illness	Physically handicapped Children	Adults
Families as part of problem	4	1	1	3
Families as resources	3	2	3	2
Families as part of the team	1	4	2	1
Families needing resources	2	3	4	4

[a]1 = highest emphasis in terms of numbers; 4 = lowest emphasis.

seling or other forms of therapy, are critical if families are to continue functioning as effective caregivers. The articles that view the family members in pathological terms were often written from a psychiatric orientation and emphasized the psychodynamic implications of having a mentally retarded child. They also tend to be found in the earlier literature, e.g., the 1950's and 1960's.

This pattern can be best understood by examining the purpose of the intervention. The major thrusts of mental retardation legislation over the past 20 years seem to be educative, and resulting programs have taken this as the primary goal. Mental retardation has come to be defined as a developmental disability. Severe mental retardation is accepted by most professionals as a noncurable condition. As such, mental retardation is a functional designation that applies at the time at which an assessment is made. Although there is ample evidence that with appropriate and adequate intervention the degree of handicap can be altered, and physical, social, and intellectual functioning can be improved, it is unlikely that a severely retarded child will improve to the point that he or she would no longer be designated as retarded. Not expecting a cure, then, the emphasis is on normalization for both the retarded child and the family, the disabled and the nondisabled. In defining retardation as a developmental disability, in arguing the relevance of educational objectives (broadly defined), and in focusing on normalization as an organizing principle, professionals identified a range of services supportive to both the retarded child and the other family members. This perspective was also consistent with the notion that parents and others were primary caregivers, could identify necessary and realistic services, and did not need therapy to overcome nonexisting pathology.

The literature dealing with mental illness is quite different. The dominant view is of families as a part of the etiology of the illness. Furthermore, when professional treatment does not produce the expected results, family members are seen as the major obstruction. Whatever the view, etiology or obstruction, family members become part of the treatment plan. They become patients. Given this, it is easier to understand why little emphasis is given to family members as part of the caregiving team. Implicit in the notion of pathology is the belief that family members are not capable of functioning in this capacity. To some extent, the professional may seek merely to neutralize the potential negative effect the family might have on the patient or to successfully treat the entire family.

The psychiatric approach, then, is significantly different from the developmental approach. As Spiegel and Bell (1959:101) suggest:

It is generally apparent that theory exercises a strong, though sometimes unavowed, influence over what is observed and how it is stated. Accordingly, effective progress must wait upon further advances in theory construction. . . . Only when such theories have been well-worked out in fine detail will students from different disciplines concerned with this area (mental health) be in a position to form and develop a scientific tradition.

In the field of mental health, most theoretical approaches begin with the assumption that the etiology is either within the psychodynamics of the patient or within the dynamics of the patient and his or her family. If the focus is on problems within the family unit, there is less chance that the family will be viewed as capable of assuming a caring role with the patient, of sharing responsibility as members of the helping team, or of needing supportive services to reduce the accompanying pressures or strains. It would seem that psychiatry has not developed an adequate theoretical base which would support the growth of professional concern about the needs of families.

The remaining area, families with physically handicapped members, offers a third approach. While the first would appear to be developmental, and the second psychiatric, the dominant approach here is the medical model. Professionals trained in this model are also conditioned to search for pathology—in this case physical. While some attention in professional education may be given to prevention and maintenance, the overriding emphasis is on the successful diagnosis, treatment, and cure of medical problems. This focus is understandable, since illness is difficult enough to measure, but health actually defies measurement. Still, in actively seeking to reverse whatever pathology (physical handicap in this case) exists, attention tends to begin and end with the patient. Families do exist and are recognized, of course, but they are viewed primarily as resources to the patient, as members of the caregiving team.

Within this framework, the family as such does not exist. It is discussed in terms of how it can contribute to the successful treatment of the patient, how it can function as an extender of the professional. The medical model does not lend itself to focusing on the needs of the other family members, to identifying services that support families by reducing the stresses they are experiencing, to recognizing the family as a unit in its own right. The major exception to this is the fairly significant number of articles identifying the family as a potential block to rehabilitation. Interestingly enough, this tends to occur only when the handicapped member is a child.

This chapter began by asking whether additional resources, if they were to become available, would filter down to families providing care for handicapped members. To answer this, the analysis attempted to identify how families were viewed by professionals. Currently, services are organized to substitute for families, to take over various caring functions. Services are not designed to be supportive to families. In fact, most services focus primarily on the handicapped person. The delivery of effective supportive services to the family requires professionals capable of doing so, or additional resources probably would result in more services that continue to substitute. A significant body of literature was reviewed around four distinct views of the family. Do professionals tend to approach the family as contributing to the problem, as resources to the handicapped person, as team members, or as needing services themselves? The review showed, first, that relatively few authors discussed the need to or value in supporting families (the last category), and, second, that shared responsibility (the third category) was not emphasized relative to the others.

It was then argued that this pattern might be understood by examining the implicit theoretical underpinnings found in the various areas of handicapping conditions. Three models or approaches were identified: The developmental (retardation), the psychiatric (mental illness), and the medical (physical). Perhaps because professionals in the developmental approach do not begin with the assumptions of pathology to be cured or family members as incapable caregivers, greater emphasis is given to supportive services and shared responsibility. The other two, the psychiatric and medical approaches, begin with these assumptions of pathology or family incapability. Such focus, by definition, tends to restrict intervention to patients, even if family members are involved in the caregiving.

If the analysis is valid, additional resources alone will not result in more services to support families caring for handicapped members. What is necessary is that professionals change their attitudes toward family members and accept the pathological approach as incomplete. The next chapter attempts to identify some of the changes that might be involved in such a shift and the barriers in the way.

7 RECOMMENDATIONS AND IMPLICATIONS FOR THE FUTURE

The previous three chapters provide a description of what families and the State, through its social welfare system, are doing to care for the handicapped. In most of the cases, handicapped persons are not residents of long-term care institutions, i.e., nursing homes, chronic illness hospitals, and institutions for the mentally ill or mentally retarded. Handicapped persons live in communities. Some live by themselves; others live semi-independently in community facilities such as boarding homes, hostels, or halfway houses; still others reside as members of their natural families or substitute families such as foster care.

The analysis then focused on two groups of handicapped persons: the frail elderly and the severely retarded children. In 1980, 2½ million elderly (12% of the total elderly population) were living with their adult children or other relatives. Most tend to be older—i.e., over 75 years of age—and are more likely to be handicapped than other elderly persons. While the percentage of the elderly living as dependents with their children has dropped over the past 30 years (from 21% in 1950), this cannot be used as an indication that families today are less willing to provide social care. What does seem to have happened is that the elderly person, preferring to live independently, has more opportunities available to do so. Twenty-five years ago, over half the elderly living with their children were under 75 and less likely to be handicapped.

The data on mental retardation show a similar pattern. Two of every three severely retarded persons and eight of ten severely retarded children live in the community. While the adult may live in a community home, the severely retarded person under age 15, if not institutionalized, usually lives with his or her family. This ratio of institutional to community (in the case of children, family) populations has not changed since 1950.

While the reasons for families deciding to provide care, to function as a social service, are unclear and need to be examined more closely, available research argues that, for the most part, family members are willing caregivers. Not only are they willing, but they give care under extreme stress and at considerable sacrifice to other family members. For most, there is a disruption of family life, less opportunity for social and leisure activities, a barrier to career and geographic mobility, and financial strain because of additional costs associated with the care of a handicapped person, compounded by the fact that these families are likely to be single-career families at a time when two earners are the norm. A less well-documented stress involving such care is related to the changing role and function of women in society and the possible ambiguity many caregivers are facing.

This willingness to care is a major reason for rates of institutionalization being as low as they are. Without this social service, demands on the formal social welfare system would probably reach intolerable levels, because no society has the resources to assume this function. Even with these stresses, few families are threatening to transfer what they perceive to be their responsibilities. They have made known what their needs are, but in nondemanding terms.

The response to families has been, at best, mixed; at worst, counterproductive. If policies and programs are categorized by purpose and function, the State has emphasized those that in essence substitute for the family, an emphasis that is expressed in both the scale of social welfare expenditures and the type of services or benefits that have been developed. The reasons are complex, and while the rationale may have changed over time, the net effect has been the same. Social services that are organized to support the family have received lower priority than those that replace the family.

In Chapter 5, 31 major programs administered by the Department of Health, Education, and Welfare and representing over $102 billion of obligated funds were analyzed. These programs were chosen because in principle they seemed to be relevant to the issue of concern to this book—families caring for handicapped members. A number of significant themes emerge from the analysis. Most policies and programs are neutral toward the family. Neutral in this sense does not mean that they neither benefited nor harmed families, for such is not the case. These policies and programs are neutral in that the family (excepting AFDC) is ignored. The explicit beneficiary in almost all instances is the individual aged or handicapped person. Existing policies recognize that an aged or handicapped person is not likely to be active in the work force or to provide financial self-support. These individuals are also likely to require medical care and other health-related services, and policies exist to pay for these. Finally, a service network of support services has been developed, since these persons often need social support if the quality of their lives is to be protected. There is no recognition, however, that when family members provide care to the aged or handicapped person, they are at risk financially, physically, socially, and emotionally.

A second emerging theme is that the preferred way to meet the needs of handicapped persons is through financial support, and while social services may be provided, their contribution relative to the income programs is secondary. This choice of strategy, as discussed earlier, seems to be based on at least two assumptions. There is an implicit belief that in providing money to dependent persons, the needs of most will be met. They either have no need for social services or they will be able to obtain them in the market. Given the level of expenditures for the social services, it would appear that the State, through its social policies, anticipates that a percentage, albeit small, of the dependent will require more than financial assistance, and services will be provided directly to them.

This interpretation is supported when the intended beneficiaries of these services are identified. By intent, most services are targeted on the poor and near poor. Even in the case of Title XX, a program that allows for services to be provided to the general population through fee schedules, most users are recipients of public assistance or are financially eligible for public assistance. Fundamental to this set of policies is the affirmation of a dual approach to social welfare, one that approves the notion of a private system for the nonpoor and a public system for the poor. While most critics of separate systems emphasize the negative and even harmful effects experienced by the poor—e.g., the arbitrariness of the system and its accompanying stigmatization— few critics argue that this dual approach has penalized the nonpoor in a number of ways. A separate system for this group assumes that the market will respond and services will be available. The private sector's response, however, has been uneven. Some communities have few private services, and others have limited private services resulting in high fees. Furthermore, in its evolution and implementation, Title XX has emerged as the major social service program nationally. It has become in many communities the only social service program, thereby excluding many families whose income is too high.

The need for additional resources to develop a system of services to support families caring for handicapped members is complicated by many service providers, the human service professionals seeming to be more comfortable in taking over the caring function than in supporting family members as caregivers. The analysis in Chapter 6 showed that professionals tend to view family members as potential barriers to successful treatment, as resources to the handicapped person, or as extenders of the professionals. Those professionals who viewed themselves as supportive to the family, who believe the family to be effective caregivers, and who see the family as needing services in their own right because of the presence of a handicapped person, are likely to operate within a developmental approach, while the others see the problem in pathological terms; i.e., from the perspective of the traditional medical or psychiatric models. It is argued that if a commitment is to be made to these families and supportive services are to be designed, some attention should be paid to reorienting these professional attitudes.

This chapter identifies arguments for and against supporting families, explores what must be done if such a support system is to become a reality, and identifies areas of research to expand the knowledge base necessary for the development of sensitive policies.

THE ARGUMENT AGAINST INTERVENTION

It has been argued in the past and will continue to be argued in the future that any unnecessary intervention in family life harms both the family and the State. The logic of the argument is unassailable. No one, regardless of his political belief, would defend the value of "unnecessary" intervention. To do so would undermine the family. Such intervention is likely to be interpreted by the family as not only an invasion of its privacy, but in a subtle fashion, a questioning of its own capability to function adequately. If the intervention grew both in scale and in areas of family life, in time anger could evolve into acceptance.

There is precedence for this result, at least in the area of mental retardation. Seventy years ago, parents of retarded children were viewed by professionals as deficient themselves, insofar as retardation was believed to be genetically transmitted. Children were removed from their homes, isolated from the community, and in some instances prevented from bearing or fathering children. Twenty-five years ago, aspects of this policy were modified, but the outcome was essentially the same. While parents were not seen as defectives in the sense that they were to blame, they were not accepted by professionals as capable caregivers. Moreover, they were still subject to a form of coercion (psychological rather than legal), and children were still likely to be placed in institutions. In today's more enlightened environment, this intervention is considered unnecessary.

Unnecessary intervention also harms the State because each intervention requires additional resources, greater levels of public expenditures, and eventually a society in which all other social institutions are secondary to the State. The financial and social costs of such action are staggering.

For these reasons, State involvement should be considered carefully before actions are taken. As discussed earlier, intervention has been limited to instances where family functioning has been clearly impaired. Policies and programs have been introduced in situations where parents are unable to carry out what is expected of them. The State has assumed rights and responsibilities when young children are in danger of being abused or neglected. The State, through its social welfare system, not only has the right to intervene to protect the child, it has the right to act in place of the parents. Even then, it proceeds with caution. Whereas in previous eras, dominated by the philosophy of the Poor Law, the State tended to discharge its responsibility rather arbitrarily and required the parents to "prove" their competency as parents, today's society places the responsibility on the State to show that the parents are inadequate. The decision to remove a child requires the presentation of evidence sufficient to demonstrate family deterioration.

This approach clearly supports the notion of intervention only when necessary. Conceptually, it is referred to as a residual approach to social welfare and undergirds most social policies. Intervention is appropriate when, and only when, there is clear pathology, i.e., when the family cannot carry out its functions.

Two important principles have emerged to shape the State's response. The first requires a case-by-case determination, and the second argues that treatment, rather than prevention or insurance against risk, is the preferred strategy. This approach is consistent with the concern that when intervention does occur, it is clearly necessary.

Only when the family cannot or will not function as the primary caregiver to handicapped members can the State step in and become the surrogate family for the handicapped person. Should the State, then, develop policies and programs to support families as caregivers? Even if families with handicapped members are experiencing considerable stress and are at risk, is the stress sufficient to break these families? Are parents of handicapped children unable to function as good parents? Are they experiencing higher divorce rates than families without handicapped children? Are the other children negatively affected?

Are they trying to divest themselves of their responsibility as parents to raise their children? Similar questions can be asked of adult children caring for an aged parent. If there were evidence that families neither wanted to continue providing care nor were capable of providing appropriate care, there might be justification for intervention. Without such evidence, intervention is inappropriate insofar as it undermines and weakens the family.

What is the evidence? As presented in Chapter 4, families are shown to be willing to assume the caregiving function and, in most instances, are capable as caregivers. While some families find the stress unmanageable and seek institutionalization for the handicapped, most learn to accommodate. Although the quality of family life may be threatened, families are "choosing" to make adjustments and are not seeking institutional care for their handicapped children or elderly parents. Rates of institutionalization (the complete transfer of the caring function to the State) have remained low, and institutional care is sought usually after the family has provided care for a relatively long time.

The State is concerned about these families, but the concern is a fundamental one. While the families may need support, intervention might result in their giving up their responsibilities, responsibilities they prefer to keep. Instead of helping families remain strong caregiving units, the "support" might result in weakening the family. Intervention becomes interference.

Perhaps the more appropriate role of the State is to become involved only when there is clear evidence of family breakdown—i.e., family pathology. By waiting until the family declares that it can no longer care for the handicapped person, the State is assured that its involvement is necessary. It is not interfering in family life. This approach should not be interpreted as one which defines the State as insensitive or uncaring. Rather, there is such a fine line between support and substitution, between intervention and interference, that caution is the preferred course.

Policies are safe when such a dichotomy operates. A broad range of services of the highest possible quality can then be provided. They should not and would not within this view be provided indiscriminately, but only when absolutely necessary. Working within the residual notion of social welfare, each case would be judged on its own merits, and decisions of appropriateness would be made by competent professionals. While such a dichotomy, either the family or the State as caregiver, may seem drastic, it does resolve the troublesome issue of noninterference in family life.

THE ARGUMENT FOR INTERVENTION

To argue for greater involvement on the part of the State requires beginning from a different set of first principles. As mentioned above, this position accepts unnecessary intervention as dysfunctional, but it rejects the conclusion that because little is known about appropriate forms of intervention, minimal intervention is the desirable course. At the heart of the disagreement is a significant difference of opinion as to the proper function of the State. The residual position discussed earlier is concerned with the elimination of poverty and the treatment of problems. Within this framework, social welfare is justified only if it is directed to those who can no longer function on their own.

Each generation defines a minimum level of welfare and develops policies and services so that at least the basic survival needs of all are met. This minimalist view suggests a reactive role for the State. The counterposition suggests that industrialization has brought with it a number of risks and consequences that potentially affect all people and not just a small percentage of the population. It is further argued that the market has not been able to achieve a just allocation of goods and services, resulting in a number of hardships for some people. It becomes necessary for social welfare services to be established as major institutions rather than residual agencies. Social services within this model are defined as essential means of correcting social inequalities. The concept of elimination of poverty needs to be replaced with the principle that the purpose of the State is to maximize the welfare of all and not just the poor. The goal then becomes one of achieving the optimum and not just guaranteeing the minimum.

The "good" society is not one in which the State intervenes as little as possible in economic and social affairs, but one in which the State effectively promotes economic activity and guides social affairs. Insofar as policies are sensitive reflectors of current societal values, the State has a major role in identifying, articulating, and shaping these values. The evolving welfare society is one built on the premise that social welfare is a collective responsibility and rests its moral claim on the ethics of mutual aid and cooperation. These are not new values, nor are they identified primarily with the more liberal sector of society. Mutual aid and cooperation are the values held by those who feel that families can only be strengthened by a return to the past.

Proponents for greater State intervention suggest that industriali- zation has weakened the earlier mutual aid systems and that the welfare state was created to support this long-standing belief in collective responsibility. It attempts to stimulate cooperation and mutual aid through various social welfare measures. Contrary to popular belief, a strong welfare state is not synonymous with the State assuming responsibility to directly meet the needs of its citizens. It does not mean that individual, family, or community responsibility is anachronistic. Furthermore, the realization of a modern, proactive welfare state does not mean the inevitable diminution of voluntarism and altruism. A welfare state concerned with collective responsibility and maximizing the welfare of all develops its policies and programs on a foundation which assumes the ethics of mutual aid and cooperation. This, at least in intent, is the rationale for the Social Security system, with its intergenerational and intragenerational exchanges. For retirement benefits, the notion of collective responsibility is clear. One generation is supported by another, and, in turn, those giving trust their needs will be met by still a younger generation. Although the support is not given directly (i.e., by a child, friend, or neighbor), the use of Social Security taxes to accomplish this end is a form of mutual aid.

Finally, this notion of a welfare state, with its emphasis on collective responsibility, mutual aid, and cooperation, is antithetical to the future development of policies that in practice suggest State involvement only after the family is unwilling or incapable of providing care—the dichotomy introduced in the previous discussion of the residual model of social welfare. It assumes, instead, that there is, or should be, a shared responsibility. Shared responsibility, moreover, implies continuous sharing and should not necessarily be limited to crisis intervention. The needs of families with handicapped members vary in time and over time, and ideally the State responds to these variations with policies that support the family when it needs support and substitutes for it when necessary. Even this postulation is incomplete, since it implies a progression from no services to support services to substitute services, the last only when the family breaks down or can no longer handle the problem.

Shared responsibility requires that a diversity of options flexible enough to meet the family's specific needs and available when required be developed. In practice, the current system restricts choice to those services that exist at the time the family seeks help. Choice, meaningful choice, suggests an emphasis on policies that would result in the development of supportive services, since so few are available. Most families need the State, through its social welfare system, to carry some responsibility. For those families in a position to function as the primary caregivers, sharing may mean that the State offers financial assistance to offset the economic stress involved in providing care. For others, it may mean the provision of practical help and advice related to home-making and physical adaptations to the home. Still others may need information and counseling. Shared responsibility may also involve the temporary takeover of the caring function so that the family has short-term relief for vacations, recreation, or shopping. At another level, sharing could mean that the family be given some assurance that if and when the stress becomes too great, when it is not in the best interest of the handicapped person nor of other family members, alternative arrangements are available. Even if this were to occur, the family would be expected to provide some care while their child or parent resides in an institution.

The choice to provide or not provide care, to provide it with or without external support, and to provide services in such a way that families and the State share the caring function, requires not only a range of services, but also services that are flexible and innovative. The next section identifies what might be done if such choices were to become a reality.

THE NEED FOR PROFESSIONAL REORIENTATION

It is pointed out in Chapter 6 that most human service professionals tend to either discount the family's ability to care for the handicapped person or, in some instances, to view the family as capable only if supervised by professional caregivers. Whether the family is seen as actually contributing to an individual family member's problem and thus requiring treatment (the psychiatric model), or is seen by professionals as an inadequate caregiver or a barrier to the successful treatment of the handicapped person (the medical model), the family is defined in pathological terms. It is deficient because of some inherent inadequacy. With the exception of those professionals interacting within a developmentally oriented framework, families only exist in terms of the handicapped person (i.e., as barrier or resource). They are not seen as the object of services in their own right. They are provided services so that they will be able to function as more effective givers of care, only under the direction of professionals. The notion that they need support because they are caregivers is not widely recognized within the psychiatric or medical models.

Professional training within these models is not conducive to recognizing the need for family support, nor does it lend itself to accepting family members as effective social services in the absence of professional supervision. Both models focus on the handicapped individual and define intervention in terms of reversing pathology. As discussed earlier, emphasis is placed on the ability to diagnose, treat, and cure, and only professionals are capable of doing so. Patients or their families may be able to articulate symptoms, to identify to the professional what they think the problem is, but only the professionally trained person can take these symptoms and translate them into a diagnosis. Patients or family members may ask for various services, but only the professional can develop an appropriate treatment plan. Given their lack of training, patients or family members see services in terms of presenting symptoms, while professionals are equipped to go beyond the symptoms and identify the cause of the problem. As Parsons (1951) pointed out, patients and family members are expected to become dependent on the professional caregiver, to rely on his or her expertise, and to follow the professional's treatment plan. The professional does not ignore the symptoms as presented, the nonprofessional "diagnosis," nor does he set aside the patient or family's perception of needed services. The professional is trained to be sensitive to them, recognizing that if they are ignored, the "real treatment plan" could be jeopardized.

The professional trained in either of these models, with their overriding emphasis on the successful treatment and reversal of problems, is conditioned to see personal satisfaction in this curative function. The need to "cure," to bring about dramatic change in a patient or client, and to feel that the change was the result of professional intervention, is normal. Having undergone many years of training and preparation to become an effective caregiver, the professionals may know more than nonprofessionals and may more successfully treat individuals and families. Continuous affirmation becomes important to the caretaker, and the most visible sign of this affirmation is a cure. Moreover, the affirmation is strongest when the professional is able to assume responsibility for the change.

Historically the professional has tended to deemphasize those areas that do not lend themselves to the possibility of cure. For years relatively few professionals were attracted to careers in the field of chronic disability, e.g., mental retardation, arthritis, and cerebral vascular accidents. Whereas cure was a real possibility in treating the acutely ill, patients with chronic disabilities were not curable. At best, the professional hoped to slow down the degenerative process or to maximize whatever functional abilities remained. Arthritis and strokes are particularly good examples of conditions professionals did not want to specialize in when little was known about successful treatment. Once new drugs were found to treat the arthritic and new techniques were discovered that did result in the rehabilitation of the stroke patient, the medical model became applicable, and professional interest grew. Only when the condition or problem fit the requirements of the medical model—i.e., the potential for diagnosis, treatment, and reversal of pathology—was there professional concern on a large scale. Only when the possibility for dramatic change existed were professionals likely to view the condition as professionally interesting, one that provided the professional a sense of personal satisfaction and even power. To put it bluntly, the general area of chronic disability was not professionally exciting.

The notion of supporting families who are the primary caregivers for such groups as the severely mentally retarded child or the frail elderly is not compatible with the medical or psychiatric models. Most of the families who care for the handicapped are not faced with acute crises. They are, more often than not, normal families who are experiencing stresses related to long-term chronic management problems. They require support and need to feel that someone is interested in them. They want someone to take the time to listen and provide them with useful information. They need relief and practical assistance. Because their needs are ordinary and even mundane, most physicians, nurses, social workers, and other professionals do not see these cases as interesting, cases from which they can receive professional satisfaction. Successful intervention with these families is not likely to cure the child with severe retardation; i.e., raise the IQ to the normal range or reverse the aging process of a 90-year-old, incontinent, bedridden parent. Moreover, there is no pathology to be reversed. Rather, success would have to be measured in terms of management, maintenance, and significantly less dramatic criteria.

As discussed in the previous chapter, the last two categories of the proposed typology seem more appropriate to guide the nature of professional-family interaction. In most instances, the families have demonstrated their ability to function as the primary caregivers, with the professionals assuming a secondary role and working through the family. The family's ability to identify relevant needs and to provide appropriate care is recognized. Moreover, to continue as primary caregivers, the family requires various supportive services in its own right; professionals should shift their current focus on the handicapped person and accept the family as a legitimate object of intervention. Again, it is not a matter of one over the other, but a concern for balance.

There is a need to move away from the pathological model and to create a service delivery system that assumes that family members are capable caregivers and that their judgment can be trusted. Such a development would, of course, require a major reorientation of profes-

sional attitude and a significant departure in current thinking. To successfully implement such an initiative, professionals would begin by
asking the caregivers what services or resources would enable them
to continue as caregivers and then provide them. What professionals
think is beneficial becomes secondary, and requests from family members are not to be translated by the professional into services which
agencies are organized to provide or services which the professional
believes are important.

Such an approach leaves many professionals uncomfortable. First,
as discussed earlier, can family caregivers really have enough knowledge to identify services that would help them? Second—a more subtle
question and to some extent more than just a professional concern—
if these families were told that they would be given what they felt was
necessary, would their request be reasonable? That is, would they ask
for too much?

Why this lack of trust? Is there evidence to support the belief that
families, if given the opportunity, would make excessive demands? Although the data are somewhat limited, families caring for handicapped
members tend to be reasonable in terms of what they perceive to be
their needs.

For example, in the early 1970's, the British government was concerned with the needs of families with thalidomide children. The special
needs of these families were not being addressed by the social welfare
system. High-ranking officials in the Department of Health and Social
Security questioned whether the existing programs were capable of
meeting these needs and were concerned, since parents had decided
not to institutionalize the children but to keep them within the family.
Discussions moved from these specific families to all families with con-
genitally handicapped children. Eventually, it was decided that the State
establish a pilot program that would operate for a limited time. The
objectives of the program were to identify this high-risk population
(families caring for children with severe congenital handicaps), find
out what the family felt its needs were, meet these needs through either
cash grants or services, and measure the impact of the intervention.
Aware of the dangers involved with establishing a program financed
and administered by the government (e.g., the possibility that the provision of services would not be flexible or innovative, that regardless
of outcome the program would become a permanent part of the social
welfare system), the State, in 1973, gave funds to a private foundation,
the Joseph Rowntree Memorial Trust, to administer the Family Fund.
Two years later the program was severely criticized. A professional human service worker raised the following concerns:

How many greedy parents there are—those who scratch around, who feel at all costs they should be given something. They do not of necessity have a precise need in mind. . . . Immense sums of money are being dissipated— thrown to the winds—where handicapped children are concerned (Fox, 1975:13).

The Family Fund responded that their experience with over 20,000 families showed that "excessive demands from greedy parents were not common."

Such demands are, in fact, extremely rare and the Fund's mail shows that they are far outnumbered by applicants who are punctilious in asking what to do with modest balances left after an article has been purchased for slightly less than the anticipated cost (Hitch, 1975:3).

Parents asked for such things as washing machines, wheelchairs, help in adapting rooms or automobiles, prostheses, and occasional respite care. Over two years, the average grant to a family was £240.

In the course of his study of families with handicapped members, the author had the opportunity to interview a number of families (Moroney, 1976). In one instance, when asked what services might support them in caring for their severely retarded daughter in her late twenties, the parents, both in their early sixties, responded initially that they were managing. Later they agreed that their greatest concern was their daughter's future after they died. They concluded that they did not need much help beyond, occasionally, some relief for a vacation (it had been years since the two had gone off together without their daughter) and, most importantly, the feeling that someone was interested in them, cared about what they were doing.

On another occasion, the author accompanied a local authority social worker carrying out a survey of handicapped persons. An elderly couple, the husband 80 years old and disabled from a stroke, the wife caring for him despite severe arthritis, was asked in the course of the interview what needs they had and what problems the local social services agency might help them with. By any number of standards, the couple had many professionally defined needs. They lived in a second-story flat with the toilet in the backyard. The apartment was heated by a single fireplace and three space heaters. They were able to move about with difficulty but were visited by their neighbors. The couple told the social worker that they would like some assistance. The wife pointed to a large tree outside the bedroom window and said that they were worried that a large overhanging branch might strike the window and break it. If this were to happen in the winter, they might freeze to death. Neither she, her husband, nor their neighbors could do anything about it, and she wondered if the social worker could arrange to have the limb cut off. The professional response was not atypical: "That's fine, but let's talk about your real needs." After returning to the office and being reminded about the tree limb, the social worker commented that he would probably do nothing, since it was not a social service need.

These three examples, the Family Fund, the aging couple caring for a severely retarded daughter, and the aging couple living alone and worrying about the coming winter, are all related to the issue of trust. In the first example, professionals question whether families are reasonable in their request or whether they make excessive demands. In the second example, the parents were asking for the intangible, a feeling that someone cared and an assurance for the future. Finally, in dealing with the elderly couple, the professional questioned the appropriateness of the identified need and searched for "more relevant" needs.

Trust, of course, is a complex process. It is more than just feeling that families can be trusted to ask for what is appropriate. The professional who is comfortable in trusting and comfortable in accepting family members as competent caregivers often finds that the services requested are not possible. As structured, most agencies are equipped to provide a distinct set of services, and needs are translated into those services a particular agency has to offer. Families, as with any other consumer, are fitted to the service as best the professional can. Flexibility may be found in the social welfare system, but usually the family and not the agency is flexible. Therefore, the professional may feel uncomfortable in asking the family to identify needs, since trust is a bilateral exchange. When a professional tells families that they are capable diagnosticians and caregivers and encourages them to request what they think is important, the family is likely to interpret this as a guarantee that the professional can provide the service. Whereas the Family Fund could respond to these requests, most agencies cannot. Discretionary social welfare does not exist on a large scale. For a professional to relate to the family as if discretionary social services were a reality when they are not can be both dangerous to the family and personally threatening to the professional.

A final possible block to trusting families to know what they need is the fact that families are more likely to request concrete services (financial assistance, appliances, respite care) and not those services that are commonly thought of as professional (counseling and other forms of therapy). If professionals spend years preparing themselves to function as therapists using the most sophisticated therapeutic methods, personal satisfaction and a feeling of worth are associated with providing these services. The more concrete services are viewed as important, but their delivery is not necessarily a professional function. While only professionals can provide therapy, paraprofessionals are capable of delivering the "hard" services. However, it is a fact that if families are allowed to choose from an unlimited array of services, most will probably opt for the latter; then the professional may feel threatened. Although many families are faced with stresses that do lend themselves to a therapeutic intervention, most do not recognize this need or are unable to articulate their concerns in these terms. The majority of families caring for handicapped persons do not need therapy, at least not long-term therapy. Furthermore, if there is no pathology to be reversed, these families are professionally uninteresting and unrewarding to the professional.

If professionals were to function in such a way that they supported families, new roles would have to be developed. The "new" expert would need to be sensitive to the family unit, to understand what it means for a family to function as a caregiver, and to be knowledgeable about community resources. To be effective in this supportive function, the professional would be required to assume the role of facilitator and intermediary. This role is not so much one of information and referral as one of advocacy for the family (at least in terms of the family being the object of intervention).

With a new emphasis on family support, the training of human service professionals would change significantly. Social workers, physicians, nurses, and others trained in the clinical model are conditioned to recognize pathology. While professional education may give some attention to preventive care and normal growth and development, its overriding concern is for the successful treatment and reversal of problems. Moreover, the emphasis placed on identifying and treating not only pathology but the more rare or exotic pathologies needs to be balanced with an appreciation of the normal and a recognition of the value of supportive services. The traditional view of the professional as primary caregiver also needs to be defined as a role with limited application. It is, of course, appropriate when pathology, whether acute or chronic, exists. It is not appropriate when families are providing care to a handicapped child or adult parent and are capable caregivers. In these instances, the role of the professional must shift to one of support, a role secondary to the primary caregiver. Such a model or approach does not imply that physicians, for example, divest themselves of the curative function. It does imply that these professionals become more adept at recognizing when pathology exists and when it does not. This more neutral preliminary diagnosis should result in appropriate "treatment." If the provider finds that in treating the handicapped person, the family could benefit from supportive services, he or she should be in a position to make the necessary referrals. Other professionals, such as social workers, nurses, therapists, or counselors, might be prepared to carry out both curative and supportive functions. This would be much more desirable than having specialists in either function. This, however, will only become possible if curricula are organized in such a way that the professional accepts both functions as professionally equal in status.

SUPPORTIVE SERVICES: RESOURCE REQUIREMENTS

While a shift in professional attitudes would be a singificant move, any meaningful effort to support families would also require additional resources. This is likely to create problems, since the present economic situation affects public expenditures for social welfare purposes. While some are arguing that current levels need to be protected, others fear that there will be retrenchment. Few are optimistic about the possibility for increases.

Although there have been considerable increases in public expenditures over the past decades, serious shortages still exist. In fact, in some services, the increases have barely kept abreast of general population growth. Currently, agencies are under pressure to concentrate their efforts on those with the most acute and immediate need. Although families caring for handicapped members are experiencing stress, their needs may not be as great as others, such as children at risk of ill treatment, the very old and severely handicapped living alone, the mentally ill and mentally retarded in urgent need of care, and individuals in families at imminent risk of breakdown.

The argument that providers concentrate their efforts on those with the greatest need assumes that those with less need have to wait until additional resources become available through the achievement of a higher rate of economic growth. While this assumption has been contested, there is an historical association between economic growth and an expanded social welfare system. During periods characterized by slow economic growth, governmental agencies tend to be reluctant to take on new responsibilities. Newly identified needs are not ignored, but the typical response is an attempt to meet these needs through greater efficiencies in the provision of services. It is hoped that better management of the system and some effective coordination of the existing programs will result in more people receiving services.

This approach is reasonable. Federal and state bureaucracies have grown substantially over the past 40 years, and new initiatives, especially since the mid-1960's, have been introduced in a haphazard fashion, resulting in much duplication and overlap. During this growth period, new policies were formulated, additional programs developed, and new service delivery systems for specific populations at risk established. Little attention was given to the possibility that existing policies and service delivery systems, if modified, would have been adequate to meet these needs.

If greater efficiencies are to be achieved, some families caring for handicapped members should be better off than they are, depending in part on how additional resources are used. Services, such as day-care, homemaking, and home health, if extended to these families, could make a significant difference, but only if current eligibility requirements are changed. Efficiencies in the income-maintenance and medical-care programs also will not provide benefits to these families without similar modifications. The development of supportive programs, then, requires additional resources and does not just happen through better management. The remainder of this chapter deals with two major supportive services: respite care and income support.

The need for respite care services is documented in Chapter 4. Families caring for handicapped children and elderly parents are experiencing physical and mental stress and find that their outside social and recreational activities are curtailed. Although the value of such services to the family is indisputable, their development has been slow and their coverage spotty. Traditionally, the major purpose of respite services has been to respond to a crisis or a need for immediate relief. More often than not, the handicapped child or aged parent was removed from the home and returned after the crisis had passed. Respite care was seen to be appropriate when the caregiver became ill or when the parents were experiencing marital difficulties. The provision of such services was associated with the occurrence of a problem and was not viewed as an ongoing supportive service. Only recently have professionals identified the value of respite services in preventing crises or problems and advocated their provision on a regular basis.

The earlier notions of crisis and pathology as they relate to respite care have been merged with the recent idea of normalization. If families are to experience any semblance of normal family life, they need time away from the handicapped person, time to be someone other than a caregiver, time to relax. Comprehensive respite care services include the provision of overnight care, babysitting during the day, and longer periods of out-of-home care for vacations. However, most families find these services in short supply or too costly, in part because of this country's apparent lack of commitment to integrate respite care into our service delivery system, as other countries have done. For example, local authorities in the United Kingdom set aside a percentage of their nursing home beds for short-term admissions. Even if the homes have waiting lists for more permanent admissions, these places are reserved so that families may have 1- or 2-week vacations. Community hostels for the mentally retarded are used in the same way.

The rationale for this policy is simple: If given regular relief, families are able to function more effectively as caregivers so that long-term admissions or complete transfers are prevented or at least delayed. In this context, the British are using their institutions to achieve social as well as health objectives. In the United States, institutional care means long-term care usually financed by Medicaid. This program, with its single emphasis on medical care, is not structured to finance respite care for family members. The institutions themselves are also not organized to provide this service. Respite care does not begin when the handicapped person is admitted to the institution. The elderly person or severely retarded child is likely to feel frightened when moving to a strange environment and needs to have contact with institutional personnel before being admitted. In the United Kingdom, this contact is feasible, since the institutions are community based, are under the local authority personal social service departments, and have a great degree of staff interaction. The family is visited before the admission, and, if feasible, the handicapped person can visit the institution. In-home respite care faces the same funding/financing problems as those of out-of-home care. As discussed in Chapter 5, most community social services are currently provided through Title XX. Respite care relative to other services has low priority and, when available, tends to be restricted to families with low income.

A second area is that of financial assistance. Current policies ignore the financial burden that caring for a handicapped person places on most families. There are programs for the handicapped person and for families with extremely low incomes (e.g., SSI and AFDC), but none to offset the costs associated with care. A number of countries have established income-maintenance programs that specifically focus on families providing care for the handicapped, rather than on the handicapped person. In 1971, the British government introduced the Constant Attendance Allowance (CAA). Initially, a sum of money was provided to the caregiver in situations where a handicapped person required frequent attention all day and most of the night. Two years later, the program was expanded to include those who needed such care either day or night, and a second benefit was established at a lower rate. The sole determinant of eligibility was the level of handicapping condition. Age of the handicapped person and family income were not material. While the benefits were not large, the program did achieve two complementary objectives: In many instances, the grant made a real difference in the family's financial status; less measurable but in the view of the program designers as important, families were told in a tangible way that their efforts were recognized, that they were not ignored. The psychological benefit of the grant outweighed the actual amount of the transfer. Also, the financial support was not given to the handicapped person but to the caregiver. Moreover, there were no requirements that the money be spent on predetermined services and goods; the recipients could use the grant in any way they wished.

The Danish social welfare system has a comparable program. Persons who are considered fully unemployable or whose earning capacity is negligible qualify for an income grant equal to the old-age pension. Two criteria are used for eligibility determination. First, the handicapped person must be between 15 and 67 years of age, after which he automatically transfers to the national old-age pension; second, family income is not a factor. If, by reason of his or her condition, the handicapped person requires constant attendance by others, a nonincome-related allowance equal to the full basic rate (pension) is paid. For children, payment may be paid to parents or other relatives for their care in their own homes. If the condition and circumstances of the child involve special expense to the home in excess of what a nonhandicapped child would cost, an allowance is paid. As with other programs, family income is not considered in determining eligibility.

Although income support to families is common in most Western countries, support that is in keeping with the notion of a modern welfare state, it has not become a part of this country's effort. For many people it is inconceivable, if not unnatural, to pay families to care for their dependent members. Parents or adult children should provide care because they are expected to do so. The normal (in the nonpathological sense) response is to want to care, whether from a sense of duty or from love. The basis of this position emerges from an historical belief in acceptable moral principles. The payment of money to carry out "natural" family functions is viewed as harmful in that the moral reasons for caring—duty, love, responsibility to care for one's own— are replaced by less altruistic motives.

Such an attitude has been instrumental in blocking attempts to initiate a family or children's allowance. Whereas most Western countries, in the belief that children can place a family in economic risk, have such policies, the United States views them as inherently harmful to family well-being. All societies are concerned with strengthening families. Other countries attempt to reduce as many stresses as possible through constant attendance allowances and family and child allowances. Allowances are major preventive measures in that, if stress is reduced, if risks are minimized, the family is more capable of functioning as a family.

The United States' position is that only weakened families need support from the social welfare system. And yet, there is an element of ambivalence in our policies. Money is given to people to function as families. Foster parents are paid to care for children without natural parents or whose parents are incapable of providing a caring environment. Others are paid to care for handicapped persons residing in institutions. The staff, in effect, functions as a substitute family by providing for the physical and, in some cases, the social needs of the residents. Recently, policies have been initiated which provide financial incentives to prospective adopting parents. Previously, many low-income families wanting to adopt a child may have found child rearing costs prohibitive.

The reluctance to support natural families but willingness to assist "substitute" families needs to be reexamined. The moral issue aside, there is no empirical evidence that providing financial support results in families that are less responsible or less caring. The European experience to date suggests the opposite. When relieved of the financial stress associated with the care of a handicapped person, when given a visible sign that someone is interested in them, most family caregivers are encouraged to continue providing care.

Although there is no national policy, many natural experiments are offering financial support to families. One such program is the MR-Family Subsidy Program administered by the Minnesota Department of Public Welfare. A Family Task Force was formed in response to a request by the Commissioner of Public Welfare to study the issues and problems of families providing for their handicapped child in the natural or adoptive home. This task force, over 75% of which was comprised of parents of handicapped children, was charged with identifying the problems faced by these families, analyzing state and local programs in terms of their support to the family unit, and identifying gaps in the service delivery system.

Based on its analysis, the task force recommended the establishment of a program which would provide financial support for all expenses related to the child's disability needs. Expenses associated with the raising of a normal child would not be covered under the program.

Eligibility would be based solely upon the disability needs of the child and not on the income of the family. The program was established in 1975 under the Minnesota Statutes, Section 252.27, Subdivision 4. The program, on an experimental basis, subsidized 50 families with a maximum of $250 per month. While the program is similar in principle to the constant attendance allowances of the United Kingdom and Denmark, the Family Subsidy Program restricts family expenditures to seven categories: (1) diagnostic assessment, medical expenses, medications; (2) special diets and clothing; (3) special devices ranging from medical to recreational equipment; (4) parental relief and child-care costs; (5) educational and training programs; (6) preschool program costs; and (7) transportation costs.

The typical child in the program was 8 years old, had an IQ below 35, and suffered from one or two additional handicapping conditions, of which cerebral palsy, seizures, difficulties in mobility, and hyperactivity were the most frequent. These children were found to be comparable to children institutionalized in the state hospitals, and yet they did not have a history of placement out of the home. Although a number of families were considering institutionalization, relatively few did once they joined the program.

The notion of a constant attendance allowance policy is long overdue in this country. While the costs are great, the benefits are potentially greater. Every day that a family continues providing care is beneficial to the State and indirectly to the general public.

The costs of institutional care are discussed in Chapter 5. Nursing-home costs are in excess of $600 per month (1976), and institutional care for the mentally retarded averages $800 (1976). The costs of institutionalization can also be singificant in terms of the handicapped person and his or her family. These costs, however, are more difficult to measure, since they are social and psychological rather than economic. A program such as the constant attendance allowance gives families more meaningful choices than they currently have.

Once the concept of family support becomes acceptable, the issue becomes one of level of benefit and eligibility. One approach is to peg the benefit to the Supplementary Security Income (SSI) grant. In 1976 dollars, this would mean a monthly allowance of $157.70, or $1,900 per year. This grant, given to the caregiver, would be provided solely on the basis of the severity of the handicapping condition and not on the basis of family income. This program might, of necessity, be limited to families caring for the very severely handicapped, as defined in Chapter 4. Approximately 500,000 noninstitutionalized adults would meet this criterion and be potential beneficiaries. These 500,000 adults would, however, be the upper limit, since many are not living with relatives but are residents of semiprotective settings, such as foster homes, boarding homes, and hostels.

The analysis presented in Chapter 4 suggests that of the 2½ million elderly living with their adult children or other relatives, 60,000 are likely to be very severely handicapped. Approximately 165,000 severely mentally retarded children are also living with their parents. A constant attendance allowance program along the lines suggested above would cost an estimated $300 million. These expenditures may seem prohibitive in the period of retrenchment, but they are likely to be cost effective in the long run.

Such a supportive strategy is, however, somewhat foreign to the social welfare philosophy of the United States. It requires developing policies that provide benefits based solely on need and not on family income. Needs-tested programs are fairly common in many Western countries. Society, through its government, recognizes that certain segments of the population are at risk. Typically, these subpopulations include, but are not limited to, the elderly and the handicapped. The concept of risk is used in a statistical sense in that not all elderly or handicapped persons are in need or have problems. Still, these subpopulations are more likely to have problems as compared to other groups within the population. To minimize the economic, phyisical, and social risks associated with the condition (being old or handicapped), benefits are made available to all members of the designated subpopulation. Once the legitimacy of the claim is determined (i.e., membership in the group) the individual or family is entitled to the benefit. The Social Security program, specifically the old-age pension program, comes closest to these concepts of universal coverage and membership in an at-risk population group. Benefits are not determined by the presence or absence of personal resources. But even under this program, individuals must not only be of retirement age, but they must also have contributed to the program while they were working.

In this country it is argued that universal provision of benefits is inherently wasteful, since some of the beneficiaries will, in fact, not "need" the benefit. It is further argued that if benefits or services were provided on a selective basis, if only those who really need services were eligible, recipients would then be given more services or higher benefit levels. On a theoretical level, this reasoning is quite appealing. For example, why should a family caring for its severely retarded child be given a constant attendance allowance of $1,900 per year if the family income is $50,000? This argument usually concludes by noting that if those whose income is above a certain level are excluded from the program, it may be possible to give more than $1,900 to those who need financial support.

On a practical level, this position becomes unsettling. A means-tested program implies that families do not have a right for a benefit, and, once benefits or services are no longer rights, their provision is usually associated with a stigmatization. Even if the income level were to be reasonable—$10,000 or even $15,000 per year—many families would not subject themselves to the eligibility screening. For many, it means an invasion of privacy; for others, it is a strong dislike for any program that seems to be charity. Furthermore, if benefits are income related, there is a danger that the income level will be lowered (e.g., from $10,000 to $8,000) in periods of retrenchment. Such was the experience with Medicaid when large groups of previously eligible individuals and families were dropped from the program. This is not possible in universal nonmeans tested programs. Benefits may be raised or lowered, but recipients are not excluded as long as they are providing care to a handicapped person. The major policy variable then becomes the identification of that level of handicap to be used in defining group membership or eligibility. Given the uncertainty of demand, it is reasonable to begin with the most severely handicapped and, at a later date, reassess whether other groups should be included. This, of course, was the experience in the United Kingdom.

These suggestions, the allocation of resources for respite care services and the inception of a constant attendance allowance, are only two of many recommendations that might have been made. It is the opinion of the author that their need and value have been established. Although it might be argued that income support alone should be sufficient and that families receiving the allowance could use it to purchase respite care if they wanted to, the market to date has not been responsive to fulfilling this need.

During the course of this study, the author attended workshops and conferences dealing with the care of the handicapped. Many of them were attended by parents of handicapped children as well as professionals in the field. A recurrent theme expressed by these parents was their frustration in trying to find respite care. Even those who were financially able to pay for the service were not able to find such care in their communities. These parents felt that respite care, especially that delivered in the home setting (e.g., periodic babysitting during the day and occasional overnight care), required people who were knowledgeable about mental retardation, sensitive to the needs of the handicapped child, and capable of providing necessary care. In general, the usual sitter was not adequate, and, therefore, a constant attendance allowance by itself would not be sufficient. The next section identifies areas of research that still need to be addressed.

A RESEARCH AGENDA

Insofar as this study relied almost exclusively on existing data sources, many questions remain unanswered. Although the analysis does counter the growing belief that the modern family is incapable or unwilling to function as caregivers to the handicapped, the evidence cannot be used to answer some of the more qualitative questions. One such area is introduced in Chapter 1—the analysis of existing social policies as they relate to the family. Although, as noted, a number of policy institutes have been established to focus on this concern, and a growing number of social scientists have committed themselves to this inquiry, the results to date are tentative and unsystematic. What is needed is a coordinated effort, intra- and interdepartmental in scope, to assess whether governmental policies are complementary, contradictory, or counterproductive to the goal of strengthening families. Such an effort, beginning on the national level and then moving to the state and local level, is a massive undertaking. This study only examined policies and programs of one federal agency—the Department of Health and Human Services. Moreover, even within this one agency, the analysis was limited to those policies that directly affect the handicapped and their families. Many program areas have an indirect impact on these families. Other agencies, such as Labor, Housing and Urban Development, Transportation, and the Internal Revenue Service have policies that directly and indirectly affect all families and thus families caring for handicapped members. A commitment to such an effort would have the benefit of firmly establishing the family as a critical object of social policy and would generate a framework to address the needs of families caring for dependent members.

A second area requiring attention is the identification of those factors that influence families to continue providing care. Handicapped persons are more likely to live in communities than in institutions. Significant numbers of the noninstitutionalized handicapped live with their families. Many of these caregivers feel neglected by the State and have expressed a need for supportive services that have historically been deemphasized in favor of services that substitute for the family.

Why is it that families want to continue the caregiving function, a function that seems out of place in light of the current value system that favors institutionalization and an economic system that often necessitates more than one wage earner per household? Or, what exchange system is operating between the caregivers and the caretakers? Given the strains and pressures involved in the care of a handicapped person, the exchange is likely to be characterized by bilateral rather than unilateral transactions. By understanding the dynamics of the exchange, policies can be developed that could support families and not interfere in family life. For example, in a given population of families with handicapped persons, there will be families who are functioning as more than adequate caregivers with minimal State intervention. There will be others who are willing to provide care but in the absence of supportive services will not be able to do so. A third group of families will be characterized by a declared willingness to provide care, but an incapacity to do so, even with support. In these situations, both the handicapped person and other family members suffer. The last group would include those families who are unwilling to carry out this function. Research along these lines, identifying the distribution of these family types and the factors associated with each pattern, could be the basis for developing a sensitive, supportive delivery system.

More studies along the lines of Sussman's project at Bowman Gray Medical School and the demonstrations conducted by the Community Service Society of New York City should be carried out. Both are offering a broad range of services, including cash grants to families caring for elderly parents. Their findings not only increase the existing understanding of the dynamics of family care, but provide important information that does not exist.

It is apparent that respite care is not available in many locations and, where available, is inadequate. Research is needed to identify the barriers associated with this low provision. These barriers may be in the regulations of the existing policies (e.g., Medicaid), or may be related to certain organizational or political factors, such as Title XX.

Although the issue of family violence is much in the forefront of public concern and considerable sums are available for research and services, little is known about the extent of violence in families with handicapped members. Whether the violence is the neglect or physical abuse of the retarded child or the frail elderly parent, information should be systematically collected on its prevalence.

The final area of research related to family support is service delivery. This study has shown that families need to have choices made available through a flexible social welfare system. The need for discretionary social services is clear, but the present system cannot respond. It is highly organized, often along categorized lines, and tends to fit recipients to existing services. The purpose of an agency becomes the sum total of its services and not the needs of its consumers.

Many today believe that the American family is far from strong. Political leaders, professionals in the human service field, and the general public have concluded that the family as a basic social institution is in a weakened state. Some go so far as to argue that there is widespread family deterioration. For any number of reasons, a loose coalition has emerged that includes representatives from the political right and left. This coalition is urging the State to find ways to reverse this pathology and restore the family to its former position of strength.

The problem with the movement is that the notion of restoring families is, in fact, more a romantic dream than a position with any historical basis. Moreover, the debate appears to be more an exercise in rhetoric than anything else. Terms are ill defined; little attempt has been made to achieve concensus on basic definitions; and "strong families" have come to mean families that are not pathological.

Present policies tend to mirror this concern insofar as they operate on the assumption that weak families are weak because of some internal deficiency. Most policies are implicitly established to rehabilitate these families. The emphasis on pathology is consistent with the residual approach to meeting social objectives, an approach that dominates the welfare state. Rather then attempting to develop mechanisms to reduce or minimize the stresses that families face, the State operates on the assumption that intervention only when clearly needed is the preferred course. Intervention is appropriate only when there is clearly defined pathology; otherwise the intervention may interfere in family life and over time weaken the family unit.

This more conservative approach may be safer than one which attempts to support families by preventing problems from occurring, but it has had serious effects on families functioning as caregivers for handicapped members. Services that substitute for the family are the rule and supportive services the exception. This reactive policy posture is discussed in Chapter 5, where expenditure patterns are analyzed. The emphasis on pathology emerges in the review of professional attitudes examined in Chapter 6. With the exception of those professionals who have begun to view the developmental model as appropriate, families are not accepted as capable caregivers in their own right. At best, they are defined as part of the professional team that may, if properly supervised, carry out a limited number of tasks. At worst, these families are seen by the professionals as barriers to the rehabilitation of the handicapped child. Families are treated as coopted but only have meaning in terms of the handicapped and the treatment plan. Reasons for these attitudes toward the family are complex; they are associated with professional training, professional needs for rewards and success, and a professional's unwillingness to assume a role secondary to the family.

This chapter offers recommendations to strengthen families who are willing to assume the function of primary caregivers. Some of these recommendations require additional resources, others modifications in existing policies, and still others changes in attitudes. At this time, these recommendations cannot be justified in cost-effective or benefit-cost terms. If families were giving up their caregiving function in growing numbers, this argument would make sense because family care would be less costly than institutional care. Fortunately for society this is not happening. If choices have to be made between at-risk groups based on the best benefit-cost ratio possible, these families will again be penalized. Other groups of at-risk populations will, more than likely, show greater returns for investments as long as the criterion continues to be economic returns.

Unless changes in priorities take place, these families will continue to be ignored and underserved. Families who transfer the caring function to the State are "rewarded" in that resources are made available. Families who maintain the caring function are penalized in that their contribution to society is ignored. To rectify this inequitable situation, to move beyond the current Welfare State to the more positive idea of as welfare society, the criterion inherent in the human investment model must be balanced with criteria evolving from the philosophical belief in justice as fairness. These families care, they are providing more care than the organized social welfare system, and are functioning as social services. To continue benefiting from this situation without attempting to be supportive, without sharing the caring responsibility, is hardly in keeping with the notion of a caring society.

8 FAMILY RESPONSIBILITY: AN EPILOG

One issue remains unresolved. In Chapter 2 we raised the question of family responsibility, care of dependent members, and dependency. The position of the New Right and the current administration —that social welfare measure create dependency and therefore should be curtailed—was introduced. The counterposition—that social welfare measures are a necessity if families are to continue to function as major social institutions in a modern society—was also explored. While the concept of reciprocity was identified as a useful framework within which to analyze the issue, the inquiry up to now has not dealt with it explicitly.

We can conclude that the State has, in some instances, prevented dependency if dependency is defined in economic terms. Various social insurance programs have protected elderly persons when they retire and workers when they are temporarily unemployed. These income programs have been instrumental in preventing some individuals from becoming financially dependent. Moreover, these programs have been designed in such a way that the recipient perceives him or herself to be in a reciprocal relationship with the giver, i.e., the State. In that the recipient, while working contributes taxes through Social Security and Unemployment Insurance, he or she is collecting what is theirs by right when they can no longer work. The fact that many recipients receive more than they contributed does not seem to affect this sense of reciprocity. Although the recipients find themselves dependent, they do not experience what Pinker (1973) describes as a "profound sense of stigma."

We have, however, also concluded that these measures are not targeted toward families but toward individuals. They are to replace the

the income of elderly individuals or workers who are temporarily unemployed. In the former instance, we assume that if the elderly person
lives with his or her adult children or even grandchildren, this income
will become a part of the family's income, or at least will reduce the
financial burden on the family. As argued earlier, this should be treated
more as a hypothesis or research question and not as a fact. There are
no data on this issue yet. In the latter instance, there is probable cause
to argue that unemployment insurance does target the family. Still, the
benefit is tied to the previous earning history of the individual worker
and not to the size or need of the family. Theoretically, a family-oriented
benefit would take into account these variations and provide differential
benefits.

The We can also conclude that the State, while not creating dependent
families, does foster a continued dependency in some families once
the initial dependency occurs. By definition, the use of a means test
assumes that a family, when it is declared eligible, is dependent. There
is no reciprocity among equals—the receivers are dependent on the
givers. In Pinker's formulation, the interaction between the family and
the State through its service providers is based on the principle of
"unilateral exchange" resulting in a "profound sense of stigma."

The State, when it operates within this formulation, is reverting to
an earlier conceptualization of the welfare state—that of the nineteenth
century Poor Law. The issue is not one of preventing dependency; it
waits until the dependency occurs. While this approach may not be as
personally dehumanizing today, the family still has to admit that it
cannot meet its own needs. Within this context, the State assumes certain family functions.

Both of these approaches to dependency deal primarily with economic dependency, one characterized by bilateral exchanges and the
other by unilateral exchanges. Neither directly deals with the major
concerns of this analysis. Can the State formulate policies that will support nondependent families in the care of dependent members? Is it
possible to develop policies that will strengthen these families in such
a way that the recipients perceive they are equal to the givers?

In the preceding chapters we identified a number of obstacles to
realizing this goal, e.g., professional attitudes toward the family's ability
to provide care and a preoccupation to provide services to poor and
low-income families. A number of policy recommendations were made
in the last chapter. They are not proposed as a comprehensive agenda;
they are offered only as examples. Furthermore, they deal specifically
with families providing care for handicapped members. We do suggest,
however, that these policies can be developed within a framework em-

phasizing reciprocity, in that the State recognizes the significant amount of social care provided by the family care that could but is not transferred to the State.

What of other families? Can the State develop similar types of policies for other families? Can families be strengthened and not weakened if social services (broadly defined) are made available?

In Chapter 2, we introduced Kamermann and Kahn's formulation of the purposes of social services and related these to the family life cycle; the stress that most, if not all, families experience in carrying out family functions; and the positive contribution of informal support systems for family well-being. The key policy question for the future may be the extent to which the State can strengthen these informal support systems.

Over the past decade, families have joined together to form support networks, and the evidence suggests that these networks will continue to grow. At a recent conference (1984) sponsored by the Bush Institute for the Study of Families and Children, Yale University invited representatives from over two hundred self-help groups to come together to share ideas. Some were organized around special needs—e.g., parents with handicapped children; others around particular problems—e.g., child abuse and other forms of family violence; still others came together to provide a service for each other —e.g., day care. Still others were neighborhood based, and provided generic social supports to each other.

These different groups had a number of common elements. First, they sensed a loss of community, a sense of belonging to others who were concerned with their well-being on a personal level. Second, they tended to agree that most social institutions (e.g., schools, social services, and medical care services) were inflexible and highly bureaucratized. Individual needs were shaped to fit existing services rather than the other way around. Finally, these representatives raised their concern for self-control of their own destiny. While they did not label it as such, they were dealing with their need to give as well as to receive—to enter into reciprocal relationships.

The isssue of dependency as opposed to self-sufficiency, then, has to be seen as a symbolic argument. It cannot be viewed as a dichotomy. We are dependent on others just as others are dependent upon us. Furthermore, we recognize the value of dependency. But, we must believe that we exist in mutually supportive networks in which some individuals are not made to feel inferior and others superior. This creates stigmatization.

Pinker (1973) suggests that a number of elements affect the nature of dependency. Two of these are related to State involvement. He points out that stigmatization and deep psychological dependency occur first when the receiver is made to feel inferior, second when the dependency is long-standing. We have dealt with the first to some extent in Chapter 6, when we discussed professional attitudes toward families. This reorientation of professionals is a prerequisite of the State is to positively interact with families and natural support networks. The second is more subtle, and perhaps more difficult to control (i.e., the length of the dependency). In practice, it would mean that the State would intervene to stimulate the growth of support networks (this might entail financial support, information, or expertise), but that the role of the State would not be intrusive and would be time limited. It would mean that families would initially share with professionals the design of the support networks and eventually control them. It can be reduced to a moral and ethical rationable. If we support families in their caring for dependent members, and if we do so in such a way that they are better equipped to carry out family functions, the State has made an investment in society's future. This has to be the basis for the intervention since it assumes reciprocity—the family receives support knowing that it will be able to give to society over the long run.

If social policies were to stimulate the development of natural support networks and provide these networks with support when necessary, would this result in more self-sufficient families? Undoubtedly. Would it result in a gradual shrinking of the welfare state? No. For the foreseeable future there will be dependent families, whether the dependency is financial, physical, or psychological, requiring the State to directly intervene. Moreover, the social welfare measures that tend to prevent economic dependency (e.g., Social Security) will continue. In their absence, older people will, in fact, become negatively dependent on their children and grandchildren.

Titmuss (1971) has offered one of the more insightful discussions of this issue. He argues that industrialization and modernization, with their emphasis on economic values and individualization, have brought about community breakdown and alienation. Historical approaches to social welfare have produced a "we-they" society; "we," the nonpoor, provide for a residual proportion of society because "they" are incapable of providing for themselves.

In Titmuss's view, social policy is concerned with different types of moral transactions embodying notions of exchange or reciprocal obligations necessary to bring about and maintain social and community relationships. Schottland (1963:iv) defines social policy as a "statement of social goals and strategy . . . dealing with the relations of people with each other, the mutual relationships of people with their government." Boulding (1967), in the same vein, argues that the objective of social policy is to build the identity of a person around some community with which he is associated.

If families are to be strengthened, if family members are to be more capable caregivers, the State, through its social welfare system, should not consider retrenchment. It needs to enter into a partnership with families, a relationship characterized by reciprocity. Otherwise, more and more families will become dependent.

BIBLIOGRAPHY

Abramowicz, H., and Richardson, S. Epidemiology of severe mental retardation in children: Community studies. *American Journal of Mental Deficiency,* 80: 18–39, 1970.

Adams, B. Isolation function and beyond: American kinship and the family. *Journal of Marriage and the Family,* 32: 575–597, 1970.

Adams, B. Interaction theory and the social network. In: Sussman, M., ed. *Sourcebook in Marriage and the Family.* 4th ed. Boston: Houghton Mifflin, 1974.

Adams, M. *Mental Retardation and Its Social Dimensions.* New York: Columbia University, 1971.

Ainsworth, M. The effects of maternal deprivation: A review of findings and controversy in the context of research strategy. *Public Health Papers,* 14: 97–165, 1962.

Aldrich, C. A. Preventive medicine and Mongolism. *American Journal of Mental Deficiency,* 52: 127–129, 1947.

Aldrich, F.; Holliday, A.; Colwell, Jr., D.; Johnson, B.; Smith E.; and Sharpley, R. The Mental Retardation Service Delivery System Project: A Survey of Mental Retardation Service Usage and Needs Among Families with Retarded Children in Selected Areas of Washington State. *Research Report,* Vol. I. Olympia, Wash.: Office of Research, 1971.

Allan, K., and Cinsky, M. *General Characteristics of the Disabled Population,* by DHEW Pub. No. (SSA)72-11713(19). Washington, D.C.: Supt. of Docs. U.S. Govt. Print. Off., 1966.

Allen, W., and Stockton, R. Black family structures and functions: An empirical examination of some suggestions made by Billingsley. *Journal of Marriage and the Family,* 35: 39–49, 1973.

Alvarez, W. Trends in the social habits of elderly Americans. *Geriatrics,* 27: 77, 1972.

Anderson, M. *Sociology of the Family: Selected Readings.* Middlesex, England: Penguin, 1971. (a)

Anderson, M. *Family Structure in Nineteenth Century Lancashire.* Cambridge: Cambridge University, 1971. (b)

Anderson, O.; Collette, P.; and Feldman, J. *Family Expenditure Patterns for Personal Health Services, 1953 and 1958: Nationwide Surveys.* Research Series No. 14. New York: Health Information Foundation, 1960.

Annual Report of the National Advisory Committee on the Handicapped. Washington, D.C., 1976.

Aponte, H. Organization treatment around the family's problems and their structural bases. *Psychiatric Quarterly,* 48: 209–222, 1974.

Appleton, W. Mistreatment of patients' families by psychiatrists. *American Journal of Psychiatry,* 131: 655–657, 1974.

Arling, G. Resistance to isolation among elderly widows. *International Journal of Aging and Human Development,* 7: 67–86, 1976.

Ashmore, R. Background considerations in developing strategies for changing attitudes and behavior toward the mentally retarded. In: Begab, M., and Richardson, S., eds. *The Mentally Retarded and Society: A Social Science Perspective.* Baltimore: University Park, 1975.

Askenasy, A. *Attitudes Toward Mental Patients: A Study Across Cultures.* The Hague: Mouton Press, 1974.

Babchuk, N., and Ballweg, J. Black family structure and primary relations. *Phylon,* 33: 334–347, 1972.

Bachrach, L. *Deinstitutionalization: An Analytical Review and Sociological Perspective.* DHEW Pub. No. (ADM) 79–351. Washington, D.C.: Supt. of Docs., U.S. Gov. Print. Off., 1976.

Back, K. Personal characteristics and social behavior: Theory and method. In: Binstock, R. and Shanas, E., eds. *Handbook of Aging and the Social Sciences.* New York: Van Nostrand Reinhold, 1976.

Bane, M. J. *Here to Stay. American Families in the Twentieth Century.* New York: Basic Books, 1976.

Bane, M. J. Discussion Paper: HEW Policy Toward Children, Youth and Families. Prepared for the Assistant Secretary for Planning and Evaluation, 1978, p. 21.

Bardis, P. Changes in the colonial and modern American family systems. *Social Science,* 38: 103–114, 1963.

Barsch, R. *The Parent of Handicapped Child.* Springfield, Ill.: Thomas, 1968.

Battle, C. Disruptions in the socialization of a young, severely handicapped child. *Rehabilitation Literature,* 35(5): 130-140, 1974.

Baumeister, A. The American residential institution: Its history and character. In: Baumeister, A., and Butterfield, E., eds. *Residential Facilities for the Mentally Retarded.* Chicago: Aldine, 1970.

Bayley, M. *Mental Handicap and Community Care.* London: Routledge and Kegan Paul, 1973.

Bayrakal, S. A group experience with chronically disabled adolescents. *American Journal of Psychiatry,* 132: 1291–1299, 1975.

Beattie, W. Aging and the social services. In: Binstock, R., and Shanas, E., eds. *Handbook of Aging and the Social Sciences.* New York: Van Nostrand Reinhold, 1976.

Bedard, E. M. (ed.). Unmet needs versus perceived needs—The effect of inadequate communication. In: *HNA Regional Clinical Conferences.* New York: Appleton-Century-Crofts, 1967, pp. 71–77.

Begab, M. Casework for the mentally retarded-Casework with parents. *The Mentally Retarded Child: A Guide to Social Agencies.* Washington, D.C.: Supt. of Docs., U.S. Govt. Print. Off., 1963.

Begab, M., and Richardson, S. *The Mentally Retarded and Society: A Social Science Perspective.* Baltimore: University Park, 1975.

Beggs, H., and Blekner, M. *Home Aide Services and the Aged: A Controlled Study.* Part II, The Service Program. Cleveland, Ohio: The Benjamin Rose Institute, 1970.

Bell, W. "Filial Responsibility, Social Provision and Social Policy." Washington, D.C.: Administration on Aging, Administrative Papers, No. 2 (undated).

Bell, W. Relatives' responsibility: A problem in social policy. *Social Work,* 12: 32–39, 1967.

Bengston, V. Generation and family effects in value socialization. *American Sociological Review,* 40: 358–371, 1975.

Bengston, V., and Cutler, N. Generations and intergenerational relations: Perspectives on age groups and social change. In: Binstock, R., and Shanas, E., eds. *Handbook of Aging and the Social Sciences.* New York: Van Nostrand Reinhold, 1976.

Berger, B.; Hackett, B.; and Millar, R. M. The communal family. In: Sussman, M., ed. *Sourcebook in Marriage and the Family.* Boston: Houghton Mifflin, 1974.

Berger, M., and Wuescher, L. The family in the substantive environment: An approach to the development of transactional methodology. *Journal of Community Psychology,* 3: 246–253, 1975.

Berger, P., and Kellner, H. Marriage and the construction of reality. In: Dreitzel, H., ed., *Recent Sociology.* London: Macmillan, 1970.

Berkman, B., and Rehr, H. Elderly patients and their families. Factors related to satisfaction with hospital social services. *Gerontologist,* 15: 524–528, 1975.

Besner, A. Economic deprivation and family patterns. *Welfare Review,* 3 (9): 20–28, 1965.

Bild, B., and Havighurst, R. Senior citizens in great cities: The case of Chicago. *Gerontologist,* 16: 4–88, 1976.

Billingsley, A. *Black Families in White America.* Englewood Cliffs, N.J.: Prentice-Hall, 1968.

Billingsley, A. Family functioning in the low-income black community. *Social Casework,* 50: 563–572, 1969.

Binger, C. M.; Albin, A. R.; Feurstein, R. C.; Kushner, J. H.; Zoger, S.; and Mikkelsen, C. Childhood leukemia: Emotional impact on patient and family. *New England Journal of Medicine,* 280: 414–418, 1969.

Binstock, J. Motherhood, an occupation facing decline. *Futurist,* 6: 99–102, 1972.

Binstock, R. Responsibility for the care of the geriatric patient: Legal, psychological, and ethical issues. Fantasies and facts about social policy and aging. *Journal of Geriatric Psychiatry,* 5: 148–173, 1972.

Birch, H., ed. *Brain Damage in Children: The Biological and Social Aspects.* Baltimore: Williams and Wilkins, 1974.

Birch, H.; Richardson, S.; Baird, D.; Horobin, C.; and Illsley, R. *Mental Subnormality: A Clinical and Epidemiologic Study in the Community.* New York: Williams and Wilkins, 1970.

Birenbaum, A. The mentally retarded child in the home and the family cycle. *Journal of Health and Social Behavior,* 12: 55–65, 1971.

Blatt, B. The executive. In: Kugel, R., and Shearer, A., eds. *Changing Patterns in Residental Services for the Mentally Retarded,* Washington, D.C.: Supt. of Docs., U.S. Govt. Print. Off., 1976.

Blau, Z. S. *Old Age in a Changing Society.* New York: Franklin Watts, 1973.

Blenkner, M. *Serving the Aging: An Experiment in Social Work and Public Health Nursing.* New York: Institute for Welfare Research, Community Service Society, 1964.

Blenkner, M. Social work and family relationships in later life with some thoughts on filial maturity. In: Shanas, E., and Streib, G., eds. *Social Structure and the Family: Generational Problems.* Englewood Cliffs, N.J.: Prentice-Hall, 1965.

Bloch, D. A. *Techniques of Family Therapy.* New York: Grune and Stratton, 1973.

Blood, R. Impact of urbanization on American family structure and functioning. *Sociology and Social Research,* 49: 5–16, 1964.

Blood, R., Jr. *The Family.* New York: Free Press, 1972.

Boggs, E. Federal legislation. In: Wortis, J., ed. *Mental Retardation. An Annual Review.* Vol. III. New York: Grune and Stratton, 1971.

Boggs, E. "Economic Costs of Family Care." Paper presented at the Conference on Family Care of Developmentally Disabled Members. Minneapolis, Minn., 1978.

Bone, M.; Spain, B.; and Martin, F. M. *Plans and Provisions for the Mentally Handicapped.* London: Allen and Unwin, 1972.

Bott, E. Urban families: Conjugal roles and social networks. *Human Relations,* 15 (8): 346, 1955.

Bott, E. *Family and Social Network.* 2nd ed. London: Tavistock, 1971.

Bould, S. Female-headed families: Personal fate control and the provider role. *Journal of Marriage and the Family,* 39: 339–350, 1977.

Boulding, K. Boundaries of Social Policy. *Social Work* 12 (No.1): 3–11, 1967.

Bowlby, J. *Maternal Care and Mental Health.* Geneva: World Health Organization, 1951.

Bowlby, J. *Attachment and Loss. Vol. I. Attachment.* New York: Basic Books, 1969.

Braakman, R.; Orbaan, I. J. C.; and Blaauwvan Dishoeck, M. Information in the early stages after spinal cord injury. *Paraplegia,* 14: 95–100, 1976.

Braceland. F. Senescence: The Inside story. *Psychiatric Annals,* 2 (10): 48–62, 1972.

Brandwein, R. A.; Brown, C. A.; and Fox, E. M. Women and children last: The social situation of divorced mothers and their families. *Journal of Marriage and the Family,* 36: 498–514, 1974.

Brearly, C. *Social Work, Aging and Society.* London: Routledge and Kegan Paul, 1975.

Brickner, P.; Janeski, J.; Rich, G.; Dugee, T.; Starita, L.; LaRocco, R.; Flannery, T.; and Werlin, S. Home maintenance for the homebound aged: A pilot program in New York City. *Gerontologist,* 16: 25–29, 1976.

Brim, O. G., Jr., and Wheeler, S. *Socialization After Childhood: Two Essays.* New York: Wiley, 1966.

Brim, O., Jr. Socialization through the life cycle. In Sussman, M., ed. *Sourcebook in Marriage and the Family.* New York: Houghton Mifflin, 1968.

Brody, E. The aging family. *Gerontologist,* 6: 201–206, 1966.

Brody, E. The etiquette of filial behavior. *Aging and Human Development,* 1: 87–94, 1970.

Brody, E. Aging and the family personality: A developmental view. *Family Process,* 13: 23–28, 1974.

Brody, S. Public policy issues of women in transition. *Gerontologist*, 16: 181–183, 1976.

Bronfenbrenner, U. The origins, of alienation. *Scientific American*, 231(2): 52–61, 1974. (a)

Bronfenbrenner, U. Developmental research, public policy and the ecology of childhood. *Child Development*, 45: 1, 1974. (b)

Bronfenbrenner, U. Toward an Experimental Ecology of Human Development. *American Psychologist*, 32: 513–531, 1977.

Bronfenbrenner, U.; Belsky, J.; and Steinberg L. *Day Care in Context: An Ecological Perspective on Research and Public Policy.* Review prepared for the Department of Health, Education, and Welfare, Office of the Assistant Secretary for Planning and Evaluation, 1976.

Brotman, H. The older population revisited: First results of the 1970 Census. *Facts and Figures on Older Americans*, DHEW Pub. No. (SRS-AOA) 182. Washington, D.C.: Supt. of Docs., U.S. Govt. Print. Off., 1971.

Brotman, H. The fastest growing minority: The aging. *American Journal of Public Health*, 64: 249–252, 1974.

Brotman, H. Life expectancy. Comparison of national levels in 1900 and 1974 and variations in State levels, 1969–1971. *Gerontologist*, 17: 12–22, 1977.

Browder, J. A. Adoption and foster care of handicapped children in the United States. *Developmental Medicine and Child Neurology*, 17: 614–620, 1975.

Brown, A. Satisfying relationships for the elderly and their patterns of disengagement. *Gerontologist*, 14: 258–262, 1974.

Brown, C., and Hellinger, M. Therapists' attitudes toward women. *Social Work*, 20: 266–270, 1975.

Bullington, B.; Sexton, D.; and White, P. Working with families of multihandicapped children in a residential institution. *Children Today*, 5(5): 13–17, 1976.

Burch, T., and Gendel, M. Extended family structure and fertility: Some conceptual and methodological issues. *Journal of Marriage and the Family*, 32: 227–236, 1970.

Burdette, M. *Personal Care and Household Help Needs of the Noninstitutionalized Disabled;* DHEW Pub. No. (SSA) 73-11713(21). Washington, D.C.,: Supt. of Docs., U.S. Govt. Print. Off., 1966.

Burgess, E.W., and Locke, H.J. *The Family: From Institution to Companionship.* New York: American Book, 1945.

Burton, L., *The Family Life of Sick Children: A Study of Families Coping with Chronic Childhood Disease.* London: Routledge and Kegan Paul, 1975.

Butler, R. *Aging and Mental Health.* St. Louis: Mosby, 1973.

Butterfield, E. Basic facts about public residential facilities for the mentally retarded. In: Kugel, R., and Wolfensberger, W., eds. *Changing Patterns in Residential Services for the Mentally Retarded.* President's Committee on Mental Retardation. Washington, D.C.: Supt. of Docs., U.S. Govt. Print. Off., 1969.

Caldwell, B.; Effects of infant care. *Review of Child Development Research.* Vol. I. New York: Russell Sage Foundation, 1964.

Caldwell, B., and Richmond, J. The Children's Center in Syracuse, New York. In: Dittman, L. ed. *Early Child Care: The New Perspectives.* New York: Atherton, 1968.

Califano, J., Jr. "American Families: Trends, Pressures and Recommendations." A Preliminary Report to Georgia Governor Jimmy Carter, 1976.

California Department of Mental Hygiene. *Annual Mental Retardation Census Tabulations, 1970–1974,* Sacramento, 1975.

Calvert, D. Dimensions of family involvement in early childhood education. *Exceptional Children*, 37: 655–659, 1971.

Cantor, M. Life space and the social support system of the inner city elderly of New York. *Gerontologist*, 15: 23–27, 1975. (a)

Cantor, M. "The Formal and Informal Social Support Systems of Older New Yorkers." Paper presented at the 10th International Congress of Gerontology, Jerusalem, Israel, 1975. (b)

Cantor, M.; Rosenthal, K.; and Wilker, L. Social and family relations of black aged women in New York City. *Gerontologist*, 15: 64, 1975.

Caplan, G. *Support Systems and Community Mental Health*. New York: Behavioral, 1974.

Caplan, G. The family as a support system. In: Caplan, G., and Killilea, M. eds. *Support Systems and Mutual Help. Multidisciplinary Explorations*. New York: Grune and Stratton, 1976.

Carisse, C. Family values of innovative women: Perspectives for the future. In: Sussman, M., and Cogswell, B., eds. *Cross National Family Research*. London: E. J. Brill, 1972, pp. 35–51.

Carpenter, J. Changing roles and disagreement in families with disabled husbands. *Archives of Physical Medicine and Rehabilitation*, 15: 272–274, 1974.

Carr, J. *The effect of the severely subnormal on their families*. In: Clarke, A. M., and Clarke, A. D., eds. *Mental Deficiency: The Changing Outlook*. 3rd ed. New York: Free Press, 1975.

Carroll, J. The inevitability of the nuclear family. *Humboldt Journal of Social Relations*, 1973.

Carson, J. *Silent Voices: The Southern Negro Woman*. New York: Delacorte, 1969.

Cherington, C., and Dybwad, G., eds. *New Neighbors: The Retarded Citizen in Quest of a Home*. President's Committee on Mental Retardation. Washington, D.C.: Supt. of Docs., U.S. Govt. Print. Off., 1974.

Children's Bureau. *Families of Mongoloid Children*, by Kramm, E. Washington, D.C.: Supt. of Docs., U.S. Gov't. Print. Off., 1963.

Chilman, C. Public social policy and families in the 1970's. *Social Casework*, 54: 575–585, 1973.

Chilman, C. Child-bearing and family relationship patterns of the very poor. In: Sussman, M., ed. *Sourcebook in Marriage and the Family*. 4th ed. Boston: Houghton Mifflin, 1974.

Christopherson, L., and Lunde, D. Selection of cardiac transplant recipients and their subsequent psychosocial adjustment. *Seminars in Psychiatry*, 3: 36–45, 1971.

Clarke, A. M., and Clarke, A. D., eds. *Mental Deficiency: The Changing Outlook*. 3rd. ed. New York: Free Press, 1975.

Clausen, J., and Yarrow, M., eds. The impact of mental illness on the family. *Journal of Social Issues*, 11(4): 49–60, 1955.

Clausen, J.; Yarrow, M.; Deasy, L.; and Schwartz, C. The impact of mental illness: Research formulation. *Journal of Social Issues*, 11(4): 6–11, 1955.

Clausen, J. *Socialization and Society*. Boston: Little, Brown, 1968.

Clavan, S. Changing female sexual behavior and future family structure. *Pacific Sociological Review*, 15: 295–308, 1972.

Clavan, S., and Vatter, E. The affiliated family: A device for integrating old and young. *Gerontologist*, 12: 407–412, 1972.

Clayton, R., and Voss, H. Shacking up: Cohabitation in the 1970's. *Journal of Marriage and the Family,* 39: 273–283, 1977.

Coale, A. *Aspects of the Analysis of Family Structure.* Princeton, N.J.: Princeton University, 1965.

Cobb, S. Social Support as a Moderator of Life Stress. *Psychomatic Medicine,* 38: 300–314, 1976.

Cobb, S. Social Support and Health Through the Life Course, In: Riley, M., ed. *Aging from Birth to Death: Interdisciplinary Perspectives.* N.Y.: American Association for the Advancement of Science, 1979.

Cogswell, B. Socialization into the family: An essay on some structural properties of roles. In: Sussman, M., ed. *Sourcebook in Marriage and the Family.* New York: Houghton Mifflin, 1968, pp. 366–377.

Cogswell, B., and Sussman, M. Changing family and marriage forms: Complications for human service systems. *Family Coordinator,* 21: 505–516, 1972.

Cohen, M. G., Alternative to institutional care. *Social Casework,* 54: 447–452, 1973.

Cohen, P. The impact of the handicapped child in the family. *Social Casework,* 43: 137–142, 1962.

Coll, B. *Perspectives in Public Welfare: A History.* Washington, D.C.: U.S. Department of Health, Education and Welfare, 1973.

Collins, A., and Pancoast, D. *Natural Helping Networks. A Strategy for Prevention.* Washington, D.C.: National Association of Social Workers, 1976.

Colman, M.; Dougher, C.; and Tanner, M. Group therapy for physically handicapped toddlers with delayed speech and language development. *Journal of American Academy of Child Psychiatry,* 15: 395–413, 1976.

Congressional Record. Message from the President of the United States Relative to Welfare Reform, Aug. 11, 1968, p. 59582.

Conine, T. Listening in the helping relationship. *Physical Therapy,* 56: 159–162, 1976.

Conley, R. *The Economics of Mental Retardation.* Baltimore: The Johns Hopkins University, 1973.

Conroy, J., and Derr, K. *Survey and Analysis of the Habilitation and Rehabilitation Status of the Mentally Retarded with Associated Handicapping Conditions.* Washington, D.C.: Department of Health, Education and Welfare, 1971.

Constantine, L.; Constantine, J.; and Edelman, S. Counseling implications of comarital and multilateral relations. *Family Coordinator,* 21: 267–273, 1972.

Council for Exceptional Children. *State Statutory Responsibilities for the Education of Handicapped Children.* Reston, VA: the Council, 1974.

Craft, M. The multiple handicapped child. *British Journal of Disorders of Communication,* 3: 182–188, 1968.

Craven, R., and Sharp, B. The effects of illness on family functions. *Nursing Forum,* 11: 186–193, 1972.

Croog, S.; Levine, S.; and Lurie, Z. The heart patient and the recovery process: A review of the directions of research on social and psychological factors. *Social Science and Medicine,* 2: 111–164, 1968.

Croog, S.; Lipson, A.; and Levine, S. Help patterns in severe illness: The roles of kin network, non-family resources, and institutions. *Journal of Marriage and the Family,* 34: 32–41, 1972.

Crouch, B. Age and institutional support: Perceptions of older Mexican-Americans. *Journal of Gerontology,* 27: 524–529. 1972.

Cruickshank, W., ed. *Cerebal Palsy, A Developmental Disability.* Syracuse, N.Y.: Syracuse University, 1976.

Daniel, J. H., and Hyde, J. N., Jr. Working with high risk families: Family advocacy and the parent education program. *Children Today,* 4: 23–25, 1975.

David, A., and Donovan, E. Initiating group process with parents of multihandicapped children. *Social Work in Health Care,* 1: 177–183, 1976.

Davis, K. Equal treatment and unequal benefits: The Medicare program. *Milbank Memorial Fund Quarterly,* 53: 449–485, 1975.

Davis, R. Family of physically disabled child. Family reactions and deductive reasoning. *New York State Journal of Medicine,* 75: 1039–1041, 1975.

Dean, A., and Lin, A. The Stress Buffering Role of Social Support. *Journal of Nervous and Mental Disease,* 165: 403–417, 1977.

Demos, J. Family Home Care: Historical Notes and Reflections. In: Perlman, R., ed., *Family Home Care: Critical Issues for Services and Polices.* N.Y.: Haworth Press, 1983, pp. 161–175.

Dempsey, J., ed. *Community Services for Retarded Children: The Consumer Provider Relationship.* Baltimore: University Park, 1976.

Deutsch, C., and Goldston, J. "Patient Attitudes and Their Relationship to Home Placement of the Severely Disabled." Paper presented at the annual meeting of the American Psychological Association, Cincinnati, September 4, 1959.

Development in Aging. 1968. Special Committee on Aging, United States Senate, 91st Congress, 1st Session, Report No. 91–119. Washington, D.C.: Supt. of Docs., U.S. Govt. Print. Off., 1968.

Dinerman, M. Catch 23: Women, work, and welfare. *Social Work.* 22: 472–477, 1977.

Diprizio, C., and Baer, S. "The Influence of the Women's Movement on the Mothers of Mentally Handicapped Children: The Issue of Personal Freedom." Paper presented at the 54th Annual Council for Exceptional Children Convention, Chicago, April 1976.

Donner, G. Parenthood as crisis: A role of the psychiatric nurse. *Perspectives in Psychiatric Care,* 10: 84–87, 1972.

Donzelot, J. *The Policing of Families.* N.Y.: Pantheon Books, 1979.

Dorenberg, N. Parents as teachers of their own retarded children. In: Wortis, J., ed. *Mental Retardation: An Annual Review.* New York: Grune and Stratton, 1972.

Dorner, S. The relationship of physical handicap to stress in families with an adolescent with spina bifida. *Developmental Medicine and Child Neurology,* 17: 765–776, 1975.

Droller, H. Does community care really reach the elderly sick? Social and medical factors accelerating admission to a geriatric unit. *Gerontologia Clinical,* 11: 169–182, 1969.

Duff, R. On deciding the use of the family commons. *Birth Defects,* 12: 73–84, 1976.

Duncan, B., and Duncan, O. Family stability and occupational success. *Social Problems,* 16: 273–285, 1969.

Dunlap, W. Services for families of the developmentally disabled. *Social Work,* 21: 220–223, 1976.

Duvall, E. Family development applications: An essay review. *Family Coordinator,* 21: 331–333, 1972.

Dybwad, G. Statement Before the U.S. Senate Subcommittee on Children and Youth. *American Families: Trends and Pressures.* Washington, D.C.: Committee on Labor and Public Welfare, 1973.

Eagle, E. Charges for care and maintenance in State institutions for the mentally retarded. *American Journal of Mental Deficiency,* 65: 199–207, 1960.

Eagle, E. Maintenance charges and costs for residents of State institutions for the mentally retarded. *Public Health Reports,* 78: 927–940, 1963.

Edgerton, R. *The Cloak of Competence.* Berkeley: University of California, 1967.

Ehrlich, S. The family structure of hospitalized adolescents. *Journal of Health and Human Behavior,* 3: 121–124, 1962.

Eiduson, B. Looking at children in emergent family styles. *Children Today,* 3(4): 2–6, 1974.

Einbinder, M. The legal family—A definitional analysis. *Journal of Family Law,* 13: 781–802, 1973.

Erickson, G., and Hogan, T. *Family Therapy. An Introduction to Theory and Technique.* Monterey, Calif.: Brooks/Cole, 1972.

Evans, E. B., and Saia, G. *Day Care for Infants.* Boston: Beacon, 1972.

Family Impact Seminar. *Toward an Inventory of Federal Programs with Direct Impact on Families.* Washington, D.C.: George Washington University, 1978.

Farber, B. Effects of a severely mentally retarded child on family integrations. *Monographs of the Society for Research in Child Development.* Vol. XXIV, 1959.

Farber, B. Family organization and crisis: Maintenance of integration in the family with a severely retarded child. *Monographs on Social Research in Child Development,* Vol. XXV, 1960.

Farber, B. *Family Relationships of Institutionalized and Non-institutionalized Retarded Children.* Children's Bureau, No. 461. Bethesda, Md.: Public Health Service, 1968. (a)

Farber, B. *Mental Retardation: Its Social Context and Social Consequences.* Boston: Houghton Mifflin, 1968. (b)

Farber, B. Family adaptations to severely mentally retarded children. In: Begab, M., and Richardson, S., eds. *The Mentally Retarded and Society: A Social Science Perspective.* Baltimore: University Park, 1975.

Farber, B., and Ryckman, J. Effects of severely mentally retarded children on family relationships. *Mental Retardation Abstracts,* 2: 1–17, 1965.

Farber, B.; Jenne, W.; and Toigo, R. "Family Crisis and the Decision to Institutionalize the Retarded Child." *Council for Exceptional Children Research Monograph,* Series A, No. 1, 1960.

Faulkner, A. The black aged as good neighbors: An experiment in volunteer service. *Gerontologist,* 15: 554–559, 1975.

Featherstone, J. Family Matters. *Harvard Educational Review,* 49: 20–52, 1979.

Federal Council on the Aging. *Report on National Policy for the Frail Elderly,* Washington, D.C., 1977.

Fein, G. Infant day care and the family: Regulatory strategies to ensure parent participation. Merrill-Palmer Institute, 1976.

Fein, G., and Clarke-Stewart, A. *Day Care in Context.* New York: Wiley, 1973.

Feldman, M.; Byalick, R.; and Rosedale, M. Parents and professionals: A partnership in special education. *Exceptional Children.* 41: 551–554, 1975.

Fellin, P. A reappraisal of changes in American family patterns. *Social Casework,* 45: 263–267, 1964.

Field, M. *The Aged, the Family and the Community*. New York: Columbia University, 1972.

Finlayson, A. Social networks as coping resources: Lay help and consultation patterns used by women in husband's post-infarction career. *Social Science and Medicine*, 10: 97–103, 1976.

Fischer, A.; Beasley, J.; and Harter, C. The occurrence of the extended family at the origin of the family of procreation: A developmental approach to Negro family structure. *Journal of Marriage and the Family*, 30: 290–300, 1968.

Fishman, C., and Fishman, D. A group training program in behavior modification for mothers of children with birth defects: An exploratory study. *Child Psychiatry and Human Development*, 6: 3–14, 1975.

Fleck, S. The role of the family in psychiatry. In: Freedman, A., and Kaplan, H., eds. *Human Behavior: Biological, Psychological, and Sociological*. New York: Atheneum, 1972.

Fleck, S.; Corneleson, A.; Norton, B.; and Lidz, T. Interaction between hospital staff and families. *Psychiatry*, 20: 343–350, 1957.

Fleming, J. *Care and Management of Exceptional Children*. New York: Appleton-Century-Crofts, 1973.

Fleming, J. The aging person in American society. A commentary on social and personal relationships. In: Fields, W., ed. *Neurological and Sensory Disorders in the Elderly*. New York: Grune and Stratton, 1975.

Foley, V. *An Introduction to Family Therapy*. New York: Grune and Stratton, 1974.

Foley, V. Family therapy with black disadvantaged families: Some observations on roles, communications and technique. *Journal of Marriage and Family Counselling*, 1: 29–38, 1975.

Ford, N. *Analysis of 1973 Participation of Handicapped Children in Local Education Programs*. Washington, D.C.: Department of Health, Education, and Welfare, Office of Assistant Secretary for Planning and Evaluation, 1975.

Foster, B. *Statistics of Public Elementary and Secondary Day Schools. Fall 1974*. Washington, D.C.: Supt. of Docs., U.S. Govt. Print. Off., 1975.

Fotheringham, J., and Creal, D. Handicapped children and handicapped families. *International Review of Education*, 20: 353–371, 1974.

Fotherington, J.; Skelton, M.; and Hoddinott, B. A. The effects on the family of the presence of a mentally retarded child. *Canadian Psychiatric Association Journal*. 17: 283-290, 1972.

Fowle, C. The effects of the severely mentally retarded child on his family. *American Journal of Mental Deficiency*, 73: 468–473, 1968.

Fox, R., and Parsons, T. Illness, therapy and the modern urban family. *Journal of Social Issues*, 8(4): 31–44, 1952.

Fox, S. Responsibility for the care of the geriatric patient: Legal, psychological, and ethical issues: The past, present and future of a child's legal responsibility for support of his parents. *Journal of Geriatric Psychiatry*, 5: 137–147, 1972.

Fox, S. Should parents pay. *Health and Social Service Journal*, Feb., 1975.

Fraiberg, S. *Every Child's Birthright: In Defense of Mothering*. New York: Basic Books, 1977.

Frank, L. A national policy for the family. *Journal of Marriage and Family Living*, 10: 1–4, 1948.

Franklin, D. The adoption of children with medical conditions: Part I, process and outcome. *Child Welfare*, 48: 459–467, 1969a.

Franklin, D. The adoption of children with medical conditions: Part II, The family today. *Child Welfare*, 48: 533–539, 1969*b*.

Freed, A. The family agency and the kinship system of the elderly. *Social Casework*, 56: 579–586, 1975.

Freeman, H., and Simmons, O. Mental patients in the community: Family settings and performance levels. *American Sociological Review*, 23: 147–154, 1958.

Freeman, H., and Simmons, O. *The Mental Patient Comes Home*. New York: Wiley, 1963.

Freeston, B. An enquiry into the effect of a spina bifida child upon family life. *Developmental Medicine and Child Neurology*, 13: 456–461, 1971.

Friend, M. R. The historical developmeent of family diagnosis. *Social Service Review*, 34: 2–18, 1960.

Furstenberg, F. Industrialization and the American family: A look backward. *American Sociological Review*, 31: 326–337, 1966.

Gatti, F., and Colman, C. Community network therapy: An approach to aiding families with troubled children. *American Journal of Orthopsychiatry*, 46: 608–617, 1976.

Gelwicks, L.; Feldman, A.; and Newcomer, R. *Report on Older Populations: Needs, Resources and Services*. Los Angeles: Gerontology Center, University of Southern California, 1971.

Gibson, G., and Ludwig, E. Family structure in a disabled population. *Journal of Marriage and the Family*, 30: 54–63, 1968.

Glasser, P., and Navarre, E. Structural problems of the one-parent family. *Journal of Social Issues*, 21: 98–109, 1965.

Glick, P. *American Families*. New York: Wiley, 1957.

Glick, P. "Updating the Life Cycle of the Family." Revision of a paper presented at the Annual Meeting of the Population Association of America. Montreal, April 30, 1976. (a)

Glick, P. Living arrangements of children and young adults. *Journal of Comparative Family Studies*, 7: 321–333, 1976 (b)

Goffman, E. *Asylums*. Garden City, N.Y.: Anchor, 1961.

Gold, J. *Child Care and the Working Woman*. A Report of the Secretary's Advisory Committee on the Rights and Responsibilities. Department of Health, Education, and Welfare. Washington, D.C.: Supt. of Docs., U.S. Govt. Print. Off., 1975.

Goldie, L. The psychiatry of the handicapped family. *Developmental Medicine and Child Neurology*, 8: 456–462, 1966.

Goldmann, F. What are social workers in general hospitals doing for the long-term patient. *Social Work*, 5(4): 68–77, 1960.

Goldstein, H. Population trends in U.S. public institutions. *American Journal of Mental Deficiency*, 63: 599–604, 1959.

Goldstein, J.; Freud, A.; and Solnit, A. *Beyond the Best Interests of the Child*. New York: Free Press, 1973.

Goode, W. *The Family*. Englewood Cliffs, N.J.: Prentice-Hall, 1964.

Goode, W. *World Revolution and Family Patterns*. Glencoe, Ill.: Free Press, 1975.

Goodell, G. Rehabilitation: Family involved in patient's care. *Hospitals*, 49(6): 96–98, 1975.

Goolsby, E. Facilitation of family-professional interaction. *Rehabilitation Literature*, 37: 332–334, 1976.

Gordon, M. *The Nuclear Family in Crisis*. New York: Harper and Row, 1972.

Gordon, M. *The American Family in Social-Historical Perspective*. New York: St. Martins, 1975.

Gore, S. "The influence of Social Support and Related Variables in Ameliorating the Consequences of Job Loss." Unpublished Dissertation, University of Pennsylvania, 1973.

Gottesman, L., and Brody, E. M. Psycho-social intervention programs within the institutional setting. In: Sherwood, S., ed. *Long Term Care*. New York: Spectrum, 1975.

Gottesman, L., and Hutchinson, E. Characteristics of institutionalized elderly. In: Brody, E. M., ed. *Social Work Guide for Long-Term Care Facilities*. Washington, D.C.: Supt. of Docs., U.S. Govt. Print. Off., 1974.

Gottlieb, J. Public, peer and professional attitudes toward mentally retarded persons. In: Begab, M., and Richardson S., eds. *The Mentally Retarded and Society: A Social Science Perspective*. Baltimore: University Park, 1975.

Government Accounting Office. *Problems in Providing Proper Care to Medicaid and Medicare Patients in Skilled Nursing Homes*. Washington, D.C.: Supt. of Docs., U.S. Govt. Print. Off., 1971.

Graliker, B.; Koch, R.; and Handerson, R. A study of factors influencing placement of retarded children in a State resident al institution. *American Journal of Mental Deficiency*, 69: 553–559, 1965.

Greenbalt, B. *Responsibility for Child Care. The Changing Role of Family and State in Child Development*. San Francisco: Jossey-Bass, 1977.

Grossman, F. *Brothers and Sisters of Retarded Children: An Exploratory Study*. Syracuse University, 1972.

Grossman, H. *Manual on Terminology and Classification in Mental Retardation*. Washington, D.C.: American Association on Mental Deficiency, 1973.

Gussow, Z., and Tracy, G. The role of self-help clubs in adaption to chronic illness and disability. *Social Science and Medicine*, 10: 407–414, 1976.

Gutherie, G.; Butler, A.; and Gorlow, L. Personality differences between institutionalized and non-institutionalized retardates. *American Journal of Mental Deficiency*, 67: 543–548, 1963.

Haber, L. Disabling effects of chronic disease and impairment. II. Functional capacity limitations. *Journal of Chronic Disease*, 26: 127–151, 1973. (a)

Haber, L. Some parameters for social policy in disability: A crossnational comparison. *Milbank Memorial Fund Quarterly*, 51: 319–340, 1973. (b)

Haley, J. Research on family patterns: An instrument measurement. *Family Process*, 3: 41–65, 1964.

Hall, J., and Bradley, A. Treating long-term mental patients. *Social Work*, 20: 383–386, 1975.

Hamilton, M. *Home based Family Services: Report of the Georgia Outreach Project*. Washington, D.C.: Day Care and Child Development Council of America, 1975.

Hareven, T. The Family as process: The historical study of the family cycle. *Journal of Social History*, 7: 322–329, 1974.

Harper, D., and Garza, J. Ethnicity, family structure and intergenerational solidarity. *Sociological Symposium*, 2: 75–82, 1969.

Harrell, J. A., ed. *Selected Readings in the Issues of Day Care.* Washington, D.C.: The Day Care and Child Development Council of America, 1972.

Harris, A. *Handicapped and Impaired in Great Britain.* London: OPCS, Social Survey Division. Her Majesty's Stationery Office, 1971.

Harris, L. *The Myth and Reality of Aging in America.* Washington, D.C.: National Council on Aging, April 1975.

Haselkorn, F., and Bellak, L. A multiple-service approach to cardiac patients. *Social Casework,* 31: 292–298, 1950.

Hauser, P. Aging and world wide population change. In: Binstock, R., and Shanas, E., eds. *Aging and the Social Sciences.* New York: Von Nostrand and Reinhold, 1976.

Hearings before the Subcommittee on Executive Reorganization. *Federal Role in Urban Affairs.* Senate Committee on Government Operations, 89th Congress, Second Session, 1966.

Heber, R. *Epidemiology of Mental Retardation.* Springfield, Ill.: Thomas, 1970.

Heinicke, C., and Strassman, L. "The Effects of Day Care on Preschoolers and the Provision of Support Services for Day Care Families." Prepared for Department of Health, Education, and Welfare, Office of Assistant Secretary for Planning and Evaluation (undated).

Heintz, P., Held, T., and Levy R. Family structure and society. *Journal of Marriage and the Family,* 37: 861–870, 1975.

Heltsley, M., and Powers, R. Social interaction and perceived adequacy of interaction of the rural aged. *Gerontologist,* 15: 533–536, 1975.

Hendrix, L. Nuclear family universals: Fact and faith in the acceptance of an idea. *Journal of Comparative Family Studies,* 6: 125–138, 1975.

Henretta, J.; Campbell, R.; and Gardocki, G. Survey research in aging. An evaluation of the Harris survey. *Gerontologist,* 17: 160–167, 1977.

Hetherington, E. M.; Cox, M.; and Cox, R. "The Development of Children in Mother Headed Family." Paper presented at the Families in Contemporary America Conference, George Washington University, Washington, D.C., June 11, 1977.

Hewett, S. *The Family and the Handicapped Child.* London: Allen and Unwin, 1972.

Hewett, S. Research on families with handicapped children—An aid or an impediment to understanding? *Birth Defects,* 12(4): 35–46, 1976.

Hill, R. Decision-making and the family life cycle. In: Shanas, E., and Streib, G., eds. *Social Structure and the Family: Generational Relations.* Englewood Cliffs, N.J.: Prentice-Hall, 1965.

Hill, R. Modern systems theory and the family: A confrontation. In: Sussman, M., ed. *Sourcebook in Marriage and the Family.* 4th ed. Boston: Houghton Mifflin, 1974.

Hill, R., and Hansen, D. The identification of conceptual frameworks utilized in family study. *Marriage and Family Living,* vol. 22, 1960, pp. 299–311.

Hill, R., and Koenig, R. *Families in East and West: Socialization Process and Kinship Ties.* The Hague, the Netherlands: Mouton, 1970.

Hill, R.; Foote, N.; Aldous, J.; Carlson, R.; and MacDonald, R. *Family Development in Three Generations: A Longitudinal Study of Changing Patterns of Planning and Achievement.* Cambridge, Mass.: Schenkman, 1970.

Hislop, H. The penalties of physical disability. *Physical Therapy,* 56: 271–278, 1976.

Hitch, D. The family fund's experience. *Health and Social Service Journal,* Apr. 1975.

Hobbs, N. A comparison of institutionalized and non-institutionalized mentally retarded. *American Journal of Mental Deficiency,* 69: 206–210, 1964.

Hobbs, N. *The Futures of Children.* San Francisco: Jossey-Bass, 1975.

Hoffman, L., and Nye, F. *Working Mothers.* San Francisco: Jossey-Bass, 1974.

Hoffman, S. Maritial instability and the economic status of women. *Demography,* 14: 67–76, 1977.

Holt, K. The home care of the severely retarded child. *Pediatrics,* 22: 746–755, 1958.

Holroyd, J.; Brown, N.; Wikler, L.; and Simmons, J. Stress in families of institutionalized and non-institutionalized autistic children. *Journal of Community Psychiatry,* 3: 26–31, 1975.

Horejsi, C. *Deinstitutionalization and the Development of Community Services for the Mentally Retarded: An Overview of Concepts and Issues.* Missoula, Mont.: University of Montana, 1975.

Horejsi, C. "Social and Psychological Factors in Family Care for Persons who are Developmentally Disabled: An Overview." Paper presented at the Conference on Family Care of Developmentally Disabled Members. Minneapolis, Minn., 1978.

Horejsi, C., and Berkley, A. *Deinstitutionalization and the Development of Community Based Services for the Mentally Retarded Youth of Western Montana.* Missoula, Mont.: Department of Social Work, University of Montana, 1975.

Hosey, C. Yes, our son is still with us. *Children Today,* 2(6): 14–17, 1973.

Houghton, L., and Martin, A. Home vs. hospital: A hospital-based home care program. *Health and Social Work,* 1(4): 88–103, 1976.

House Committee on Ways and Means. Hearings. Office Memorandum. "Administrative Actions Necessary to Improve Our Welfare Programs." 87th Congress, 2nd Session, 1962. p. 161.

House of Representatives. *Background Materials Concerning Child and Family Services Act, 1975, HR 2966.* Washington, D.C.: Supt. of Docs., U.S. Govt. Print. Off., 1976.

Howell, M. Employed mothers and their families. *Pediatrics,* 52: 252–263, 1973.

Howell, M. *Helping Ourselves: Families and the Human Network.* Boston: Beacon, 1975.

Howells, J. *Theory and Practice of Family Psychiatry.* New York: Brunner/Mazel, 1971.

Hunt, J. Parent and child centers: Their basis in the behavorial and educational sciences. In: Shore, M., and Mannino, F., eds. *Mental Health and Social Change.* New York: AMS, 1975.

Hunt, R. Homemaker service. *Encyclopedia of Social Work,* 16th Issue, Vol. I. New York: National Association of Social Workers, 1971.

Hurd, G. *Preprimary Enrollment Trends of Children Under Six: 1964–1968.* Washington, D.C.: Supt. of Docs., U.S. Govt. Print. Off., 1970.

Infant Day Care: An Abstract Bibliography. Available from College of Education, University of Illinois, Urbana, Ill., 1976.

Irving, H. Relationships between married couples and their parents. *Social Casework,* 52: 91–96, 1971.

Ismail, H. Considerations in the provision of comprehensive care for children with severe visual handicap. *Child Care and Health Developments,* 2: 99–106, 1976.

Jackson, J.J. Comparative life styles and family and friend relationships among older black women. *Family Coordinator,* 21: 477–485, 1972.

Jackson, J.K. The role of the patient's family in illness. *Nursing Forum,* 1: 118–128, 1962.

Jenkins, W.; Anderson, R.; and Dietrich, W., eds. *Rehabilitation of the Severely Disabled.* Dubuque, Iowa: Kendall/Hunt, 1976.

Jew, W. Helping handicapped infants and their families. The delayed development project. *Children Today,* 3(3): 7–10, 1974.

Johnson, E., and Bursk, B. Relationships between the elderly and their adult children. *Gerontologist,* 17: 90–96, 1977.

Johnson, G.; Fox, J.; Schaefer, H.; and Ishikawa, W. Predicting rehospitalization from community placement. *Psychological Reports,* 29: 475–478, 1971.

Jones, F. "Maternal Attachment to Infants during Post-natal Period." Paper presented at the 84th Annual Meeting of the American Psychological Association, Washington, D.C., September 3–7, 1976.

Jorgensen, J.A., and Brophy, J.J. Psychiatric treatment modalities in burn patients. *Current Psychiatric Therapies,* 15: 85–92, 1975.

Joseph, Sir Keith. Britain: A decadent new utopia. *The Guardian,* October 21, 1974.

Justice, R.; Bradley, J.; and O'Connor, G. Foster family care for the retarded: Management concerns of the caretaker. *Mental Retardation,* 9(4): 12–15, 1971.

Kadis, A. Current theories and basic concepts in family therapy. In: Goldman, G., and Milman, S., eds. *Innovations in Psychotherapy.* Springfield, Ill.: Thomas, 1972.

Kahana, E., and Coe, R.M. Alternatives in long-term care. In: Sherwood, S., ed. *Long-term Care: A Handbook for Researchers, Planners, and Providers.* New York: Spectrum, 1975.

Kahn, A. *Social Policy and Social Servies.* New York: Random House, 1973.

Kahn, A., and Kammerman, S., *Not for the Poor Alone.* Philadelphia: Temple University, 1975.

Kahn, R.L. The mental health system and the future aged. *Gerontologist,* 15: 24–31, 1975.

Kalish, R. Four score and ten. *Gerontologist,* 14: 129–135, 1974.

Kamerman, S., and Kahn, A. *Social Services in the United States.* Philadelphia: Temple University Press, 1976.

Kanter, R. M. Work in America. *Daedalus,* 107: 47–48, 1978.

Kanthor, H.; Pless, B.; Satterwhite, B.; and Myers, G. Areas of responsibility in the health care of multiple handicapped children. *Pediatrics,* 54: 779–785, 1974.

Kantor, D., and Lehr, W. *Inside the Family: Toward a Theory of Family Process.* San Francisco: Jossey-Bass, 1975.

Kaplan, A., and Wolf, L. The role of the family in relation to the institutionalized mental patient. *Mental Hygiene,* 38: 634–639, 1954.

Kaplan, B.; Cassell, J., and Gore, S. Social Support and Health. *Medical Care,* 15: 47–58, 1977.

Kaplan, D.; Smith, A.; Grobstein, R.; and Fischman, S. Family mediation of stress. *Social Work*, 18(4): 60–69, 1973.

Kaplan, D.; Grobstein, R.; and Smith, A. Predicting the impact of severe illness in families. *Health and Social Work*, 1(3): 71–82, 1976.

Kaplan, J., and Ford, C. Rehabilitation for the elderly: An eleven-year assessment. *Gerontologist*, 15: 545–549, 1975.

Karnes, M, and Zehrbach, R. Matching families and services. *Exceptional Children*, 41: 545–549, 1975.

Kaseman, C. The single-parent family. *Perspectives in Psychiatric Care*, 12(3): 113–118, 1974.

Katz, S.; Halstead, L.; and Wierenga, M. A medical perspective of team care. In: Sherwood, S., ed. *Long-Term Care*. New York: Spectrum, 1975.

Keith, P. Evaluation of services for the aged by professionals and the elderly. *Social Service Review*, 49: 271–278, 1975.

Keller, S. Does the family have a future? *Journal of Comparative Family Studies*, 2: 1–14, 1971.

Kelman, H. Some problems in casework with parents of mentally retarded children. *American Journal of Mental Deficiency*, 61: 595–598, 1957.

Kempler, H. Extended kinship ties and some modern alternatives. *Family Co-ordinator*, 25: 143-149, 1976.

Kent, D. Social and family contexts of health problems of the aged. In: Crawford, C., ed. *Health and the Family*. New York: MacMillan, 1971.

Kerchoff, A. G. Conjugal relationships in industrial societies. In: Sussman, M., and Cogswell, B., eds. *Cross National Family Research*. London: E. J. Brill, 1972, pp. 54–65.

Kern, R. Emotional problems in relation to aging and old age. *Geriatrics*, 26(6): 82–93, 1971.

Kerr, J. Income and expenditures the over-65 age group. *Journal of Gerontology*, 23: 79–81, 1968.

Kershaw, J. The handicapped child and his family. *Public Health*, 80: 18–26, 1965.

Kirk, S. Clients as outsiders: Theoretical approaches to deviance. *Social Work*, 17(2): 24–33, 1972.

Kirkland, M. *Retarded Children of the Poor. A Casebook*. DHEW Pub. No. (SRS) 72-23003. Washington, D.C.: Supt. of Docs., U.S. Govt. Print. Off., 1971.

Kirstin, H.; Harris, E.; and Morris, R. *An Alternative to Institutional Care for the Elderly and Disabled: A Proposal for a New Policy*. Waltham, Mass.: Florence Heller School, Brandeis University, 1971.

Kisly, C. Striking back at stroke. *Hospitals*, 47(22): 64–72, 1973.

Klaber, M. Institutional programming and research: A vital partnership in action. In: Baumeister, A., and Butterfield, E., eds. *Residential Facilities for the Mentally Retarded*. Chicago: Aldine, 1970.

Klaus, M., and Kennell, J. *Maternal-infant Bonding: The Impact of Early Separation or Loss on Family Development*. St. Louis: Mosby, 1976.

Kleba, E. *Key Facts on the Handicapped*. Washington, D.C.: Congressional Research Service, Library of Congress, 1975.

Knudsen, W. Mental retardation—Who should pay the bill for resident care in public institutions? *Family Law Quarterly*, 3: 331–343, 1969.

Kobrin, F. The fall in household size and the rise of the primary individual in the United States. *Demography*, 13: 127–138, 1976.

Koch, R., and Dobson, J., eds. *The Mentally Retarded Child and His Family: A Multidisciplinary Handbook.* New York: Brunner/Mazel, 1971.

Kogan, K., and Tyler, N. Mother-child interaction in young physically handicapped children. *American Journal of Mental Deficiency,* 77: 492–497, 1973.

Kohut, S. The abnormal child: His impact on the family. *Physical Therapy,* 46: 160–167, 1966.

Kossoris, P. Family therapy: An adjunct to hemodialysis and transplantation. *American Journal of Nursing,* 70: 1730–1733, 1970.

Kostick, A. A day care program for the physically and emotionally disabled. *Gerontologist,* 12: 134–138, 1972.

Kramer, M.; Taube, C.; and Starr, S. Patterns of use of psychiatric facilities by the aged: Current status, trends, and implications. *Psychiatric Research Reports of the American Psychiatric Association,* 23: 89–150, 1968.

Kramm, E. *Families of Mongoloid Children.* Washington, D.C.: Supt. of Docs., U.S. Govt. Print. Off., 1963.

Krapf, E. Family mental health and the older generation. *World Health Organization Public Health Papers,* 28: 90–94, 1965.

Kraus, A.; Spasoff, R.; Beattie, E.; Holden, E.; Lawson, J.; Rodenburg, M.; and Woodcock, G. Elderly applicants to long-term care institutions: Their characteristics, health problems, and state of mind. *Journal of the American Geriatrics Society,* 24: 117–125, 1976. (a)

Kraus, A.; Spasoff, R.; Beattie, E., Holden, E.; Lawson, J.; Rodenburg, M.; and Woodcock, G. Elderly applicants to long-term care institutions: The application process, placement and care needs. *Journal of the American Geriatrics Society,* 24: 165–172, 1976. (b)

Kreisman, D., and Joy, D. Family response to the mental illness of a relative: A review. *Schizophrenia Bulletin,* 10(Fall): 34–57, 1974.

Kreps, J. The Economics of intergenerational relationships. In: Shanas E., and Streib, G., eds. *Social Structure and the Family: Generational Relations.* Englewood Cliffs, N.J.: Prentice-Hall, 1965.

Kreps, J. The economy and the aged. In: Binstock, R., and Shanas, E., eds. *Handbook of Aging and the Social Sciences.* New York: Van Nostrand Reinhold, 1976.

Kugel, R. Introduction. In: Kugel, R., and Shearer, A., eds. *Changing Patterns in Residential Services for the Mentally Retarded.* Washington, D.C.: Supt. of Docs., U.S. Govt. Print. Off., 1976.

Kugel, R., and Shearer, A., eds. *Changing Patterns in Residential Services for the Mentally Retarded.* Washington, D.C.: Supt. of Docs., U.S. Govt. Print. Off., 1976.

Kugel, R., and Wolfensberger, W., eds. *Changing Patterns in Residential Services for the Mentally Retarded.* Washington, D.C.: Supt. of Docs., U.S. Govt. Print. Off., 1969.

Kulczki, L. Adequate home care for patients with cystic fibrosis. *Clinical Proceedings of the Children's Hospital,* Washington, D.C., 26(3): 97–103, 1970.

Kushlick, A. The Prevalence of Recognized Mental Subnormality of IQ Under 50 Among Children in the South of England with References to the Demand for Places for Residential Care. *Proceedings of the International Copenhagen Congress on the Scientific Study of Mental Retardation,* 1964.

Laing, R. *The Politics of the Family.* New York: Pantheon, 1971.

Lasch, C. The Family in History. *The New York Review of Books,* 22(18): 35–38, 1975.

Lasch, C. *Haven in a Heartless World: The Family Besieged.* N.Y.: Basic Books, 1977.

Laslett, P. Societal Development and Aging. In: Binstock, R., and Shanas, E., eds. *Handbook of Aging and the Social Sciences.* New York: Van Nostrand Reinhold, 1976.

Laslett, T. R. *The World We Have Lost.* London: Methuen, 1965.

Laury, G. Some reflections on aging in the United States. *Geriatrics,* 28: 178–182, 1973.

LaVor, J., and Callender, M. Home health cost effectiveness: What are we measuring? *Medical Care,* 14: 866–872, 1976.

Lawton, M. The relative impact of congregate and traditional housing on elderly tenants. *Gerontologist,* 16: 237–242, 1976.

Lawton, M., and Cohen, J. The generality of housing impact on the well-being of older people. *Journal of Gerontology,* 29: 194–204, 1974.

Lazar, I., and Darlington, R.D. *Lasting Effects After Preschool* Washington, D.C.: Education Commission of the States. 1978.

Leake, C. Family care program for older people. *Geriatrics,* 22(7): 75–76, 1967.

Leavitt, M. The discharge crisis: The experience of families of psychiatric patients. *Nursing Research,* 24: 33–44, 1975.

Leichter, H. *The Family As Educator.* New York: Teachers College, 1975.

Leichter, H., and Mitchell, W. *Kinship and Casework.* New York: Russell Sage Foundation, 1967.

Lemkau, P., and Impre, P. Results of a field epidemiologic study. *American Journal of Mental Deficiency,* 73: 858–863, 1969.

Lerner, P. *Social Security Disability Applicant Statistics/1969.* DHEW Pub. No. (SSA) 74–11914. Washington, D.C.: Supt. of Docs., U.S. Govt. Print. Off., 1973.

Leslie, G. *The Family in Social Context.* New York: Oxford University, 1973.

Levitan, S., and Alderman, K. *Child Care and ABC's Too.* Baltimore: The Johns Hopkins University, 1975.

Levy, L., and Rowitz, L. *The Ecology of Mental Disorder.* New York: Behavioral Publications, 1973.

Lewis, J. The Family and Physical Illness. *Texas Medicine,* 22 (2): 43–49, 1976.

Liebman, R.; Minuchin, S.; and Baker, L. The use of structural family therapy in the treatment of intractable asthma. *American Journal of Psychiatry,* 131: 525–540, 1974.

Linn, M. W., and Gurel, L. Family attitudes in nursing home placement. *Gerontologist,* 12: 220–224, 1972.

Linton, R. *The Study of Man.* New York: Appleton-Century-Crofts, 1936.

Lipman-Blumen, J. The implications for family structure of changing sex roles. *Social Casework,* 57(2): 67–79, 1976.

Litman, T. Health Care and the family: A 3-generational analysis. *Medical Care,* 9: 67–81, 1971.

Litman, T. The family as a basic unit in health and medical care: A social-behavioral overview. *Social Science and Medicine,* 8: 495–519, 1974.

Little, V. Open day care for the aged: A Swedish model. *Social Work,* 23: 284, 1978.

Litwak, E. Extended kin relations in an industrial democratic society. In: Shanas, E., and Streib, G., eds. *Social Structure and the Family.* Englewood Cliffs, N.J.: Prentice-Hall, 1965.

Litwak, E. The use of extended family groups in the achievement of social goals. In: Sussman, M., ed. *Sourcebook on Marriage and the Family.* New York: Houghton Mifflin, 1968.

Litwak, E., and Szelenyi, I. Primary group structures and their functions: Kin, neighbors, and friends. *American Sociological Review,* 34: 465–481, 1969.

Livsey, C., and Lindenbaum, S. A family-oriented psychiatric clinic in a general hospital. *Hospital and Community Psychiatry,* 23: 371–374, 1972. (a)

Livsey, C. Physical illness and family dynamics. *Advances in Psychosomatic Medicine,* 8: 237–251, 1972. (b)

Lowenthal, M., and Robinson, B. Social networks and isolation. In: Binstock, R., and Shanas, E., eds. *Handbook of Aging and the Social Sciences.* New York: Van Nostrand Reinhold, 1976.

Lowther, C., and Williamson, I. Old people and their relatives. *The Lancet,* December 31, 1966.

Lund, H., and Kaufman, M. The matrifocal family and its relationship to mental retardation. *Journal of Mental Subnormality,* 14: 80–83, 1968.

Lystad, M. Family patterns, achievements, and aspirations of urban Negroes. *Sociology and Social Research,* 45: 281–288, 1961.

McAllister, R.; Butler, E.; and Lei, T. J. Patterns of social interaction among families of behaviorally retarded children. *Journal of Marriage and the Family,* 35: 93–100, 1973.

McAndrews, I. Children with a handicap and their families. *Child Care and Health Development,* 2: 213–218, 1976.

McCollum, A., and Gibson, L. *Family Adaptation to the Child with Cystic Fibrosis.* White Plains, N.Y.: National Foundation—March of Dimes, 1970.

McConkey, R., and Jeffree, D. Partnership with parents. *Special Education: Forward Trends,* 2(3): 13–15, 1975.

MacKeith, R. The feelings and behavior of parents of handicapped children. *Developmental Medicine and Child Neurology,* 15: 524–527, 1973.

Mackie, R. *Special Education in the United States: Statistics 1948–1966.* New York: Teachers College, 1969.

MacMillan, C. Physiotherapy for the handicapped in the community. *Physiotherapy,* 60: 230–231, 1974.

McTavish, D. Perceptions of old people: A review of research methodologies and findings. *Gerontologist,* 11 (Supplement): 90–101, 1971.

Maddox, G. The patient and his family. In: Sherwood, S., ed. *The Hidden Patient: Knowledge and Action in Long-term Care.* New York: Spectrum, 1975.

Maddox, G. Families as context and resource in chronic illness. In: Sherwood, S., ed. *Long-Term Care.* New York: Spectrum, 1975.

Magraw, R. M. Interdisciplinary teamwork for medical care and health services. *Annals of Internal Medicine,* 69: 821–835, 1968.

Maldonado, D. The Chicano aged. *Social Work,* 20: 213–216, 1975.

Malpass, J. Family orientation program. *American Corrective Therapy Journal,* 29: 17–21, 1975.

Malzberg, B. Some statistical aspects of first admissions. *American Journal of Mental Deficiency,* 57: 27–37, 1952.

Mannino, F., and Shore, M. Family structure, aftercare, and post-hospital adjustment. *American Journal of Orthopsychiatry,* 44: 76–85, 1974.

Marciano, T. The variant family forms in a world perspective. *The Family Coordinator,* 24: 407–420, 1975.

Marmo, N. Discovering the lifestyle of the physically disabled. *American Journal of Occupational Therapy,* 29: 475–478, 1975.

Marshner, C. The Pro-Family Movement and Traditional Values. In: Kagan, L. ed. *What is Pro-Family Policy.* New Haven, Conn.: Yale University Bush Center, 1981.

Martin, H. Parental response to handicapped children. *Developmental Medicine and Child Neurology,* 17: 251–252, 1975.

Martindale, D., and Martindale, E. *The Social Dimensions of Mental Illness, Alcoholism, and Drug Dependence.* Westport, Conn.: Greenwood, 1971.

Matheny, A., and Vernick, J. Parents of the mentally retarded child—Emotionally overwhelmed or informationally deprived. *Journal of Pediatrics,* 74: 953–959, 1969.

Mattson, A. Long-term physical illness in childhood: A challenge to psychosocial adaptation. *Pediatrics,* 50: 801–811, 1972.

May, J. *Family Health Indicators: Annotated Bibliography.* DHEW Pub. No. (ADM) 75–135. Rockville, Md.: National Institute of Mental Health, 1974.

Mead, M. Statement before the U.S. Senate Subcommittee on Children and Youth. *American Families: Trends and Pressures.* Washington, D.C.: Committee on Labor and Public Welfare, 1973.

Meadow, K., and Meadow, L. Changing role perceptions for parents of handicapped children. *Exceptional Children,* 38: 21–27, 1971.

Meissner, W. Family process and psychosomatic disease. *International Journal of Psychiatry in Medicine,* 5: 411–430, 1974.

Mendes, H. Single fatherhood. *Social Work,* 21: 308–312, 1976.

Menolascino, F., and Pearson, P. *Beyond the Limits: Innovations in Services for the Severely and Profoundly Retarded.* Seattle: Straub, 1974.

Mercer, C. Interrelations among family stability, family composition, residence and race. *Journal of Marriage and the Family,* 29: 456–460, 1967.

Mercer, J. Patterns of family crisis related to the reacceptance of the retardate. *American Journal of Mental Deficiency,* 71: 19–32, 1966.

Mercer, J. *Labeling the Mentally Retarded.* Berkeley: University of California, 1973.

Mesibov, G. Alternatives to the principle of normalization. *Mental Retardation,* 14(5): 30–32, 1976.

Meszaros, A., and Meszaros, E. Integration of the discharged schizophrenic patient within the family. In: Greenblatt, M., et al., eds. *Mental Patients in Transition.* Springfield, Ill.: Thomas, 1961.

Meyen, E., ed. *Planning Community Services for the Mentally Retarded.* Scranton, Pa.: International Textbook, 1967.

Meyer, W. *Staffing Characteristic and Child Outcomes.* Prepared for Department of Health, Education, and Welfare, Office of the Assistant Secretary for Planning and Evaluation, 1977.

Meyerowitz, J., and Kaplan, H. Cystic fibrosis and family functioning. *Journal of Thanatology,* 1: 244–266, 1971.

Miller, M., and Harris, A. The chronically ill aged: Paradoxical patient-family behavior. *Journal of the American Geriatrics Society,* 15: 480–495, 1967.

Miller, M.; Bernstein, H.; and Sharkey, H. Denial of parental illness and maintenance of familial homeostasis. *Journal of the American Geriatrics Society,*
21: 278–285, 1973.

Miller, M.; Bernstein, H.; and Sharkey, H. Family extrusion of the aged patient: Family homeostasis and sexual conflict. *Gerontologist,* 15: 291–296,
1975.

Miller, N., and Cantwell, D. Siblings as therapists: A behavioral approach.
American Journal of Psychiatry, 133: 447–450, 1976.

Millis, J. S. A reexamination of assumptions in medical education. Supplement
to *G.P. Magazine,* August 1967, pp. 44–47.

Minde, K.; Hackett, J.; Killou, D.; and Silver, S. How they grow up: 41 physically
handicapped children and their families. *American Journal of Psychiatry,* 128:
1554–1560, 1972.

Minuchin, S. A conceptual model of psychosomatic illness in children: Family
organization and family therapy. *Archives of General Psychiatry,* 32: 1031–
1038, 1975.

Mitchell, R. Chronic handicap in childhood: Its implications for family and
community. *Practitioner,* 211: 763–768, 1973.

Mizio, E. Impact of external systems on the Puerto Rican family. *Social Casework,*
55: 76–83, 1974.

Moncreiff, J. *Mental Subnormality in London: A Survey of Community Care.*
London: PEP. 1966

Moroney, R. "Family Policy and the Handicapped." Paper presented at the
Colloquium, *Strengthening Informal Supports for* American Federation of
the Blind, New York, November 13–14, 1975. (a)

Moroney, R. "Family Support Systems: A New Focus." Paper presented at the
Colloquium, *Strengthening Informal Supports for the Aging.* Sponsored by
the Community Service Society of New York and Hunter College School of
Social Work, 1975. (b)

Moroney, R. *The Family and the State: Considerations for Social Policy.* New
York: Longmans, 1976.

Moroney, R. The need for a national family policy. *Urban and Social Change
Review,* 10(1): 10–14, 1977.

Moroney, R. The family as a social service: Implications for policy and practice.
Child Welfare, 57(4): 211–220, 1978. (a)

Moroney, R. "Families, Social Services and Social Policy." Paper presented at
the Annual Meeting of the National Conference on Social Welfare, Los Angeles, 1978. (b)

Moroney, R. "Economic Factors and Family Care." Paper presented at the International Conference, *Family Care of Developmentally Disabled Members,*
Minneapolis, 1978. (c)

Morris, R. Alternative forms of care for the disabled: Developing community
services. *Birth Defects,* 12(4): 127–136, 1976. (a)

Morris, R., et al. *Community Based Maintenance Care for the Long-Term Patient.*
Waltham, Mass.: Levinson Policy Institute, Brandeis University, 1976. (b)

Morris, R.; Leschier, I. E.; and Withorn, A. *Analysis of Federally Supported
Social Services: Options and Directions.* Waltham, Mass.: Florence Heller
School, Brandeis University, 1977.

Morrissey, J. Family care for the mentally ill: A neglected therapeutic resource.
Social Service Review, 39: 63–71, 1965.

Moss, M., and Kaplan-Dénour, A. Reactions of families of chronic hemodialysis. *Psychotherapy and Psychosomatics,* 26: 20–26, 1975.

Mowrer, O. New hope and help for the disintegrating American family. *Journal of Family Counseling,* 3: 17–23, 1975.

Mueller, A. Family care and post-discharge community adjustment. *Journal of the Fort Logan Mental Health Center,* 5: 85–99, 1968.

Murdock, C. Civil rights of the mentally retarded—Some critical issues. *Family Law Quarterly,* 7: 1–74, 1973.

Murdock, G. P. *Social Structure.* New York: Macmillan, 1949.

Nathan, R., ed. *Mental Retardation: Trends in State Services.* Washington, D.C.: Supt. of Docs., U.S. Govt. Print. Off., 1976. (a)

Nathan, R., ed. *Mental Retardation: Century of Decision. Report to the President.* Washington, D.C.: Supt. of Docs., U.S. Govt. Print. Off., 1976. (b)

National Advisory Committee on the Handicapped. *The Unfinished Revolution: Education for the Handicapped.* Washington, D.C.: Supt. of Docs., U.S. Govt. Print. Off., 1976.

National Association of Coordinators of State Programs for the Mentally Retarded. *Day Training Services for Mentally Retarded Children: A State by State Survey.* Arlington, Va.: The Association, 1974.

National Association for Retarded Citizens. *NARC Research News.* Arlington, Texas: Research Advisory Council, NARC, 1974.

National Center for Health Statistics. *Characteristics of Patients in Nursing and Personal Care Homes.* National Health Survey, 1969.

National Center for Health Statistics. *Characteristics of Residents in Nursing Homes and Personal Care Homes.* National Health Survey, Series 121, No. 19, 1973.

National Center for Social Statistics. *Findings of the 1967 AFDC Study.* Washington, D.C.: Department of Health, Education, and Welfare, 1970.

National Center for Social Statistics. *Findings of the 1970 APTD Study, Part I, Demographic and Program Statistics.* Washington, D.C.: Department of Health, Education, and Welfare, 1972.

National Institute of Mental Health. *Patients in Mental Institutions. I. Public Institutions for the Mentally Retarded.* Washington, D.C.: Survey and Reports Section, Office of Biometry, 1966.

Newman, S. *Housing Adjustments of Older People.* Ann Arbor: Institute for Social Research, University of Michigan, 1976.

Nimkoff, M. F. *Comparative Family Systems.* Boston: Houghton Mifflin, 1965.

Nimkoff, M. F., and Middleton, R. Types of family and types of economy. *American Journal of Sociology,* 66: 215–217, 1960.

Nirje, B. The normalization principle: Implications and comments. *Journal of Mental Subnormality,* 16: 62–70, 1970.

Nirje, B. The normalization principle. In: Kugel, R., and Shearer, A., eds. *Changing Patterns in Residential Services for the Mentally Retarded.* Washington, D.C.: Supt. of Docs., U.S. Govt. Print. Off., 1976.

Noland, R., ed. *Counseling Parents of the Mentally Retarded.* Springfield, Ill.: Thomas, 1970.

Nooe, R. Toward independent living for the mentally retarded. *Social Work,* 20: 286–290, 1975.

Norton, A. The family life cycle undated: Components and uses. In: Winch, R. F., and Spanier, G. B., eds. *Selected Studies in Marriage and the Family.* New York: Holt, Rinehart and Winston, 1974, pp. 162–170.

Norton, A., and Glick, P. Marital instability: Past, present and future. *Journal of Social Issues,* 32: 8–12, 1976.

Nuckolls, J.; Cassell, J.; and Kaplan, B. Pyschosocial Aspects, Life Crisis, and Prognosis of Pregnancy. *American Journal of Epidemiology,* 95: 431–441, 1972.

Nye, F. Values, family and a changing society. *Journal of Marriage and the Family,* 29: 241–248, 1967.

Nye, F. *Role Structure and Analysis of the Family.* Beverly Hills: Sage, 1976.

Office of Child Development. *Head Start Services to Handicapped Children: Second Annual Report.* Washington, D.C.: Department of Health, Education, and Welfare, 1974.

Office of Education. *The Unfinished Revolution: Education for the Handicapped.* Washington, D.C.: Supt. of Docs., U.S. Govt. Print. Off., 1976.

Office of Human Development. *A Summary of Selected Legislation Relating to the Handicapped, 1963–1967.* Washington, D.C.; Supt. of Docs., U.S. Govt. Print. Off., 1969.

Office of Human Development. *Day Care: A Statement of Principles.* DHEW Publication No. (OHD) 72-10. Washington, D.C.: Supt. of Docs., U.S. Govt. Print. Off., 1971.

Office of Human Development. *The Problem of Mental Retardation.* DHEW Publication No. (OHD) 75-2203. Washington, D.C.: Supt. of Docs., U.S. Govt. Print. Off., 1975.

Office of Human Development. *Child Welfare in 25 States: An Overview.* Washington, D.C.: Department of Health, Education, and Welfare, 1976.

Office of Human Development. *The State of Children 1977,* by Snapper, K., and Ohms, J. DHEW Publication No. (OHDS) 78-30133. Washington, D.C.: Supt. of Docs., U.S. Govt. Print. Off., 1978.

Office of Management and Budget. *Social Indicators 1976.* Washington, D.C.: Supt. of Docs., U.S. Govt. Print. Off., 1977, p. 69.

Office of Mental Retardation Coordinator. *Mental Retardation Sourcebook of the Department of Health, Education, and Welfare.* DHEW Publication No. (05) 73–81. Washington, D.C.: Supt. of Docs., U.S. Govt. Print. Off., 1972. (a)

Office of Mental Retardation Coordinator. *Programs for the Handicapped.* Washington, D.C.: Department of Health, Education, and Welfare, 1972. (b)

Office of Mental Retardation Coordinator. *Mental Retardation Sourcebook of the Department of Health, Education, and Welfare,* Table 14. Washington, D.C.: 1973.

Office of Mental Retardation Coordinator. *Mental Retardation Source Book.* Washington, D.C.: Department of Health, Education, and Welfare, 1974.

Office of Research and Statistics. *Report Number 1 from the Social Security Survey of Institutionalized Adults, 1967.* Washington, D.C.: Supt. of Docs., U.S. Govt. Print. Off., 1971.

Office of Research and Statistics. *SSI Recipients in Domiciliary Care Facilities: States with Federally Administered Optional Implementation.* Washington, D.C.: Supt. of Docs., U.S. Govt. Print. Off., 1976.

Ogburn, W. F. *The Family and Its Functions.* New York: McGraw-Hill, 1933.

Ogburn, W.F., and Nimkoff, M. H. *Technology and the Changing Family*. Boston: Houghton Mifflin, 1955.

Olshansky, S. Chronic sorrow: A response to having a mentally defective child. *Social Casework*, 43: 191–194, 1962.

O'Neill, N., and O'Neill, G. Open marriage: The conceptual framework. In: Sussman, M., ed. *Sourcebook in Marriage and the Family*. 4th ed. Boston: Houghton Mifflin, 1974.

Osmond, M. W. cross-cultural analysis of family organization. *Journal of Marriage and the Family*, 31: 302–310, 1969.

Palisi, B. Ethnic generation and family structure. *Journal of Marriage and the Family*, 28: 49–50, 1966.

Pannbacker, M., and Schneiderman, C. Rehabilitation of cleft palate: Parents and professionals, a unifying model. *Rehabilitation Literature*, 38: 178–187, 1977.

Parfit, J. Siblings of handicapped children. *Special Education: Forward Trends*, 2: 19–21, 1975.

Parsons, T. The kinship system of the contemporary United States. *American Anthropologist*, 45: 22–38, 1943.

Parsons, T. Illness and the role of the physician: A sociological perspective. *American Journal of Orthopsychiatry*, 21(3): 452–460, 1951.

Parsons, T. The normal American family. In: Sussman, M., ed. *Sourcebook in Marriage and the Family*. New York: Houghton Mifflin, 1968, pp. 36–46.

Parsons, T., and Bales, R. *Family, Socialization and Interaction Process*. Glencoe, Ill: Free Press, 1955.

Pattison, E. A psychosocial kinship model for family therapy. *American Journal of Psychiatry*, 132: 1246–1251, 1975.

Patton, R., and Weinstein, A. Changing characteristics of the population in the New York State schools for mental defectives. *American Journal of Mental Deficiency*, 64: 625–635, 1960.

Paul, J.; Stedman, D.; and Neufeld, G., eds. *Deinstitutionalization. Program and Policy Development*. Syracuse, N.Y.: Syracuse University, 1977.

Pearce, D. The feminization of poverty: Women, work and welfare. *The Urban and Social Change Review*, 11: 28–36, 1978.

Pearson, J. Family support and counseling in Huntington's disease. *Psychiatric Forum*, 4: 46–50, 1973.

Peck, B. B. Physical medicine and family dynamics: The dialectics of rehabilitation. *Family Process*, 13: 469–479, 1974.

Peck, J., and Stephens, W. A Study of the relationships between the attitudes and behavior of parents and that of their mentally defective child. *American Journal of Mental Deficiency*, 64: 839, 1960.

Perrin, J.; Rusch, E.; Pray, J.; Wright, G.; and Bartlee, G. Evaluation of a ten-year experience in a comprehensive care program for handicapped children. *Pediatrics*, 50: 793–800, 1972.

Pickett, R. The American family: An embattled institution. *Humanist*, 35(3): 5–8, 1975.

Pinker, R. *Social Theory and Social Policy*. London: Heinemann, 1973.

Pinkerton, P. Parental acceptance of the handicapped child. *Developmental Medicine and Child Neurology*, 12: 207–212, 1970.

Pless, I. Individual and family needs in the health care of children with developmental disorders. *Birth Defects*, 12: 91–102, 1976.

Pless, I.; Roghmann, K.; and Haggerty, R. Chronic illness, family functioning, and psychological adjustment: A model for the allocation of preventive mental health services. *International Journal of Epidemiology*, 1: 271–277, 1972.

Pollak, O. A family diagnosis model. *Social Service Review*, 34: 19–31, 1960.

Pollak, O. The outlook for the American family. *Journal of Marriage and the Family*, 29: 193–205, 1967.

Pollak, O. Family structure: Its implications for mental health. In Pollak, O., and Friedman, A., eds. *Family Dynamics and Female Sexual Delinquency.* Palo Alto, Calif.: Science and Behavior, 1969.

Poloma, M. "The Myth of the Egalitarian Family: Familial Roles and the Professionally Employed Wife." *Paper presented at the Sixty-fifth Annual Meeting of the American Sociological Association.* Washington, D.C., 1970.

Poznanski, E. Emotional issues in raising handicapped children. *Rehabilitation Literature*, 34: 322–326, 1973.

Poznanski, E. Parental adaptations to maternal employment. *Journal of American Academy of Child Psychiatry*, 13: 319–334, 1974.

President's Committee on Mental Retardation. M R 72. *Islands of Excellence.* Washington, D.C.: Supt. of Docs., U.S. Govt. Print. Off., 1973.

President's Committee on Mental Retardation. *Mental Retardation . . . The Known and the Unknown.* Washington, D.C.: Supt. of Docs., U.S. Govt. Print. Off., 1975. (a)

President's Committee on Mental Retardation. *People Live in Houses. Profiles of Community Residences for Retarded Children and Adults.* Washington, D.C.: Supt. of Docs., U.S. Govt. Print. Off., 1975. (b)

President's Committee on Mental Retardation. *Mental Retardation: Trends in State Service.* Washington, D.C.: Supt. of Docs., U.S. Govt. Print. Off., 1976.

President's Panel on Mental Retardation. *Report to the President: A Proposed Program for National Action to Combat Mental Retardation.* Washington, D.C.: Supt. of Docs., U.S. Govt. Print. Off., 1962.

Presidential Veto Message of the Comprehensive Child Development Act of 1971. December 10, 1971.

Prock, V. Effects of institutionalization: A comparison of community, waiting list, and institutionalized aged persons. *American Journal of Public Health*, 59: 1837–1844, 1969.

Provence, S.; Naylor, A.; and Patterson, J. *The Challenge of Day Care.* New Haven: Yale University, 1977.

Rabb, T., ed. *The Family in History: Interdisciplinary Essays.* New York: Harper and Row, 1975.

Rabkin, J. Opinions about mental illness: A review of the literature. *Psychological Bulletin*, 77: 153–171, 1972.

Ramey, J. Emerging patterns of innovative behavior in marriage. In: Sussman, M., ed. *Sourcebook in Marriage and the Family.* 4th ed. Boston: Houghton Mifflin, 1974.

Rao, L. Industrialization and the family: A world view. *International Journal of Sociology of the Family*, 3: 179–189, 1973.

Raphael, B. Preventive intervention with the recently bereaved. *Archives of General Psychiatry*, 34: 1450–54, 1977.

Rapoport, R. The family and psychiatric treatment. *Psychiatry*, 23: 53–62, 1960.

Rapoport, R. and Rapoport, R. Patients' families: Assets and liabilities. In: Greenblatt, M., et al., eds. *Mental Patients in Transition*. Springfield, Ill.: Thomas, 1961.

Rapoport, R., and Rapoport, R. *Dual-Career Families*. Harmondsworth, England: Penguin, 1971.

Reid, E. Helping parents of handicapped children. *Children*, January/February 1958, pp. 15–19.

Rein, M. *Social Policy: Issues of Choice and Change*. New York: Random House, 1970.

Rein, M., and Miller, S. M. Social action on the installment plan. In: Meyer, E., ed. *Planning Community Services for the Mentally Retarded*. Scranton, Pa.: International Textbook, 1967.

Report of the Poor Law Commission of 1832. Cd. 2728, 1905.

Report to the President, White House Conference on Children, 1970. Washington, D.C.: Supt. of Docs., U.S. Govt. Print. Off., 1970.

Retchless, M. Rehabilitation programs for chronic patients: II. Stepping stones to the community. *Hospital and Community Psychiatry*, 18: 377–378, 1967.

Ricciuti, H. "Effects of Infant Day Care Experience on Behavior and Development: Research and Implications for Social Policy." Prepared for Department of Health, Education, and Welfare, Office of the Assistant Secretary for Planning and Evaluation, 1976.

Ridley, J. C. Demographic change and the role and status of women. *Annals of the American Academy of Political and Social Sciences*, 375: 15–23, 1968.

Riley, L., and Nagi, S., eds. *Disability in the United States. A Compendium of Data on Prevalence and Programs*. Columbus, Ohio: Ohio State University, 1970.

Riley, M., and Foner, A. *Aging and Society. Vol. I: An Inventory of Research Findings*. New York: Russell Sage Foundation, 1968.

Riley, M.; Riley, J.; and Johnson, M., eds. *Aging and Society. Vol. II: Aging and the Professions*. New York: Russell Sage Foundation, 1969.

Riskin, J., and Faunce, E. An evaluative review of family interaction research. *Family Process*, 11: 365–455, 1972.

Robinson, L. Basic concepts in family therapy: A differential comparison with individual treatment. *American Journal of Psychiatry*, 132: 1045–1048, 1975.

Roby, P., ed. *Child Care. Who Cares?* New York: Basic Books, 1973.

Rockmore, M. Social work responsibility in mental illness. *Social Work*, 5(3): 70–76, 1960.

Rockmore, M., and Feldman, R. The mental hospital patient in the community. *Mental Hygiene*, 40: 285–294, 1956.

Rodman, H.; Nichols, F.; and Voydanoff, P. Lower-class attitudes toward "deviant" family patterns: A cross-cultural study. *Journal of Marriage and the Family*, 31: 315–321, 1969.

Roghmann, K.; Hecht, P.; and Haggerty, R. Family coping with everyday illness: Self reports from a household survey. *Journal of Comparative Family Studies*, 4: 49–62, 1973.

Roos, P. *Trends in Residential Institutions for the Mentally Retarded. Trends in Education Series*. Columbus, Ohio: University Council for Educational Administration, 1976.

Rose, A., and Peterson, H., eds. *Older People and Their Social World*. Philadelphia, Pa.: F. A. Davis, 1965.

Rosen, B. Family structure and value transmission. *Merrill-Palmer Quarterly, 10:* 59–76, 1964.

Rosen, D., and Callan, L. *Report of Trends in Residential Services for the Mentally Retarded.* Sterling Heights, Mich.: National Association of Superintendents of Public Residential Facilities, 1972.

Rosenberg, A. *Appropriateness of the Continued Institutionalization of the State School Population in New York State.* New York: Department of Mental Hygiene, 1969.

Rosencranz, H. A.; Pihlblad, C. T.; and McNevin, T. E. *Social Participation of Older People in the Small Town.* Columbia, Mo.: University of Missouri, 1968.

Rosenheim, M. Social welfare and its implications for family living. In: Shanas, E., and Streib, G., eds. *Social Structure and the Family: Generational Relations.* Englewood Cliffs, N.J.: Prentice-Hall, 1965.

Rosenzweig, N. Some differences between elderly people who use community resources and those who do not. *Journal of the American Geriatric Society.* 23: 224–233. 1975.

Roskies, E. *Abnormality and Normality: The Mothering of Thalidomide Children.* Ithaca, N.Y.: Cornell University Press. 1972.

Rosow, I. *Social Integration of the Aged.* New York: The Free Press, 1967.

Rosow, I. *Socialization to Old Age.* Berkeley, Calif.: University of California Press, 1974.

Rosow, I. The aged in a post-affluent society. *Gerontology,* 1(4): 9–22, 1975.

Rossi, A. Family development in a changing world. *American Journal of Psychiatry,* 128: 1057–1066, 1972.

Rothman, T., ed. *Changing Patterns in Psychiatric Care. An Anthology of Evolving Scientific Psychiatry in Medicine.* New York: Crown Publishers, 1970.

Rowitz, L. Social factors in retardation. *Social Science and Medicine,* 8: 405–412, 1974.

Rubenstein, D. Rehospitalization versus family crisis intervention. *American Journal of Psychiatry,* 129: 715–720, 1972.

Ruderman, F. *Child Care and Working Mothers. A Study of Arrangements Made for Daytime Care of Children.* New York: Child Welfare League of America, 1968.

Saenger, G. *Factors Influencing the Institutionalization of Mentally Retarded Individuals in New York City.* Albany, N.Y.: State Interdepartmental Health Resources Board, 1960.

Safirstein, S. Psychiatric aftercare including home visits. *New York State Journal of Medicine,* 71: 2441–2445, 1971.

Sainsbury, P., and Grad de Alarcón, J. The psychiatrist and the geriatric patient: The effects of community care on the family of the geriatric patient. *Journal of Geriatric Psychiatry,* 4(1): 23–41, 1971.

Samerotte, G., and Harris, M. Some factors influencing helping: The effects of a handicap, responsibility, and requesting help. *Journal of Social Psychology,* 98: 39–45, 1976.

Sanders, K.; Mills, J.; Martin, F.I.R.; and Del. Horne, D. J. Emotional attitudes in adult insulin-dependent diabetics. *Journal of Psychosomatic Research,* 19: 241–246, 1975.

Sawhill, I. Discrimination and poverty among women who head families. *Journal of Women in Culture and Society,* 1, 2, and 3: 201–221, 1976.

Scheerenberger, R. *Public Residential Services for the Mentally Retarded.* Washington, D.C.: National Association of Superintendents of Public Residential Facilities for the Mentally Retarded, 1976.

Schlesinger, B. *The One-Parent Family. Perspectives and Annotated Bibliography.* Toronto: University of Toronto, 1970.

Schonell, F., and Watts., B. A first survey of the effects of a subnormal child on the family unit. *American Journal of Mental Deficiency,* 61: 210–219, 1956.

Schooler, C. Childhood family structure and adult characteristics. *Sociometry,* 35: 255–269, 1972.

Schorr, A. *Filial Responsibility in the Modern American Family.* Washington, D.C.: Department of Health, Education, and Welfare, 1960.

Schorr, A. Family values and real life. *Social Casework,* 57: 397–401, 1976.

Schorr, A., and Moen, P. "Single Parents: Public and Private Image." *Paper presented for the Task Force on Mental Health and The Family.* President's Commission on Mental Health, 1977.

Schottland, C. *The Social Security Program in the United States.* New York: Appleton-Century-Crofts, 1963.

Schreiber, M. *Social Work and Mental Retardation.* New York: John Day, 1970.

Schulz, D. *Coming Up Black: Patterns of Ghetto Socialization.* Englewood Cliffs, N.J.: Prentice-Hall, 1969.

Schulz, J. *The Economics of Aging.* Belmont, Calif.: Wadsworth, 1976. (a)

Schulz, J. Income distribution and the aging. In: Binstock, R., and Shanas, E., eds. *Handbook of Aging and the Social Sciences.* New York: Van Nostrand Reinhold, 1976. (b)

Schutt, W. Critical issues in the management of adolescents with handicaps. *Proceedings of the Royal Society of Medicine,* 68: 309–310, 1975.

Schwab, L. Rehabilitation of physically disabled women in a family-oriented program. *Rehabilitation Literature,* 36(2): 34–43, 1975.

Seelback, W. "Adult Children as Caretakers for Aged Parents: Toward a Theoretical Formulation." Paper presented at the annual meeting of the National Council for Family Relations, American Association of Marriage and Family Counselors, St. Louis, Mo., October 1974.

Segal, R. "Current Trends in Services for the Aged Mentally Retarded." Paper presented at the 54th Annual Council for Exceptional Children Convention, Chicago, Ill., April 1976.

Segre, S. Family stability, social classes and values in traditional and industrial societies. *Journal of Marriage and the Family,* 37: 431–436, 1975.

Seidl, F.; Austin, C.,; and Greene, D. Is home health care less expensive? *Health and Social Work,* 2(2): 5–19, 1977.

Selan, B. Psychotherapy with the developmentally disabled. *Health Social Work,* 1: 73–85, 1976.

Sewell, W. H. Some recent developments in socialization theory and research. *Annals of the American Academy of Political and Social Science,* 349: 163–181, 1963.

Shanas, E. *The Health of Older People: A Social Survey.* Cambridge: Harvard University, 1962.

Shanas, E. Some observations on cross-national surveys of aging. *Gerontologist,* 3: 7–9, 1963. (a)

Shanas, E. "The Unmarried Old Person in the United States: Living Arrangements and Care in Illness, Myth or Fact." Paper presented at the International Social Service Research Seminar in Gerontology, Markaryo, Sweden, August, 1963. (b)

Shanas, E. Family help patterns and social class in three countries. *Journal of Marriage and the Family*, 29: 257–266, 1967.

Shanas, E., et al., eds. *Old People in Three Industrial Societies*. New York: Atherton Press, 1968.

Shanas, E. Measuring the home health needs of the elderly in five countries. *Journal of Gerontology*, 26: 37–40, 1971.

Shanas, E. Factors affecting care of the patient: Clients, government policy, role of the family and social attitudes. *Journal of the American Geriatric Society*, 21: 394–397, 1973.

Shanas, E., and Hauser, P. Zero population growth and the family life of old people. *Journal of Social Issues*, 30: 79–92, 1974.

Shanas, E., and Maddox, G. Aging, health and the organization of health resources. In: Binstock, R., and Shanas, E., eds. *Handbook of Aging and the Social Sciences*. New York: Van Nostrand Reinhold Co., 1976.

Shanas, E., and Streib, G., eds. *Social Structure and the Family: Generational Relations*. Englewood Cliffs, N.J.: Prentice-Hall, 1965.

Shea, M. Planning for psychotic patients at home. *Social Casework*, 31: 420–423, 1950.

Shiakin, D., and Frate, D. *The Extended Family in Black Societies*. The Hague: Mouton, 1975.

Shimkin, D., and Shimkin, E. The extended family in U.S. black societies: Findings and problems. Urbana, Ill.: University of Illinois. Mimeo, 1975.

Shochet, B., and Lisansky, E. New dimensions in family practice. *Psychosomatics*, 10: 88—93, 1969.

Shoemaker, W.; Tindell, H.; Schubert, J.; Hoke, H.; and Argires, J. Chronic invalidism in a young woman: A study of family dynamics. *Journal of Family Practice*, 4: 155–157, 1977.

Sholevar, G. P. Families of institutionalized children. *American Journal of Orthopsychiatry*, 45: 269–270, 1975.

Shore, M., and Mannino, F. *Mental Health and Social Change: 50 Years of Orthopsychiatry*. New York: AMS Press, 1975.

Shorter, E. *The Making of the Modern Family*. New York: Basic Books, 1975.

Simmons, L. Social participation of the aged in different cultures. In: Sussman, M., ed. *Sourcebook in Marriage and the Family*. 3rd ed. Boston: Houghton Mifflin, 1968.

Simon, A.; Lowenthal, M.; and Epstein, L. *Crisis and Intervention: The Elderly Mental Patient*. San Francisco: Jossey-Bass, 1970.

Simos, B. Adult children and their aging parents. *Social Work*, 18(3): 78–85, 1973.

Sirjamaki, J. *The American Family in the 20th Century*. Cambridge: Harvard University, 1959.

Skarnulis, B. "Residential Services: Support Not Supplant the Natural Home." Paper presented at the South Western Region Deaf-Blind Center, Special Study Institute, San Diego, Calif., 1978.

Skolnick, A., and Jerome, H. *Family in Transition*. Boston: Little, Brown, 1971.

Slipp, S. Family therapy with disorganized poor families. *Groups: A Journal of Group Dynamics and Psychotherapy,* 5: 3–13, 1973.

Smits, S. The role and function of the rehabilitation counselor serving the severely disabled. In: Jenkins, W., et al., eds. *Rehabilitation of the Severely Disabled.* Dubuque, Iowa: Kendall/Hunt, 1976.

Soldo, B., and Lauriat, P. Living arrangements among the elderly in the United States: A loglinear approach. *Journal of Comparative Family Studies,* 7: 351–366, 1976.

Somerville, R. M. The future of family relationship in the middle and older years. *Family Coordinator,* 21: 487—498, 1972.

Sorokin, P. *The Crisis of Our Age.* New York: E. P. Dutton and Company, 1941.

Southard, S. *The Family and Mental Illness.* Philadelphia: Westminister, 1957.

Soyka, P. Homemaker-home health aide services for handicapped children. *Child Welfare,* 55: 241–251, 1976.

Spark, G. Grandparents and intergenerational family therapy. *Family Process,* 13: 225–237, 1974.

Spiegel, J., and Bell, N. The family of the psychiatric patient. In: Arieti, S., ed. *American Handbook of Psychiatry.* New York: Basic Books, 1959.

Stack, C. B. *All Our Kin. Strategies for Survival in a Black Community.* New York: Harper and Row, 1974.

Stack, C., and Semmel, H. Social insecurity: Breaking up poor families. In: Mondell, B. R., ed. *Welfare in America: Controlling the Dangerous Classes.* Englewood Cliffs, N.J.: Prentice-Hall, 1974.

Stanton, E. *Clients Come Last. Volunteers and Welfare Organizations.* Beverly Hills, Calif.: Sage, 1970.

Staples, R. The Mexican-American family: Its modification over time and space. *Phylon,* 32: 179–192, 1971.

Staton, R. A comparison of Mexican and Mexican-American families. *Family Coordinator,* 21: 325–330, 1972.

Steele, T.; Finkelstein, S. H.; and Finkelstein, F. O. Hemodialysis patients and spouse: Marital discord, sexual problems and depression. *Journal of Nervous and Mental Disease,* 162: 225–237, 1976.

Stein, Z., and Susser, M. Change over time in the incidence and prevalence of mental retardation. In: Hellmuth, J., ed. *The Exceptional Infant.* New York: Brunner/Mazel, 1971.

Stein, Z., and Susser, M. The epidemiology of mental retardation. In: Arieti, S., ed. *American Handbook of Psychiatry.* 2nd ed. New York: Basic Books, 1974.

Stein, Z., and Susser, M. Public health and mental retardation: New power and new problems. In: Begab, M., Richardson, S., eds. *The Mentally Retarded and Society: A Social Science Perspective.* Baltimore: University Park, 1975.

Steiner, G. *The Futility of Family Policy.* Washington, D.C.: Brookings Institute, 1981.

Steiner, G. Y. *The State of Welfare.* Washington, D.C.: Brookings, 1971.

Steiner, G. Y. *The Children's Cause.* Washington, D.C.: Brookings, 1977.

Steinfels, M. *Who's Minding the Children? The History and Politics of Day Care in America.* New York: Simon and Schuster, 1973.

Sternlicht, M., and Deutsch, M. *Personality Development and Social Behavior in the Mentally Retarded.* Lexington, Mass.: Heath, 1972.

Stetson, D. The two faces of policy: Divorce reform in western democracies. *Journal of Comparative Family Studies,* 6: 15–30, 1975.

Streib, G. Family patterns in retirement. In: Sussman, M., ed. *Sourcebook in Marriage and the Family.* Boston: Houghton Mifflin, 1968.

Streib, G. Older families and their troubles: Familial and social responses. *Family Coordinator,* 21: 5–19, 1972.

Stokes, B. Helping parents to accept. *Child Care and Health Development,* 2: 29–33, 1976.

Sultz, H.; Schlesinger, E.; Mosher, W.; and Feldman, J. *Long-Term Childhood Illness.* Pittsburgh: University of Pittsburgh, 1972.

Sussman, M., ed. *Sociology and Rehabilitation.* Washington, D.C.: American Sociological Association, 1965. (a)

Sussman, M. Relationships of adult children with their parents in the United States. In: Shanas, E., and Streib, G., eds. *Social Structure and the Family: Generational Relations.* Englewood Cliffs, N.J.: Prentice-Hall, 1965. (b)

Sussman, M. The isolated nuclear family: Fact or fiction. In: Sussman, M., ed. *Sourcebook in Marriage and the Family.* 3rd ed. New York: Houghton Mifflin, 1968.

Sussman, M. "The Methodological Problems in the Study of the Family." Paper presented at the 81st Annual Convention of the American Psychological Association, Montreal, August 30, 1973.

Sussman, M. *Sourcebook in Marriage and the Family.* 4th ed. Boston: Houghton Mifflin, 1974.

Sussman, M. The four f's of variant family forms and marriage styles. *Family Coordinator,* 24: 563–576, 1975.

Sussman, M. The family life of old people. In: Binstock, R., and Shanas, E., eds. *Handbook of Aging and the Social Sciences.* New York: Van Nostrand Reinhold, 1976.

Sussman, M., and Burchinal, L. Kin family network: Unheralded structure in current conceptualizations of family functioning. In: Sussman, M., ed. *Sourcebook in Marriage and the Family.* 3rd ed. New York: Houghton Mifflin, 1968.

Taft, L. The care and management of the child with muscular dystrophy. *Developmental Medicine and Child Neurology,* 15: 510–518, 1973.

Talabere, L., and Graves, P. A tool for assessing families of burned children. *American Journal of Nursing.* 76: 225–227, 1976.

Tallman, I. Spousal role differentiation and the socialization of severely retarded children. *Journal of Marriage and the Family,* 27: 37–42, 1965.

Tallman, I. The family as a small problem solving group. *Journal of Marriage and the Family,* 32: 94–104, 1970.

Tallman, I., and Miller, G. Class differences in family problem solving: Effects of verbal ability, hierarchial structure, and role expectations. *Sociometry,* 37: 13–37, 1974.

Tarjan, G., et al. The natural history of mental deficiency in a State hospital. I. Probabilities of release and death by age, intelligence quotients, and diagnosis. *Journal of Diseases of Children,* 96(July): 64-70, 1958.

Tarjan, G.; Wright, S.; Eyman, R.; and Keeran, D. Natural history of mental retardation: Some aspects of epidemiology. *American Journal of Mental Deficiency,* 77: 369–379, 1973.

Teicher, J. Psychological aspects of cystic fibrosis in children and adolescents. *California Medicine*, 110: 374, 1969.

Tew, B., and Laurence, K. Mothers, brothers, and sisters of patients with spina bifida. *Developmental Medicine and Child Neurology*, 15 (Supplement Number 29): 69–76, 1973.

Tew, B.; Payne, H.; Laurence, K. Must a family with a handicapped child be a handicapped family? *Developmental Medicine and Child Neurology*, 16 (Supplement Number 32): 95–98, 1974. (a)

Tew, B.; Payne, H.; Laurence, K.; and Rawnsley, K. Psychological testing: Reactions of parents of physically handicapped and normal children. *Developmental Medicine and Child Neurology*, 16 (Supplement Number 4): 501–506, 1974. (b)

Thompson, P. The personal physician, the psychiatrist, the family, and the older patient. *Journal of the American Geriatrics Society*, 16: 984–993, 1968.

Thurlow, M.; Bruininks, R.; Williams, S.; and Morreau, L. *Deinstitutionalization and Residential Services: A Literature Survey*. Minneapolis: Information and Technical Assistance Project in Deinstitutionalization, University of Minnesota, 1978.

Titmuss, R. *Social Policy*. London: Allen and Unwin, 1963.

Titmuss, R. *The Gift Relationship*. London: Allen and Unwin. 1971.

Tizard, J. The epidemiology of mental retardation: Implications for research on malnutrition. In: Hambraeus, L., and Vahlquist, B., ed. *Early Malnutrition and Mental Development*. Symposia of the Swedish Nutrition Foundation, No. 12. Uppsala: Almquist and Wiksell, 1974.

Tizard, J., and Grad de Alarcon, J. *The Mentally Handicapped and Their Families: A Social Survey*. Cambridge: Oxford University, 1961.

Tomlin, W. Rehabilitation of the severely disabled. Serving the severely disabled. In: Jenkins, W., et al., eds. *Rehabilitation of the Severely Disabled*. Dubuque, Iowa: Kendall/Hunt, 1976.

Townsend, P. The effects of family structure on the likelihood of admission to an institution in old age: The application of a general theory. In: Shanas, E., and Streib, G., eds. *Social Structure and the Family*. Englewood Cliffs, N.J.: Prentice-Hall, 1965.

Townsend, P. The emergence of the four generation family in industrial society. In: Neugarten, B., ed. *Middle Age and Aging*. Chicago: University of Chicago, 1968.

Townsend, P. Policy strategies for the vulnerable minority of the aged. *Proceedings of the Royal Society of Medicine*, 66: 885–887, 1973.

Townsend, P., and Flanagan, J. Experimental preadmission program to encourage home care for severely and profoundly retarded children. *American Journal of Mental Deficiency*,80: 562–569, 1976.

Townsend, P., and Wedderburn, D. *The Aged in the Welfare State*. London: Bell, 1965.

Travis, G. *Chronic Illness in Children. Its Impact on Child and Family*. Stanford, Calif.: Stanford University, 1976.

Tretakoff, M. Counseling parents of handicapped children: A review. *Mental Retardation*, 7(4): 31–34, 1969.

Tymchuk, A. Training parent therapists. *Mental Retardation*, 13(5): 19–22, 1975.

Urban, Institute. *Child Support Payments in the United States*. Washington, D.C.: The Institute, 1976.

U.S. Bureau of the Census. *Census of Population: 1950*. Washington, D.C.: Supt. of Docs., U.S. Govt. Print. Off., 1953.

U.S. Bureau of the Census. *Historical Statistics of the United States, Colonial Times to 1957*. Washington, D.C.: of Supt. of Docs., U.S. Govt. Print. Off., 1960.

U.S. Bureau of the Census. *Census of Population: 1960*. Washington, D.C.: Supt. of Docs., U.S. Govt. Print. Off., 1963.

U.S. Bureau of the Census. *Census of Population: 1970*. Washington, D.C.: Supt. of Docs., U.S. Govt. Print. Off., 1973.

U.S. Bureau of the Census. *Nursery School and Kindergarten Enrollment: October 1973*. Series P-20, No. 268. Washington, D.C.: Supt. of Docs., U.S. Govt. Print. Off., 1974.

U.S. Bureau of the Census. Demographic aspects of aging and the older population in the United States. *Current Population Reports*. Special Studies, Series P-23, No. 59. Washington, D.C.: Supt. of Docs., U.S. Govt. Print. Off., 1976. (a)

U.S. Bureau of the Census. Daytime care of children: October 1974 and February 1975. *Current Population Reports*. Series P—20, No. 298. Washington, D.C.: Supt. of Docs., U.S. Govt. Print. Off., 1976. (b)

U.S. Bureau of the Census. Marital status and living arrangements. *Current Population Reports*. Series P-20, No. 306. Washington, D.C.: Supt. of Docs., U.S. Govt. Print. Off., 1977, p. 15. (a)

U.S. Bureau of the Census. *Statistical Abstracts of the United States*. Washington, D.C.: Supt. of Docs., U.S. Govt. Print. Off., 1977. (b)

U.S. Bureau of the Census. 1976 Survey of Institutionalized Persons. *Current Population Reports*. Special Studies, Series P-23, No. 69. Washington, D.C.: Supt. of Docs., U.S. Govt. Print. Off., 1978.

U.S. Bureau of the Census. *Census of Population: 1980*. Washington, D.C.: Supt. of Docs., U.S. Government Printing Office., 1984.

U.S. Bureau of Labor Statistics. *Marital and Family Characteristics of the Labor Force in March 1973*. Special Labor Force Report No. 164. Washington, D.C.: Supt. of Docs., U.S. Govt. Print. Off., 1973. (a)

U.S. Bureau of Labor Statistics. *Children of Working Mothers, March 1973*. Summary/Special Labor Force Report. Washington, D.C.: Supt. of Docs., U.S. Govt. Print. Off., 1973. (b)

U.S. Bureau of Labor Statistics. Department of Labor. *Earnings and Employment*. Vol. IXX. Washington, D.C.: Supt. of Docs., U.S. Govt. Print. Off., 1973. (c)

U.S. Department of Health, Education, and Welfare. *Home Health Care: Report of the Regional Public Hearings of the Department of Health, Education, and Welfare, September 20—October 1, 1976*. DHEW Pub No. 76-135. Washington D.C.: Supt. of Docs:, U.S. Govt. Print. Off., 1976.

U.S. Department of Health, Education, and Welfare. *Long-Term Care: A Challenge to Service Systems*, by Lavor, J. Washington, D.C.: Supt. of Docs., U.S. Govt. Print. Off., 1977.

U.S. Government Accounting Office. *Problems in Providing Proper Care to Medicaid and Medicare Patients in Skilled Nursing Homes*. Washington, D.C.: Supt. of Docs., U.S. Govt. Print. Off., 1971.

Van den Ban, A. Family structure and modernization. *Journal of Marriage and the Family,* 29: 771–773, 1967.

Veevers, J. Voluntary childlessness and social policy: An alternative view. *Family Coordinator,* 23: 397–406, 1974.

Vincent, C. Mental health and the family. *Journal of Marriage and the Family,* 29: 18–39, 1967.

Walker, J.; Thomas, M.; and Russell, I. Spina bifida and the parents. *Developmental Medicine and Child Neurology,* 13: 462–476, 1971.

Walz, T. The family agency and post-industrial society. *Social Casework,* 56: 13–20, 1975.

Warner, F.; Golden, T.; and Henteleff, M. Health insurance: A dilemma for parents of the mentally retarded. In: Dempsey, J., ed. *Community Services for Retarded Children.* Baltimore: University Park, 1975.

Warren, B., and Ferman, P. *Analysis of Agency Placement of Handicapped Children.* Vols. I, II. Ypsilanti, Mich.: Eastern Michigan University, 1974.

Warren, R. The interdependence between functional requisites of groups and individual problem-solving skills: The case of the nuclear family. *Proceedings of the American Sociological Association,* 1969.

Warren, R. *The Community in America.* Boston: Houghton, Mifflin, 1978.

Weber, R. E., and Blenkner, M. The social service perspective. In: Sherwood, S., ed. *Long-term Care: A Handbook for Researchers, Planners, and Providers.* New York: Spectrum, 1975.

Weigart, A., and Thomas, D. Family as a conditional universal. *Journal of Marriage and the Family,* 33: 188–196, 1971.

Weinstein, F., and Platt, G. *The Wish to Be Free: Society, Psyche and Value Change.* Berkeley: University of California, 1977.

Weller, S. Points of view. Co-operation in the care of handicapped children. *Public Health,* 90: 187–190, 1976.

Wells, R.; Dilkes, T.; and Trivelli, U. The results of family therapy: A critical review of the literature. *Family Process,* 11: 189–207, 1972.

Werkman, S.; Washington, J.; and Oberman, J. Symposium: The physician and mongolism. *Clinical Proceedings of the Children's Hospital,* 17(2): 42–49, 1961.

Wertheim, E. The science and typology of family systems II. Further theoretical and practical considerations. *Family Process,* 14: 285–309, 1975.

Wilensky, H. *The Welfare State and Equality.* Berkeley: University of California, 1975.

Wilensky, H., and Lebeaux, C. N. *Industrial Society and Social Welfare.* New York: Free Press, 1965.

Williams, G.; Fu-tong, H.; and Tsung-yi, L. Prediction of the burden of released mental patients. *Community Mental Health Journal,* 9: 303–315, 1973.

Wills, G. *Inventing America: Jefferson's Declaration of Independence.* New York: Doubleday, 1978.

Wilson, A. Effects of health problems on the family life of older people. In: Crawford, C., ed. *Health and the Family.* New York: MacMillan, 1971. (a)

Wilson, A. Family life among elderly persons. In: Crawford, C., ed. *Health and the Family.* New York: MacMillan, 1971. (b)

Wing, L. A handicapped child in the family. *Developmental Medicine and Child Neurology,* 11: 643–644, 1969.

Winston, E. A national policy on the family. *Public Welfare,* 27: 54–58, 1969.

Wolf, L., and Whitehead, P. The decision to institutionalize retarded children: Comparison of individually matched groups. *Mental Retardation*, 13(5): 3–7, 1975.

Wolfensberger, W. Counseling the parents of the retarded. In: Baumeister, A., ed. *Mental Retardation: Appraisal, Education and Rehabilitation*. Chicago: Aldine, 1967.

Wolfensberger, W. Will there always be an institution? I. The impact of epidemiological trends. *Mental Retardation*, 9(5): 14–20, 1971. (a)

Wolfensberger, W. Will there always be an institution? II. The impact of new service models. *Mental Retardation*, 9(6): 31–38, 1971. (b)

Wolfensberger, W. *Normalization. The Principle of Normalization in Human Services*. Toronto: National Institute on Mental Retardation, 1972.

Wolfensberger, W., and Kurtz, R., eds. *Management of the Family of the Mentally Retarded*. Chicago: Follett Educational, 1969.

Wolock, I.; Geisman, L.; Brobery, M.; Taylor, J.; and Goldstein, H. Evaluation of programs of services to children in their own homes as an alternative to placement. *American Journal or Orthopsychiatry*, 43: 249–250, 1973.

Women's Bureau. Department of Labor. *Day Care Facts*. Employment Standards Administration Pamphlet 16. Washington, D.C.: Supt. of Docs., U.S. Govt. Print. Off., 1973.

World Health Organization. The mentally subnormal child. In: Wolfensberger, W., and Kurtz, R., eds. *Management of the Family of the Mentally Retarded*. Chicago: Follett Educational, 1969.

Wright, B. *Physical Disability—A Psychological Approach*. New York: Harper and Brace, 1960.

Yankelovich, Skelly, and White. *Raising Children in a Changing Society*. Minneapolis: The General Mills American Family Report, 1977.

Yannet, H. Mental deficiency. *Advances in Pediatrics*, 8: 217–257, 1957.

Yorburg, B. The nuclear and the extended family: An area of conceptual confusion. *Journal of Comparative Family Studies*, 6: 5–14, 1975.

Young, D., and Nelson, R. *Public Policy for Day Care of Young Children*. Lexington, Mass.: Lexington, 1973.

Young, L. *The Fractured Family*. New York: McGraw-Hill, 1973.

Young, M., and Wilmott, P. *The Symmetrical Family*. London: Routledge and Kegan Paul, 1973.

Young, M., and Wilmott, P. *Family and Kinship in East London*. London: Routledge and Kegan Paul, 1975.

Zigler, E. Social deprivation and rigidity in the performance of feebleminded children. *Journal of Abnormal and Social Psychology*, 62: 413–421, 1961.

Zigler, E. Research on personality structure in the retardate. In: Ellis, N., ed. *International Review of Research in Mental Retardation*. New York: Academic, 1966.

Zill, N., and Brim, O., Jr. *Childhood Social Indicators*. New York: Foundation for Child Development, 1975.

Zimmerman, C. Basic changes in the contemporary world family systems. *Indian Journal of Social Research*, 10: 1–16, 1969.

Zimmerman, C. The atomistic family—Fact or fiction. *International Journal of Contemporary Sociology*, 8: 112–124, 1971.

Zimmerman, C. Family influence upon religion. *Journal of Comparative Family Studies*, 5(2): 1–16, 1974.

INDEX

Carroll, J., 39
Carter, J., 17
Cassells, J., 26, 27
Child welfare, 110
Childrens allowances, 161, ff
Clausen, J., 134
Coale, A., 41
Cobb, S., 26, 27
Cogswell, B., 39
Cohen, P., 82, 127, 130
Coll, B., 21
Colman, M., 127
Community Care Corps, 118
Community Service Society,
    167
Conley, R., 78, 84, 106
Conroy, J., 79
Constant attendance allowance,
    119, 160 ff
Cox, M., 53
Cox, R., 53
Crippled Childrens Services, 111

D

Davis, R., 128
Dean, A., 27
Demos, J., 20
Dependency, 18, 23, 24, 171 ff
    ratio of, 59 ff
Derr, K., 79
Divorce rates, 52 ff
Donzelot, J., 19
Dorenberg, N., 133
Duff, R., 134
Dunlap, W., 80, 137

E

Ecology, 26
Ehrlich, S., 126
Employed mothers, 49 ff

F

Family
    allowances, 161 ff
    broken, 37
    definitions, 34 ff
    female headed, 37, 54
    idealized, 36
    industrial, 55, 83
    modified extended, 44
    nuclear, 4, 38 ff
    postindustrial, 55, 83
    size, 45 ff
    stages, 42 ff
    traditional, 55, 83
Family Fund, 155 ff
Family Impact Seminar, 98
Farber, B., 82, 127
Featherstone, J., 23
Federal Council on Aging, 105
Fertility rates, 48
Filial responsibility, 11, 12, 20
Fowle, C., 82, 131
Fox, S., 155
Fragmented services, 117
Freeston, B., 138

G

Gatti, F., 127
Generic services, 117 ff
Glick, P., 35, 36, 42, 48, 52, 53
Goffman, E., 132
Goldie, L., 127
Goode, W., 55
Goodell, G., 135
Goolsby, E., 134
Gordon, M., 59
Gottesman, L., 70
Grad de Alarćon, J., 75, 79, 80
Graliker, B., 88
Grossman, H., 77